The World of Politics
A Concise Introduction

The World of Politics

A Concise Introduction

James F. Barnes
Marshall Carter
Max J. Skidmore

St. Martin's Press • New York

For our mothers

Library of Congress Catalog Card Number: 80–50413
Copyright © 1980 by St. Martin's Press, Inc.
All Rights Reserved.
Manufactured in the United States of America.
43210
fedcb
For information, write St. Martin's Press, Inc.,
175 Fifth Avenue, New York, N.Y. 10010

Cover design by Mies Hora

Maps by Clarice Borio, New York City

cloth ISBN: 0–312–89225–X
paper ISBN: 0–312–89226–8

Preface

In these days of proliferating textbooks, authors should have good reasons for undertaking another introduction to politics. We wrote *The World of Politics* because we could find no concise, inexpensive text that introduced the fundamental concepts of politics in a truly comparative perspective. In a time when events halfway around the globe have immediate impact locally, the lack of such a text seems especially unfortunate. This book, then, seeks to fill the gap.

The fundamental theme of the book is politics, the ways in which human beings collectively organize their affairs. The approach is comparative: our intention is to present the basic concepts of politics and show how they are perceived variously according to time, place, and cultural setting. We three authors ourselves represent differences of age, race, sex, home region, professional experience, and opinion. But we share a belief that the political life of the human community is important for every person—never more so than now—and we have tried to show why this is so. Our focus is on the principles of politics rather than on the discipline of political science, although we do discuss political science as a field of study.

Many books intended for use in introductory courses in politics seem to us to help perpetuate a narrow, ethnocentric view. By using a comparative approach, we invite students to see how the political process functions in one form or another throughout the human community, to understand the implications of regional and national differences, and to recognize the importance of political frameworks other than those of nation-states.

Many introductory texts are so long that they leave little or no time for the assignment of other readings, and they are frequently so expensive that to require other books works a financial hardship on students. *The World of Politics* has been designed to fill the need for a core text which is comprehensive and can provide an adequate framework for a course, yet which is brief and inexpensive so that students can work with a variety of materials. In addition to providing a nucleus for an introduction to politics course, it may serve as collateral reading in comparative government and perhaps American government. It should also be useful to supply the political dimension in an introductory survey of the social sciences.

We owe much to the many friends—teachers, students, and colleagues at home and abroad—who have helped us to understand something of the workings of politics in many places. The credit is theirs if we have succeeded here in sharing that understanding with others.

James F. Barnes
Marshall Carter
Max J. Skidmore

Contents

Part One

THE PRINCIPLES OF POLITICS

This alone should serve as a warning to people;
an end that is infinitely remote is not an end, but,
if you like, a trap . . . Each age, each generation,
each life has its own fullness.

—Alexander Herzen

1

Perspectives on Politics

Government is necessary, not because man is
naturally bad . . . but because man is by nature
more individualistic than social.

—Thomas Hobbes

But what is government itself but the greatest of
all reflections on human nature?

—James Madison

The political process helps make it possible for this book to be published,
and possible—or even necessary—for you to read it. The freedom and
motivation to write and publish books, the existence of educational institutions—along with reading requirements for individuals in those institutions—are reflections of political decisions and values of particular
communities. Making decisions that support preferred values, and then
making new decisions to confirm or reject what has been done, *is* the political process. Politics is not just "what politicians do." Even the lowli-
est subject of an absolute monarch has some role in political life. Even
those of us who say that we are not interested in politics and want nothing to do with it play a part in the process by believing and acting on that
opinion.

Politics is a little like being in love: something that is very hard to define, but you still know what it is, especially if it happens to you. Many
writers have tried over many centuries to capture the essence of politics in

3

a short sentence or two. A sample of what they have said about politics will give you an idea of how many different definitions there can be:

Politics is who gets what, when, where, how, and why.
Politics is the pursuit of the good.
Politics is the means by which some men tell others what to do.
Politics is binding decisions about who shall have what, when, and how.
Politics is the superstructure of the material base of life.
Politics is the process by which binding policies are made and carried out for a society.
Politics is prices, police, and preachments.
Politics is the translation of values into public policy.
Politics is the art of human happiness.

Some of these explanations are argumentive. They try to convince you that politics is either good or bad. Others seem to be neutral, describing without judging. A key idea in all of them is that politics somehow involves the fundamental values of a community. As people decide how to rank their values they create priorities for action. The community decides how to create, or find, and use resources to realize individual and collective goals. Moreover, these are not idle agreements. They are binding decisions that require compliance—voluntarily if possible—by members of the community, whether or not they participated in the decision making and whether or not they agree with the outcome. As James Madison wrote during the early days of the United States, "If men were angels, no government would be necessary"—but since they are not, governments exist to produce compliance by persuasion or by force.

Some of the confusion about what politics is comes from the differing emphases and concerns of particular writers, especially those who lived and wrote in very different centuries or places from our own. One large group, dominated by philosophers, has tended to think of politics as the means for obtaining the *Good*—whether this means the public interest, justice, realization of religious aims, individualism, or the withering away of the state. Great numbers of people in history have been prepared, or forced, to fight and to sacrifice for various ideas of the Good. This particular conception of what politics is all about became dramatically visible in Iran in 1979, as the political community was rapidly reshaped in the service of a religious ideal. The association of politics with the pursuit of the Good has been strong in many times and places.

This concept alone cannot, however, tell us all we need to know to understand the political process. Another element of politics is *structural*: the formal institutions and rules, the institutionalizing process, which is

nes called government to distinguish it from politics as a whole.
dy of these institutions is very old. In the nineteenth century this
became so dominant in Western political science that it tended to
any writers to other aspects of politics. They forgot, or ignored,
that many kinds of communities other than nation-states exist.
do not have visibly separate institutions and rules which can be
as their government, but all have political life. For example,
no world government, but we can observe world politics. Indians
Amazon basin do not have parliaments and prime ministers, but
vern their communities.

roughout history some writers have called attention to the need to
er the actual *behavior* of different groups of people as they con-
he requirements for communal survival. Each community finds
arshals resources, decides what to do with what it has, and how to
th goals and resources that do not match. Each has to respond to
l contacts, supportive or hostile; each has internal challenges,
ial or destructive. These activities may be informal and irregular;
y be hard to separate from other activities that have an economic
ous character. Two communities may have political institutions
e the same names but function for very different reasons and
. But if we look at the whole pattern of life in any community,
re we will find common processes operating by which this
choice of directions and channeling of energies goes on. Thus politics
may be seen as a moral question, a structural problem, or a matter of
how people behave, how they do things. One approach looks at what
should be; another at visible *forms*; and the third at process or *actions*.
Each of these is a part of the puzzle, and they must all be combined to get
a complete picture.

We can put these together by saying that *politics is an activity by
which the community is established, given order through certain structures, and given direction*. It is a search for goals and the attempt to
reach them. This is continuous since circumstances will change, goals will
be rethought, individual members of the community will come and go. A
particular community may break up, or join with another, or be con-
quered—but the political process then continues in new configurations.
Even if the state as a dominant form of community should wither away,
as Marx hoped and predicted, politics itself will not end.

Politics is a collective matter. One person, alone, choosing for himself or herself, is not taking political action. Two or more, and the political begins. As more are added, something else often happens: a small
number in the group will gradually emerge as disproportionately influential and perhaps even begin to claim that they alone can decide what is
important. Some students of human organization have argued that this is

inevitable, that there is an "iron law" of oligarchy that a few will rule over the many and that all political systems will take this form—even if they give themselves names such as "democracy" that imply otherwise. Certainly we can see many communities, past and present, in which the great mass of the people seems to have no role in the making of decisions, other than serving as resources for the generals and the tax collectors or as a chorus praising the wisdom of the rulers. Some influential writers, such as the English philosopher Thomas Hobbes, have proposed that people must live with either brutal chaos or despotic rule, and that of these order under stringent rule is the better choice. Others agree with the Greek author, Aesop, who said simply in one of his fables that "no rule is better than cruel rule." If we look around at events in the world today, we find people everywhere apparently ready to challenge the proposition that rule by some minority is the best and also the only possible form of politics.

Clearly, the idea of participation by all has a great appeal. If any states exist in which there is complete separation of the people from their government, they are exceedingly rare. Even in the most tyrannical regimes of the modern world, the people have some minimal role in the survival of the government and at least a minimal influence upon public policy. It is probably true, in fact, that no modern government can exist without this minimum consent of the people, at least as expressed in the absence of organized, continuous majority opposition to that government. Determined and sustained hostility from the people would topple the rulers of any state, as the Shah of Iran, Somoza in Nicaragua, and the Greek colonels discovered. In this sense, governments everywhere must consult the people to some degree, or at least appear to do so. If they cannot gain active support, they must at least avoid open hostility. They may do this by giving the people certain things they want, or by persuading them that what they are getting is what they want. Governments may encourage solidarity by creating hatred or fear of some group, internal or external. Modern governments, even the poorest, have techniques of propagandizing their views and manipulating the opinions of the public that were never dreamed of by even the most wealthy and powerful states of the past. They also have means of force available that would have astounded Confucius or Machiavelli or Moctezuma. But force and propaganda, without some minimum of service to and consultation with the people, is not enough to sustain a modern regime indefinitely. The compensations offered the people may be more apparent than real. They may be fraudulent. But they must be enough to check public hostility.

Therefore, in this minimal sense of consultation and public reward, every lasting community has some kind of community-wide political process or participatory rule. Even if the people fail to participate active-

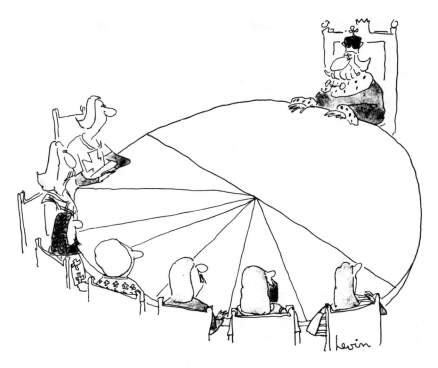

Drawing by Levin; © 1978 The New Yorker Magazine, Inc.

ly in the making of public policy, the fact that they accept the situation is of itself significant—although it is a lurking threat to the regime, for acceptance can melt in a single hot day.

In the simpler societies, many of which (such as the Bedouin of the Sinai) are now dying as they are forcibly incorporated by the nation-states of the world, there is often a very active community political process. Extensive politics can exist with little or no government as people of more complex societies think of it. Nevertheless, recognizable institutions of government, with very similar names and apparent functions, are found almost everywhere in the modern world. The most widespread of these is the nation-state, with its elaborate apparatus of hundreds of agencies and many thousands of staff members, comprising a formal structure that channels the informal operations of politics on a large scale. For several hundred years a process of state formation has been going on, by which the world has been divided into territorial segments, each with its own set of rulers and institutions. Some of these systems emerged on their own, sometimes by violence; others were imposed upon the people by outsiders. Virtually no part of the globe is outside the system of nation-states today. Formal political systems pervade the lives of us all. If we are to have any understanding of our own problems and prospects as individuals and as groups, we must understand these structures of government and how they affect the other decision-making processes of our communities; and we must understand how these communities affect each other.

In any human activity, the attitudes, values, prejudices, whims, backgrounds, and aspirations of individuals are important. *Personalities* shape government and politics as they shape all other human actions. It is just as necessary to understand the people who staff the institutions, or challenge them, as it is to understand the institutions—as structures—themselves. Structure helps to pattern outcomes; but those who occupy positions within these structures actually produce the results. Structures are changed or altered by the particular individuals who fill them, just as the individuals are themselves changed by the structures—expectations, values, opinions are shaped to some extent by the context in which we work.

Whether the community we are considering is large or small, almost certainly we will see competition at work as well as cooperation. Greed as well as charity runs the political machine. Some will participate in the community only to serve themselves, seeking to influence results for their immediate personal benefit even though it means the deprivation (or even destruction) of the community. We can easily recognize this selfishness in time of war, when some are willing to sell the safety of their country for wealth or position. It is often present in less dramatic forms, such as the manipulation of tax laws for personal gain, or the sale of defective materials to the government. For some, money is not important; power over others is all that matters. It is harder to see this, for such motives may be hidden behind a cloud of deception about "wanting only to serve." But the search for power is not inherently bad; good aims cannot be accomplished by the powerless.

And so we return to the problem of "what is politics" and ask the question that has been asked for thousands of years: "What is politics for?" The ancient Greeks concluded that through politics human beings were enabled to lead the good life. In contemporary times we tend to call this the public good, the public interest. Not everyone agrees about the content of the good life, or the public good, and this insures that there will be continuing disagreement about the best form of the political system as well.

For the Greeks, and for many other students and practitioners of politics, the good life, and the best political system, seemed possible only in an orderly, compact community in which the physical size of the territory, as well as the number of citizens, was limited to what would constitute a village today. Many writers who have described ideal societies, or utopias, have echoed this need for manageable size. Thomas Jefferson and many of his contemporaries had a similar view, although their ideal number of people and size of territory were somewhat larger. Such opinions reflected a basic belief that the purpose of human communities is to achieve individual human purpose and fulfillment through human interaction. The scale of many communities is now vast in both population and territory, and, as in past eras too, many thinkers and rulers care nothing for individuals and see some other vision of the good, in which superhuman ends—"the fatherland" or "the empire," for example—are served.

Political life, within and between communities, is to some extent a battle of these opposed conceptions of the good. But let us note that both are directed to the realization of values. Politics is not aimless; it seeks to make things better, or at least to prevent them from getting worse. It is not always easy to say what a people or a government considers "better" or "worse," particularly when the community is very large or is undergoing transition and uncertainty. Nonetheless, even when they are hidden, values always underlie the process of politics.

Human communities vary enormously; historians and social scientists around the world daily turn out thousands of pages describing these differences in time and place. Yet certain core problems and issues recur, and these form the background for this introductory book. We might reduce them to a two-part question: What are human rights, and how are they to be realized in human society? Looking a little more closely, what do we think that human beings, as human individuals and as members of human societies, are entitled to? All of us can suggest answers: the right to survival, to physical integrity, to equality, to possession and use of property—to the pursuit of happiness, as Jefferson put it. Then we must ask: What are their boundaries? Do some conflict with others? If so, which have priority? How do we organize our societies to promote these rights for each person and for the group? This in turn leads to questions that are clearly political. Is there to be a government? How is it to be organized? Who will operate it? What general powers should it have; what specific powers should its agents have? Who will carry out specific functions? How will conflicts between these functions, or those who perform them, be settled? What are the rights and obligations of the governed in their dealings with the government and with each other?

These issues, and others like them, are fundamental to politics, as they are to human society itself. Because political life deals with some of the most basic needs, relationships, and values, the Greeks assigned it the highest importance. They argued that politics was the basic or "architechtonic" science, superior to all others. We agree. Observing and participating in the political life of the community can be rewarding, exciting, even joyful. Economics is sometimes called the "dismal science." It often seems that politicians and political scientists are trying to win that label for their own field. Certainly there are many dreary, ugly, horrifying tales to be told by students of politics. But there is also the pleasure of seeing human beings attempting—often successfully—to rise above their cruel or selfish or lazy motives, individually and communally achieving richer and happier lives. And throughout history people have been drawn irresistibly into the political arena. Politics is part of the very essence of being human.

SELECTED READINGS

Almond, Gabriel, and G. Bingham Powell, Jr. *Comparative Politics: System, Process, and Policy.* 2nd ed. Boston: Little, Brown, 1978.*

Cohen, Ronald, and John Middleton, eds. *Comparative Political Systems.* Garden City, N.Y.: Natural History Press, 1967.*

Crick, Bernard. *Basic Forms of Government: A Sketch and a Model.* London: Macmillan, 1972.

_____. *In Defence of Politics.* rev. ed. Chicago: University of Chicago Press, 1972.*

Davies, James C. *Human Nature in Politics.* New York: Wiley, 1963, 1975.

Deutsch, Karl, et al. *The Nerves of Government.* rev. ed. New York: Free Press, 1966.*

Easton, David. *The Political System.* New York: Knopf, 1953.

Edelman, Murray. *Politics as Symbolic Action.* Chicago: Markham, 1971.

Karpat, Kemal H., ed. *Political and Social Thought in the Contemporary Middle East.* New York: Praeger, 1968.

Kornhauser, William. *The Politics of Mass Society.* New York: Free Press, 1959.

Lasswell, Harold D. *Politics: Who Gets What, When, How.* New York: Meridian Press, 1958.

Lindblom, Charles E. *Politics and Markets.* New York: Basic Books, 1977.

Spencer, Robert F., ed. *Religion and Change in Contemporary Asia.* Minneapolis: University of Minnesota Press, 1971.

Swartz, Marc J., Victor W. Turner, and Arthur Tuden, eds. *Political Anthropology.* Chicago: Aldine, 1966.

Watt, William Montgomery. *Islamic Political Thought.* Edinburgh: The University Press, 1968.

Weber, Max. *The Theory of Social and Economic Organization.* Trans. A. M. Henderson. Talcott Parsons, ed. New York: Free Press, 1964.

*Indicates a paperback edition is available.

SOME TOOLS FOR THE STUDENT

There are several useful books which the student of politics is advised to have at hand or know where to find in the library. If you become familiar with these, your understanding of politics and your ability to speak and write about it will be much greater and much easier.

Political References

Banks, Arthur S., ed. *Political Handbook of the World*. New York: McGraw-Hill. Yearly editions of this work are published.

Elliott, Florence. *A Dictionary of Politics*. 7th ed. Baltimore: Penguin, 1978.

Frank, Charles R., Jr., and Richard C. Webb, eds. *Income Distribution and Growth in the Less-Developed Countries*. Washington, D.C.: Brookings, 1977.*

Greenstein, F. I., and Nelson W. Polsby. *Handbook of Political Science*. Reading, Mass.: Addison and Wesley, 1975.

Mackie, Thomas T., and Richard Rose. *The International Almanac of Electoral History*. New York: Free Press, 1974.

Morrison, Donald, et al. *Black Africa: A Comparative Handbook*. New York: Free Press, 1972.

Plano, Jack C., and Milton Greenberg. *The American Political Dictionary*. 5th ed. New York: Holt, Rinehart and Winston, 1978.*

The Statesman's Yearbook, 1978-1979. New York: St. Martin's, 1978.

Taylor, Charles Lewis, and Michael C. Hudson. *World Handbook of Political and Social Indicators*. 2nd ed. New Haven: Yale University Press, 1972.*

General References

A world atlas—Rand McNally's, Webster's, or any other good one—will help you locate the nations you read about and become familiar with their relationship to each other. Second, a good desk encyclopedia, such as the *New Columbia Encyclopedia*, will answer many questions about the details of world political history. A fact handbook such as *World Facts and Figures*, by Victor Showers (New York: Wiley-Interscience, 1978), is also useful. Most countries also have at least one annual factbook, usually published by the government, a major newspaper, or a private firm. Find out about these, and about those published by the United Nations and other international organizations.

2

The Nature of Communities

The most universal quality is diversity.
                    —*Michel de Montaigne*

I am a citizen, not of Athens or Greece, but of the
world.
                    —*Socrates*

Who is here so vile that will not love his country?
                    —*William Shakespeare*

Each human being is a unique entity. The science of genetics has confirmed what most philosophers have long argued, that no individual person is an exact duplicate of any other in physical terms, and that even if this near-impossibility should occur, the divergent, particular experiences of each individual would begin at birth to differentiate such identical persons. At the same time we recognize in philosophy and in science that we are not only individuals, and we measure ourselves by our similarities to others. From the moment of birth we form a close relationship with at least one other person and most of us will spend our lives in association with many others, sometimes in amity, sometimes in hostility.

Friendships are one such affiliation: unpredictable, often accidental bondings of two or three people, in linkages that are peculiar to those particular individuals and which may end only with their deaths. Some few, such as the biblical David and Jonathan, may become so famous that they survive for centuries in history and literature. On occasion such relationships may turn into deep hatred through the real or imagined betrayal or rejection by one friend of another; powerful emotions may cause other friends or families to ally or feud as a consequence.

Most of our affiliations are more extensive and more permanent, not dependent upon the life span of any single member of the group. These affiliations are the communities that are the focus of this study. They are sometimes the subject of emotions as powerful as those involved in love and friendship. If friends or lovers (or enemies) meet across rather than within these groups, and there are important taboos against such contacts, great personal and communal turmoil may ensue. Individuals sometimes ignore or transcend condemnation by the community, as Shakespeare's Romeo and Juliet did, but if the group associations are valued, the dilemmas and costs are real. The individuals will have to reorient their conceptions of themselves, even if they are not entirely ostracized. Communities help shape our perceptions of ourselves and of others. They in turn are created and shaped by the multiple perceptions and associations of their members as these individuals adjust to changing physical and social space. From these perceptions emerges a "common thing," a "community," which seems to take on a life of its own.

The natural world presents us with many examples of groups or bonding; wolves and whales and chimpanzees all form such clusters, and humans recognize them by special names—pack, school, troop, band. In that sense we do not differ from other animals; but in a more fundamental way, human groups are unique. The distinction is based upon speech, the means by which human beings communicate with each other and record that communication, so that experience and ideas can be shared and accumulated. To be human is to speak; and speech is social behavior. (Speech, to be meaningful, requires more than one person.) We form some groups through the process of filling essential biological needs—food, shelter, reproduction—but we enrich these associations, and create others that are entirely nonbiological, by our infinitely variable perspectives, shared through language and speech. We apply those special human capacities to the groups themselves, naming them—Americans, Igbos, Muslims—and we deck ourselves with symbols or totems—flags, songs, perhaps even animals—eagles, bears, lions, whose qualities we hope we match. Thus to be human is to be a unique self and yet not to be self-sufficient, for we must speak, and share, with others.

The process of establishing, maintaining, and changing communities, which we call the political process, is central to human life. As Aristotle pointed out thousands of years ago, man is a political animal. The Greeks believed that individual potential was incompletely realized if participation in the political life of the community was denied. Much of world history reflects a conscious or unconscious agreement, as people have fought and died to expand the right of participation for themselves and for others.

Defining Identity: Places and People

Can Themba, a South African writer, expressed the sense of place or home well in "Requiem for Sophiatown":

> Somewhere here, and among a thousand more individualistic things, is the magic of Sophiatown. It is different and itself. You don't just find your place here, you make it and you find yourself.

While groups are relationships of people, they often have a specific physical setting. People living in a particular space, inhabiting a particular kind of territory, make up one important kind of community. "Mountain people" have long seen themselves as different from "lowlanders." Another obvious example is island peoples, bound together by their common life on a miniature continent. Physical surroundings impose certain requirements on a group's way of life. Desert dwellers, for example, must adopt food and clothing very different from those of people who live in tropical rain forests. When groups living in different kinds of territory become aware of each other, the variations based on these differences of terrain will form part of their definition of themselves.

The importance of nature in human communities goes beyond these distinctions. The majority of the world's people live in territorially defined groups and also in a complex set of such groups, ranging in size from a village or neighborhood to a very large region such as North America, sub-Saharan Africa, or Eastern Europe. Part of the attraction that pulls these clumps of people together is a common relationship to their terrain, which may be manmade as well as natural, cities or sections of cities—such as Soho or London, the Left Bank, or Paris itself. This may be the place where one was born or it may be chosen later as one moves from country to city or migrates to other parts of the world. We can observe these attachments in our own and others' lives and yet be unable to explain any particular one. Indeed, we may be quite unable to understand why anyone should love a crowded, dirty section of Lagos, a stretch of unbroken prairie in Kansas, or a frozen city in the Arctic Circle. Yet these attachments remain and are strong enough to be called love—love for a country, an isolated oasis town, a city square. This is perhaps one of the most powerful elements in human history. (The word "human" has the same root as the word "humus" or earth.) It plays a very large role in political life because it shapes people's definitions of themselves and their relations to others and also focuses their daily concerns on what happens in this particular special place. Governments that try to destroy such spaces—perhaps for objectively "good" reasons such as sanitation needs—often find themselves in trouble. Such intrusions, to the regime's surprise, may be met with much wider resistance than national edicts against, for example, political activity. Destruction of one group's place by another has been historically regarded as particularly cruel, from the razing of Carthage to the leveling of European cities and the atomic bombing of Japanese ones during World War II. The same is true of the "slum clearance" and "urban renewal" programs that destroy neighborhoods today.

Some writers have called these attachments to place the "territorial imperative." Others find this term unacceptable because it implies that such behavior represents a kind of instinct. But few thoughtful people deny that a relationship to territory is a very powerful element in human associations, even when the group in question is nomadic, constantly shifting its position on the land. We recognize this in our perception of refugees and displaced peoples as having been dispossessed of something very important—and we need only think of the claims and counterclaims of Israelis and Palestinians to realize the force of the relationship to land and to particular land.

Defining Identity: Behavior and Belief

In the creation of extended families, bands, clans, or "nations," the territorial imperative—which is certainly social and economic, whether instinctive, or not—is reinforced by other characteristics which both unify and divide peoples. Distinct languages develop and intensify the communality of those speaking the same or similar tongues. The boundaries of group identity become more explicit as different gods, beliefs, and customs emerge. An important dimension of these developments is the idea of "strangers" to identify those whose speech, appearance, or religious practices vary from those of the group. Many of the names that human societies give themselves literally mean "we, the people." Outsiders are some different order of being, "strange," "foreign," and their inferiority is often implied by the words "barbarian," "alien," "vandal."

The development of communal bonds is further intensified by rites and rituals that mark individual entrance into the group as a full member (perhaps on reaching adulthood), or reaffirm individual loyalty, or prepare the members for defense of the group—pledges of allegiance, national anthems, creeds, flags. Some of these rites refer specifically to biological survival and enhancement. The universal taboo against incest is thought to have evolved as a defense against genetic deterioration, and it also serves to limit conflict and competition within the group. All groups

© 1974 Playboy

"The people are not in a mood to be trifled with, your Majesty. I really think you'd better go out there and sing 'Melancholy Baby.'"

attempt to channel sexual contacts and family structures to promote cohesion, continuity, and survival, if not expansion, of the group.

These intricate processes of "belonging" are the source of much turmoil as well as harmony. Contemporary feminist concerns about sex roles and their biological and cultural antecedents are based in the conflicts that emerge as historical patterns of identity and roles are challenged by new perceptions of social status and individual fulfillment in response to economic, social, and technological development. The roles and statuses assigned to various age groups are now being tested in similar ways.

The differentiation of individuals into collective or communal entities is not a simple linear process. Communities—or in the broadest sense, civilizations—may disintegrate, leaving only vast earthworks, ruined cities, or pyramids as signs of their passage. Disease or conquest may destroy the basis of community. Jealousies and hatreds, inflamed by competition for land or gold or souls, may signal the physical destruction of one group—and perhaps its land and dwellings—by another. The demand for more physical space or the presumption of cultural or national superiority may provide an excuse for one group to displace or annihilate another. Societies as different as the Norsemen, the Apaches, and the Prussians have seen war and destruction as means of purifying and improving the community. Within these processes of change, absorption, destruction, and expansion, identities shift or are reinterpreted as a result of war or slavery or independence from colonial rule. Gold Coast Africans became black Americans. Nigeria, Guinea, and Indonesia emerged in the sunset of the British, French, and Japanese empires.

Yet what remains with unique and striking clarity is the universal impulse for community; the apparent need for external identities that distinguish us as groups and as individuals defined by groups. The title of Edward Everett Hale's famous nineteenth-century story, "The Man Without a Country," is a telling metaphor for those who cannot find the security and comfort of shared experiences and the possibility of immortality through a collective memory. In our time, belonging to a nation-state has become an even more critical element of individual security. "Stateless" or "dispossessed" persons are a suffering class, literally helpless without a badge of national identity. The threat of such dispossession is a powerful sanction against which the individual has few defenses. The Supreme Court of the United States has recognized this in holding such punishment to extremely limited use, and internationally there are agreements, not yet fully honored, that the right to a nationality is basic to many other rights.

Change and Stability in Defining Communities

Although the specifics vary, a pattern of change can be seen throughout history, continually disrupting the search for a meaningful, settled identity. The evolution of the species from its minimal social groups—bands of hunters, clusters of nomadic herders or gatherers, barely more than large families—to the nation-states of the nineteenth and twentieth centuries has been influenced by profound developments in the external world, especially the discoveries of science and their application through technology: airplanes, microscopes, cotton gins, and generators. These things are products of change and they symbolize its direction and consequences. Traditional identities are challenged when time and space become relative rather than absolute influences. Airplanes and steamships bring change as they transport South Vietnamese refugees to Ohio and Texas. The electronic revolution provided the Beatles a worldwide audience, creating what Marshall McLuhan called "the global village."

Such events make us realize that almost any community's stability is precarious. Westernized Iran collapsed apparently overnight, forcibly replaced by a militant Islamic revolution, which in turn found itself challenged by tumultuous internal dissent. In the Arab world traditional conservative kingdoms coexist with the regimes of Marxist colonels. Meanwhile a Communist regime in China has embraced the Protestant ethic and the profit motive in order to catalyze modernization.

What explains these erosions or redefinitions of communal continuity? In part, the simple fact of contact; the Industrial Revolution and the development of a global economic system have changed the outer limits of group coherence. Such forces as religion and ethnicity create and sustain communities, but exposure to a broader experience often threatens them. Family gods are challenged by the symbols and power of new theologies, secular or religious. This is not a new phenomenon. In Old Testament times monotheism overthrew a host of idols, and the Greek playwright Sophocles chronicled for us Antigone's pain in her dilemma of allegiance to the gods of family or to the authority of the king. Similarly, the power of nationalism deflects attachment to region or clan toward identification with the larger image of the country. Predictable results occur when the exotic foreigner is master in a strange land. The impulse to conserve, to retain the old identity, is often seduced by curiosity about the larger world and by the spell of progress.

The Rise of Nations and States

How do modern states arise, and how do they sustain themselves? Julius Nyerere, president of Tanzania, has stressed the importance of nationhood:

> If the present states of Africa are not to disintegrate, it is essential that deliberate steps be taken to foster a feeling of nationhood.

Dean Inge, on the other hand, views the idea of nationhood with cynicism:

> A nation is a society united by a delusion about its ancestry and by common hatred of its neighbors.

Human history shows an overall pattern of the development of increasingly complex and heterogeneous human organizations. With each stage in this development there is a period of consolidation and realignment of loyalties. In this sense the world changes as boundaries shift and "new" names (often ancient ones) are used to describe "new" places. When Africa was the shared economic preserve of European powers, it was carved into territories with names and boundaries meaningful only to cartographers. Indigenous perceptions rarely coincided with the spheres of influence decided upon at the Congress of Berlin (1884–1885). In the Middle East and Asia similar events took place. The colonial administrations of the French, Dutch, and British created new political and economic entities: Ivory Coast, Indonesia, Malaya. Within this shifting and often warring context, relationships both persevered and changed. New loyalties and outlooks struggled with older ones; colonial rule introduced disturbing new influences—railways, primary schools, radios. New literatures and languages were imposed upon the local cultures. As French and English became the world's languages, movements for autonomy arose within these colonial empires and westernized elites often led the struggle to restore local control. In the late nineteenth century European empires began to feel the blows of powerful new demands for communal separation and autonomy, together called *nationalism*.

Nationalism in its nineteenth-century manifestation was essentially an effort to give expression to preexisting communal ties (language, literature, common heroes or enemies, music, food), the trappings of a people's cultural history. It demanded and often got a state as the political recognition of the people. There are similar peoples in twentieth-century situations (such as the Igbo of Nigeria and the Lunda of south-central Africa) who are certainly as large as the nineteenth-century groups and as firmly conscious of themselves, although this to some extent is a new identity promoted by the confrontation during colonialism with other indigenous groups and with the European ruler. However, contemporary nationalism in those areas is not really concerned with these identities, which often overlap the new state boundaries. (See maps on pp. 20–21 and 24–25 for current national boundaries.) It is in a curious sense nineteenth-century nationalism turned upside down. The colonial period drew the lines and set the mechanisms of the state in motion; now the elites in these states are attempting to create nations to fit them, combin-

NORTHERN HEMISPHERE

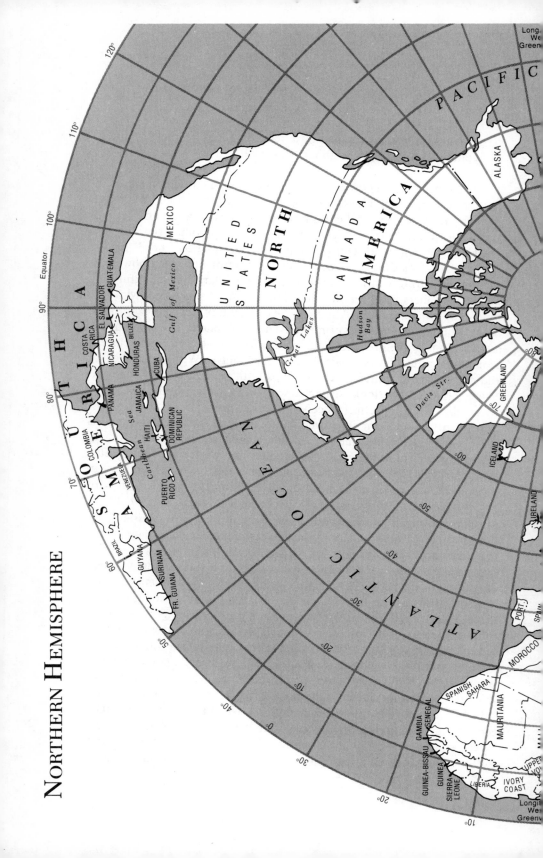

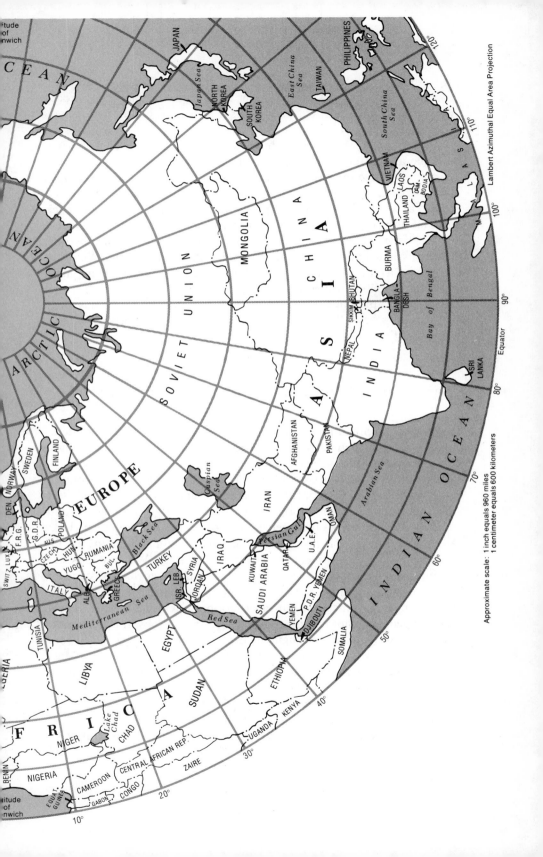

Approximate scale: 1 inch equals 960 miles
1 centimeter equals 600 kilometers

Lambert Azimuthal Equal Area Projection

ing reluctant peoples into poorly defined networks. The new leaders are constrained to take this course rather than begin the dangerous process of altering boundaries. As Nyerere puts it, they must build a nation and a state simultaneously.

Throughout this intricate process, the propensity to conserve is as notable and striking as the persistence of change. And herein lies the paradox. We see the inexorable movement toward larger, more complex social organizations in the creation of "Nigerians" out of Igbos and Yorubas, as we saw it in the making of "Americans" from a polyglot background of nearly all the world's populations. We marvel at the capacity of Alsatians to change national identities as the fortunes of war between Germany and France produced different winners and losers. Yet Alsatians have a cultural tenacity that retains qualities uniquely theirs, along with the indelible influences of both their historical masters. In North America the province of Quebec is a good example, and many other communities have that same tenacity, despite their incorporation into larger entities.

Perception and Choice in the Formation of Identities

Beyond the minimal grounding in physical reality and externally determined reality, the shaping of identities is as free and as wide-ranging as the human mind and will can make it. These identities form and re-form as part of a vast network of other identities that are also being continuously re-created and reconfirmed. As communal awarenesses intersect, the opportunities or imperatives to reaffirm, renew, or re-form communities within and across their perceptual boundaries are presented. There are no absolutes in this process. No elements of human bonding are immutable, fixed for all time as the center of identity. We may look at a communal sense of identity from outside and discover that there are apparent utilitarian purposes to it—the emphasis changes as the source of jobs changes, for instance. But this is not preordained either. If the values of a people do not fit with competition for such jobs, if new forms of education are culturally repugnant, then they will not necessarily compete for the new types of employment by reshaping their identity. Much is accidental. External circumstances bring new forms of communications, immigrants, tools, skills, war, but people respond to these in different ways. Out of a huge array of attributes, some are selected for emphasis and others ignored. There is not always any "rhyme or reason" to the process; the governing response may be to emotional, "nonrational" needs. For outsiders to judge is very difficult because we are by definition not sharing the experiences that lead to this particular sense of identity. What we can comment about from outside is the impact that certain kinds of identity have, or have had, as compared with others. An emphasis on race or other ethnic characteristics, rather than on shared territory or occupation, brings different allegiances, perhaps different tactics and styles of political behavior.

Consider, for example, what might be the bases of communal identity in a West African town when the first European explorer arrives. The traveler might describe it as a small village inhabited by people of pagan beliefs, sharing many distinctive physical characteristics, speaking a dialect of the southeastern Bantu group and living in a semitropical forest in the style of nonmechanized farmers. The community itself knows nothing of this; it cannot think of itself as pagan or animist because it has not encountered other religions, nor is the concept "villager" meaningful when there are no cities to be seen. The similarities of its language to the one spoken next door are less obvious than the differences; no one in the village has ever heard the markedly different languages farther west, much less those of Europe. The measures of race are similarly meaningless. Exactly how this group perceived itself in this past time we cannot now know, for its self-perceptions began to change upon the traveler's arrival, and it is impossible to restore or even fully remember the old bases of identity.

Identity is a mental construct. Color of skin, language, or other features that seem absolutely obvious to an outsider, will not form part of this identity if they are not part of the community's awareness of itself. But if it is confronted by outsiders who emphasize these differences, self-awareness may come to include these features in reaction. White settlers who emphasized skin color in the structure of colonial African society heightened African racial consciousness. Where Asians were also part of African colonialism, racial identity was sharpened among all three races. Much the same thing occurs in the American Southwest, where much of the Mexican-American population identifies itself with the Anglos and sees black Americans as utterly different. At the same time many in the Anglo community view themselves as having little in common with the Mexican-Americans, generally classing brown with black (except perhaps for one or two wealthy, well-educated friends who happen to have Spanish names). Mexican-Americans themselves have been regarded as a separate and sometimes inferior people by the Mexicans. While Mexican-Americans have increasingly emphasized their Mexican heritage in recent years, they have also been uneasily aware of the contempt from across the border. If it should become convenient for Mexico to develop linkages with these Spanish-speaking Americans, however, these identities might be reshaped.

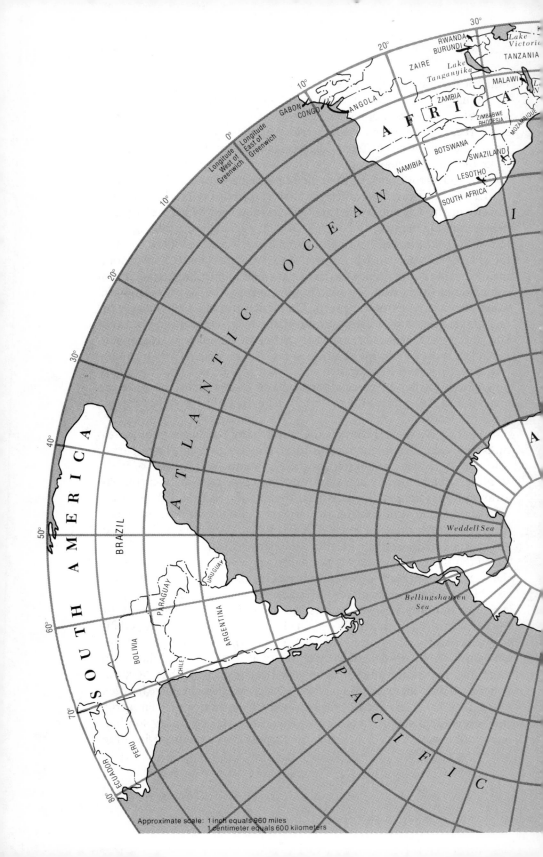

Approximate scale: 1 inch equals 960 miles
1 centimeter equals 600 kilometers

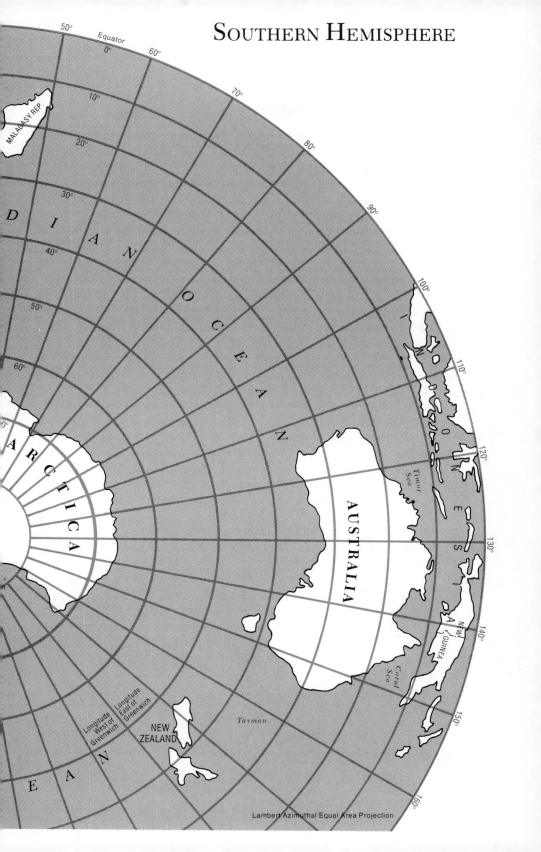

SOUTHERN HEMISPHERE

City, Factory, and Community

In the relatively recent past, two factors have combined to produce profound changes in the patterns of communal life: the "invention" of the factory system, or industrialization; and the increased urbanization of society. We see this in its most advanced form in the so-called developed nations. The rise of industrial towns, and ultimately nations, meant a severe strain on the social and economic relationships that characterized feudal Europe. The magnetic attraction of labor toward factories and the accumulation of capital in cities combined to produce a decline in traditional loyalties and identities. The clannishness of villages and small towns was subverted by the open, less personal character of the city. Intimacy in social relationships declined as the division of labor led to more specialized and formal contacts. Milk and bread and meat were provided by unknown deliverymen and sold across anonymous counters. The functional integrity of the family was challenged as family members found their fortunes without each other, in school, office, or factory. Small-town familiarity was replaced by bureaucratic neutrality. The scope of human contact was expanded but qualitatively limited. We know more people but we know only that side of them which is related to our specific needs.

The development of modern cities, stimulated and nourished by an expanding technology, pulled people away from each other and away from themselves as well. The sociologist Emile Durkheim and the psychologist Sigmund Freud both noted this from their different perspectives, and Karl Marx commented on this paradox of industrialism:

> The mutual and universal dependence of individuals who remain indifferent to one another constitutes the social network that binds them together.

Our vocabulary is enriched by their ideas of anomie and alienation, conditions of the mind that reflect the human need for dependable relationships, for limits and boundaries, which help provide a sense of selfhood. The movement to cities is uprooting. Familiar habits and relationships disappear, and the new ones are often less satisfying and more difficult to sustain.

At the same time, however, this uprooting can be a liberation. The narrow, prying parochialism of the town or village is replaced by the anonymity and freedom of the city. Political and economic alternatives appear, and individuals previously trapped by caste or racial prejudices sometimes encounter a more open, rational environment. Not only have people changed residence, the style of existence and the intellectual concept of life has changed. But for some, as Erich Fromm argues, this new freedom requires an "escape from freedom." There is a need to reimpose narrow, authoritarian limits that will give some clear, externally defined sense of purpose and identity.

In many areas of the world, organizations and associations representing old identities appear, providing a link between past and present and cushioning the shock for many who perceive ethnic or national differences for the first time. These "urban villagers" are the immigrants of the world, often trapped in the gray or twilight zone between rural ways and the rapid tempo of the city. New groups or communities develop, such as labor guilds or professional associations. The Japanese, for example, have modeled their new social and economic institutions on the older "organic" family-based structures. The spatial or territorial component is reinforced in the new environment, as ethnic or religious groups find themselves residents of the same neighborhood, either by choice or because of racial or ethnic discrimination.

All these instances could be viewed as destructive of community, but that view would be a static one. Along with cities and industrialization come opportunities for individual growth. Urban dwellers can unite to demand public education and improved health care more easily than rural people. Technological developments provide more occupational choices and these can lead to improvements in living standards. In many cases immigration to the city is an economic calculation; with luck, the newcomer can send money to relatives who remain in the smaller towns and villages. This is a worldwide phenomenon, contributing to both solidarity and disruption as family separations often become permanent and new relationships develop.

From another perspective, as Marx indicated, there is also political and economic exploitation of one group by another and the development of another order of identities—proletariat, bourgeoisie, capitalists, and communists. The industrialized world is a world of contradictions: the slums and tenements of industrial workers coexist uneasily with the conspicuously opulent neighborhoods of their employers.

In the midst of these changes, there is concern about the spiritual and ethical direction of individuals and societies. Secularism developed as the explanatory power of science successfully competed with traditional theology. In our time the existential questions of Camus challenge the certainties of St. Paul, while competition continues between capitalism and communism for intellectual and territorial hegemony.

The pattern of change is an intricate one, in which the breakdown of old community form and content overlaps the development of the new. New myths dispel old ones, and science continually forces reexamination and reconsideration of accepted truths. The period between the rejection of the old and the acceptance of the new is always one of turmoil and often violence. Martin Luther challenged the orthodoxy of Rome and families fled their ancestral places as theological disputes led to intracommunal warfare. Loyal Frenchmen became refugee Huguenots and the Puritan dissenters in England set sail for the New World. Their descendants in the New World fought several revolutionary wars as they redefined their relationships to those left behind. The French, Russian, and Chinese revolutions were each based on new ideals about power and equality.

Human existence is simultaneously static and changing, and its changes, at least over the short term of a human life span, are not necessarily forward or progressive. A new Dark Age appeared in the 1930s under Hitler and other totalitarian rulers, when accumulated grievances and some fundamental perversion of the human spirit led to mass murder by modern methods. Are the causes of such inhumanity natural? Is it capitalism or materialism or Fascism or Stalinism that converts friends into enemies, and families as well as nations into warring factions? The answer is both yes and no. Yes, in that the bases of communal integrity are in some ways inherently fragile and a collective sense of revenge or anger can lead to excesses, even barbarism. The basis for unity is all too often a shared enemy. No, in that there appears to be a human impulse to construct collective limitations and establish rules of conduct. Even in warfare the use of certain weapons is considered inhumane. While the League of Nations and the UN have not made the world "safe for democracy," the shared, continuing effort makes an important point.

Communities in Contemporary Politics: Affirmation of the Old, Creation of the New

One of the most interesting dimensions of the contemporary era is the formation of pluralistic nation-states. Many countries throughout the world are composed of many separate and distinct communities. Politics in these settings—Africa, Asia, North America—is a balancing act that requires respect for communal integrity combined with concern for the coherence of the whole. In recent years a number of these "experiments" have failed. The compromise between Christians and Moslems in Lebanon has disintegrated, the détente between the Greek and Turkish Cypriots is extremely fragile, and the Kurds and Baluchis have tried to detach themselves from the dominant Farsi (Persian) rule in Iran. In Belgium the union between Flemish and Walloons is under great stress, and in Spain the Basques pose a militant threat to traditional Castilean domination. In the United States, the ambiguous position of the "black community" poses a harsh intellectual and political question: What is the price of membership in a national community? What is the effect on one's self and collective identity when the tug of integration threatens a loss of heritage?

The fundamental issue is the meaning of identity, what we think about ourselves and how others think about us. How we coexist with others and the arrangements we make for that coexistence are important dimensions of contemporary politics. In all these examples, human communities are dissatisfied with the arrangements for their coexistence.

Identity is tied to the way we think about ourselves in spatial, material, and psychological terms. In the nation-states of today, and in areas where they are forming, land and language are important dimensions of multicommunal coexistence. In the United States the complexity of the land aspect is easily seen in American Indian history. Land is an integral part of the Indians' sense of identity. It is not simply a field to be plowed or a mountain to be climbed, but a dimension of the Indians' being and self-perception. To be deprived of ancestral lands is not only a physical and economic loss but a distortion of a way of life, a deprivation of identity.

In a variety of settings and a variety of ways, a similar conflict exists for many peoples. Modern industrial societies create new notions of land. We speak of land use and planning. Municipalities zone and control the patterns of work and living spaces. Industrial parks are reserved. In the countryside there are tensions between those who want to farm the land or preserve it as it is and those who want to exploit it for industrial or commercial reasons. This too is a dimension of identity, for we define ourselves in our mind's eye and others define us by perceptions of where we live and what we do. The demands of "progress" do not always sit well with our perceptions about how we wish to live; in other words, how we might think about our relationship to nature and, ultimately, ourselves.

The language we speak, how we communicate with others, enters this picture as well. The issue may be, as in France, an effort to maintain the purity of the language, in hopes of keeping a national identity intact. Or it may be the problem of Spanish speakers in Manhattan, Los Angeles, or Houston, Texas. Should Spanish be a first or second language in public education? Should the claim for Black English as a separate language be dismissed as the demand of a radical few? Throughout the world questions like these are posed daily. All have to do with the relationship of people to each other and the claims of some for hegemony and dominance over others in political, economic, and cultural life. The age-old enmity between Vietnamese and Chinese, or between Nilotic and

Bantu peoples in East Africa, or French and Germans in Europe are other instances of this universal problem.

As communities undergo external contacts, new perceptions arise. For example, differences in skin color lead to racial theories, rarely benign and usually, as in the antebellum American South and present-day South Africa, designed to justify the privileges of the few. Identity, in this context, is a pretext for oppression. Blackness, redness, brownness are objects of derision and exploitation as color joins class, religion, or caste as the basis for intercommunal strife.

On a worldwide scale, the paramount human goal is a way in which all human interactions may be harmoniously conducted, enriching rather than enslaving the lives of individuals and groups. In the most basic sense we are looking for political solutions to problems that result from the differences in the human species. Vastly different conceptions of life's meanings and its rewards exist among the billions of human beings who inhabit this planet. Some of us use and demand more of its resources than others. A few strive to create the conditions in which these conflicts need not end in war and destruction. Since the aim is a system of human interaction that creates the possibility of intercommunal harmony, the solutions must be as varied and changing as the specific troubles. What they will share is a common context. The realization of a wider, even global human community through the interaction of all the smaller groups that humans create lies in the realm of the political, the ideas and institutions we employ to govern ourselves.

SELECTED READINGS

Ake, Claude. *A Theory of Political Integration.* Homewood, Ill.: Dorsey Press, 1967.

Barth, Fredrik. *Ethnic Groups and Boundaries: The Social Organization of Cultural Difference.* Boston: Little, Brown, 1969.

Batten, Thomas R. *Communities and Their Development.* New York: Oxford University Press, 1957.*

Bendix, Richard. *Nation Building and Citizenship: Studies of Our Changing Social Order.* Garden City, N.Y.: Doubleday, 1969.*

Das Gupta, Jyotirindra. *Language Conflict and National Development.* Berkeley: University of California Press, 1970.

Deutsch, Karl W. *Nationalism and Social Communication.* New York: Wiley, 1953.

*Indicates a paperback version is available.

_____, and William J. Foltz, eds. *Nation-Building*. New York: Atherton, 1963.* Western and Third World studies.

Dinnerstein, Leonard, Roger L. Nichols, and David M. Reimers. *Natives and Strangers: Ethnic Groups and the Building of America*. New York: Oxford University Press, 1979.

Durkheim, Emile. *Sociology and Philosophy*. Glencoe, Ill.: Free Press, 1953.

Enloe, Cynthia H. *Ethnic Conflict and Political Development*. Boston: Little, Brown, 1973.* Political and social functions of ethnicity; its variability.

Foster, George M. *Culture and Conquest*. Chicago: Quadrangle, 1967. Latin American studies.

Freud, Sigmund. *Civilization and Its Discontents*. London: Hogarth Press, 1955.

Fromm, Erich. *Escape from Freedom*. New York: Holt, Rinehart and Winston, 1963.*

_____. *The Sane Society*. New York: Holt, Rinehart and Winston, 1955.*

Hartz, Louis. *The Founding of New Societies: Studies in the History of the United States, Latin America, South Africa, Canada, and Australia*. New York: Harcourt, Brace and World, 1964. An examination of communities that are "fragments" of the Old World.

Homans, George C. *The Human Group*. New York: Harcourt, Brace and World, 1950.

Isaacs, Harold. *Idols of the Tribe*. New York: Harper & Row, 1975.

Kedourie, Elie. *Nationalism*. London: Hutchinson, 1960.

Kotler, Milton. *Neighborhood Government: The Local Foundations of Political Life*. Indianapolis: Bobbs-Merrill, 1969.

Kuper, Leo, and M. G. Smith, eds. *Pluralism in Africa*. Berkeley: University of California Press, 1969.*

Lasch, Christopher. *Haven in a Heartless World: The Family Besieged*. New York: Basic Books, 1977.

Link, Werner, and Werner J. Feld, eds. *The New Nationalism*. New York: Pergamon, 1979.

Marx, Karl. *Early Writings*. Trans. and ed. by T. B. Bottomore. New York: McGraw-Hill, 1964.

Mazrui, Ali A. *Cultural Engineering and Nation-Building in East Africa*. Evanston, Ill.: Northwestern University Press, 1973.

Nisbet, Robert. *The Quest for Community*. New York: Oxford University Press, 1962.*

Novak, Michael. *The Rise of the Unmeltable Ethnics*. New York: Macmillan, 1971.

Olorunsola, Victor A., ed. *The Politics of Cultural Sub-Nationalism*. Garden City, N.Y.: Doubleday, 1972.*

Seton-Watson, Hugh. *Nations and States*. Boulder, Colo.: Westview Press, 1977.

Shafer, Boyd C. *Faces of Nationalism*. New York: Harper & Row, 1971.

Smock, David R., and Kwamena Bentsi-Enchill, eds. *The Search for National Integration in Africa*. New York: Free Press, 1976.

Tilly, Charles, ed. *The Formation of National States in Western Europe.* Princeton: Princeton University Press, 1975.*

Tilman, Robert O. *Communalism and the Political Process.* Boston: Houghton Mifflin, 1967.

_____, ed. *Man, State and Society in Southeast Asia.* New York: Praeger, 1969.

van den Berghe, Pierre. *Race and Ethnicity.* New York: Basic Books, 1970.

Wheeler, Thomas C., ed. *The Immigrant Experience.* Baltimore: Penguin, 1972.*

Young, M. Crawford. *The Politics of Cultural Pluralism.* Madison: University of Wisconsin Press, 1976. Comprehensive study of community and identity and their political roles.

3

Political Culture and Socialization

Nothing changes more constantly than the past;
for the past that influences our lives does not
consist of what actually happened but of what
men believe happened.
> —*Gerald White Johnson*

Men will sooner surrender their rights than their
customs.
> —*Moritz Guedemann*

We have spoken of communities and their identity and cohesion in terms of broad patterns. These patterns form what is generally called *culture*, the way of life of a community. Culture is a complex of beliefs and behaviors that the community expresses in all its affairs. When the community acts politically, we may speak of this as the *polity*. The aspects of culture that shape the polity we designate as the *political culture*. This is the aggregate of beliefs, values, and feelings that condition the way politics is conducted, giving a distinctive character to a particular polity. A community's political culture is commonly defined by focusing upon *attitudes*, following the definitions used by Lucian Pye and Sidney Verba, and Gabriel Almond and G. Bingham Powell, Jr., in their classic books on politics. In a sense this is a narrow focus, but attitudes express themselves in behavior. They shape the institutions, create customs or norms, and appear in the symbols that help to identify a polity, such as its flag or anthem. When we discuss the establishment, maintenance, and character of political cultures in the sections that follow, it is important to remember these connections to the total political process. A community's political culture is important, for it is the key both to the continued survival and cohesion of the community and to what kind of community it is and how it changes.

The Community Setting and the Individual

A number of *situational factors* help to shape a political culture. Individuals and groups are influenced by the historical context as they perceive it. A group will have a set of general values. For example, is status important? Is nonviolence preferred? Its technological capacity—the presence or absence of computers, mechanized farming, mass production—will affect how it perceives the world and what it therefore thinks is possible in the community. The size, physical shape, and location (how large is the whole community? how great an area, of what kind, does it inhabit? what are its neighbors like?) will obviously set certain limits.

We can illustrate the impact of situational variables on the political culture by considering the tremendous changes in political life that began when Johann Gutenberg invented movable type in the fifteenth century. Movable type made the mass production and mass distribution of books possible, and in turn mass literacy began to spread. These changes, flowing from what is at first glance just an alteration in technology, shattered the existing religious and political authority in Europe, and ushered in the age of the individual. Ideas of contracts, rights of participation, limited authority, even justified rebellion against tyranny, came to be accepted norms in many political cultures. The reverberations of this explosive change in printing technology are still being felt. Available reading material is now in fact a situational variable for communities everywhere. This century's revolution in communication—electronic transmission and telecommunications—is a simiiarly dramatic shift in technology. This second revolution both supports and counteracts the effects of the printing revolution, as demagogues and dictators rise to power through the use of mass media. No political culture today is entirely free of the influence of these two great technologies.

The people who make up a community determine what form the polity actually takes within their environmental freedoms and constraints. Each individual has a complex set of ideas, feelings, attitudes, perceptions, motives, needs, skills, and knowledge. These are sometimes spoken of as three basic groups of variables: *cognitive, affective*, and *evaluative*. Cognitive aspects are knowledge and skills. These include erroneous ideas and untrue information. Inaccurate beliefs can be as powerful a force in human affairs as accurate ones. Affective variables comprise feelings—emotions, loyalties, "the things of the heart." They include love of country and attachment to a leader. Evaluative variables are judgments, assessments, values, and priorities: a sense that the UN or the Organization of African Unity is a good organization, or that control of nuclear weapons is the first order of world business. In transitional societies a great many of these personal factors may be undergoing rapid transformation, but in any community the unique aspects of individual human behavior will make the overall patterns somewhat unpredictable. Nonetheless, we can discern certain regularities in the way personal variables are shaped by the polity, which helps to both explain and predict the behavior of individuals and the community.

Political Socialization

"Society attacks early when the individual is helpless," the controversial sociologist B. F. Skinner wrote, suggesting a conflictual relationship between the whole and its constituent parts. Anthropologist Ruth Benedict, however, offers a different perspective:

> The problem of the individual is not clarified by stressing the antagonisms between culture and the individual, but by stressing their mutual reinforcement.

Personal behavior, in political life as in any other aspect of social life, is almost entirely learned behavior. It is infinitely variable, but by the same token some regularities, some common features, can be imposed through the learning process. The induction of new members—by birth or conquest or immigration—into the ways of behavior that are preferred in a society is known as socialization, so when we refer to the particular knowledge, attitudes, and judgments that affect politics we speak of *political socialization*. How do we *learn* to be citizens, or rebels, or voters?

We may learn political behavior and attitudes in an open and direct fashion, which is called *manifest socialization*. This is the formal learning of political culture through civics classes, by listening to discussions or reading wall posters, from official government statements and procedures of indoctrination, or from the media. There is also a process of *latent socialization*, a more subtle acquisition of values and attitudes that are politically significant while we are doing or learning about other things. We may, for example, acquire an attitude toward all authority by the way we learn to act toward parents, teachers, or religious leaders.

Both latent and manifest political socialization occur throughout our lives, whether or not we ever have formal schooling. Certain periods can be identified that seem distinctive and that are common to most societies. At each period there are certain dominant agents, or environments, for socialization. In early childhood the family has the major role. Long before we become mature enough to pay attention to politics, we have absorbed a great deal of our family's attitude to the world around it. We acquire general perspectives, and we may also learn specific beliefs. In the United States, for example, a child of six will have some general beliefs about the political system, and probably an imprecise but not totally inaccurate conception of the role of the President. In terms of family structure the President is a kind of father figure. Some influence of this early approach can be seen in adult Americans' expectations about presidential action. If his parents have strong feelings, a child may also have an identification with a political party, though not understanding much about the party itself. As a result, family identifications with parties may continue for generations.

The way the family treats the children has a major role in shaping their general attitudes to the world as well as their feelings about themselves. These two together have great significance for the later development of political trust, sense of personal competence, and willingness to compromise. Perhaps the most basic influence of the family ever proposed was put forward by Geoffrey Bateson in a now famous anthropological hypothesis about Russian political behavior. This argument identified the cause of aggression in Russian political life as the consequence of overly restrictive clothing (tight swaddling clothes) in infancy, which led to hostility toward the world in adulthood.

Family influences are supplemented by those of one's peers in the second period, late childhood and youth. Now there are at least as many contacts with one's age group as with the family. Young people spend a great deal of time with each other in and out of school. They pass through the history of their time together, and when we speak of "generations" in politics we are referring to the cohesion that common experience at a common age gives to a group of otherwise dissimilar people. These peer influences will continue to affect us as we reach adulthood, the third period. This stage of life, however, brings a whole range of new contacts, including work groups, interest groups, parties, and families of our own.

The period of transition from youth to adult may be very traumatic. One famous description of this is the "identity crisis," as Erik Erikson calls it in his *Young Man Luther*, during which previous experiences are "pulled apart" and a new orientation to one's self, one's society, and the entire world is painfully constructed. This is often the stage of life from which revolutionaries are born—whether they are religious, social, or political challengers of the status quo. Luther, Lenin, and Jefferson were all young men when they confronted the established order.

Political socialization, in general and in specific terms, thus arises from a constellation of influences which we can summarize and illustrate:

> *Socialization Agents*
> Family: parents and siblings
> Peer groups: fellow students, workmates
> Formal structures: schools, parties
> Communication systems: the press, radio and television
> Events: depressions, assassinations, elections, wars, independence
> Individuals: heroes, political officeholders

The development of a public figure's political behavior and role can be traced through *political biography*. Individuals who stand out in a community's political history are often studied in great detail to illuminate what happened to them and to their communities in relation to their individual political histories. If we are not interested in or convinced of the importance of "Great Men," we may look at general patterns of individual behavior, an approach called *micropolitics*. We can examine why people vote, or vote only for the Conservative Party, or why they do not vote at all. We may ask why people believe they should vote, or why they choose to rebel, or why they take bribes. This does *not* mean that we can predict or determine the behavior of any particular person. But we can begin to have some general understanding of why people behave the way they do, and how and why various groups differ from each other. Such studies of individuals, even if they are represented by nameless statistics, are essential for a full understanding of a community and its political process.

Styles of Political Culture

The combination of individual attitudes and their consequent patterns of behavior, in the social context, along with their historical and physical setting, is the *political culture* of the polity. There may be a number of these combinations in a single political system, and they can be described as subcultures reflecting particular regional, ethnic, generational, or frontier groups within the larger entity. If these subcultures have some underlying unity then we can reasonably speak of a common political culture. If they do not, or if the divisions appear as great as the similari-

ties, there may be great stress in the polity as a result. This is the problem of plural, or pluralist, societies.

Looking at an individual political culture—perhaps examining our own, which is often the most difficult—we can identify certain things about it as characteristic of its collective form and functioning. A number of *typologies,* or classifications, have been devised into which we may fit aspects of many different cultures. All these efforts are unsatisfactory to some extent, because they emphasize generalities and blur distinctions; classification is always more clear-cut than reality. Yet we quite often make such comparisons in an unsystematic way by speaking of ourselves or others as, for example, competitive, submissive, lazy, or individualistic. It is useful for description and analysis to turn to some more carefully defined typologies. We should remember that they are neither absolute nor perfect, but comparisons help us understand our own culture as well as others.

One important typology raises the question of "individual orientation to the polity" and sets out three general styles: *parochial, subject,* and *citizen* or participant, with corresponding kinds of polities. The "parochial" attitude is essentially nonparticipatory, conceived of in terms of preordained status, and the resulting polity is a traditional or feudal order. "Subjects," on the other hand, are more aware of their political lives, although not primarily in terms of individual rights or popular sovereignty. Political machines, monarchies, and other hierarchical systems fit this kind of attitude. Finally there is the "citizen" orientation, which emphasizes individual participation as a right, and from which political systems arise that are expected to be agents for the citizens and accountable to them, such as democracies. Although all three varieties of political culture and system are obviously very much alive in the world, citizen orientation is becoming the dominant mode. Much of the political change in this century can be described as the "revolution of rising participation," which has forced communities to respond, at least formally, to demands for greater involvement by the whole citizenry, and has led to fundamental changes in the distribution of social and economic rewards.

A second kind of classification makes a distinction between "open" and "closed" political cultures through answers to three questions. First, are the patterns of behavior and beliefs focused on what we will call traditional explanations and motives, or are they modern in outlook? (These are general terms which we will explore in more detail in the following chapter.) Second, is the overall attitude to the surrounding world one of tolerance or of confrontation; that is, relativist or absolutist? Third, is the general emphasis on individual or collective roles and values? We will give all three of these orientations more attention when we consider political change, for "open" or "closed" culture plays an important role in it.

There are other important aspects of political culture that we can look for, which we might classify under *political style*. For example, is the dominant mode of behavior aggressive or conciliatory? Are most people apathetic or "involved," confident or diffident? Do people have a general sense of competence, or are they uncertain and insecure about their ability and right to take part in politics? Is there a general sense of trust in the motives and purposes of others, and therefore a willingness to act together, or does general suspicion prevent action in concert? For instance, some studies of Mexico have found that the average person is likely to assume that people outside the family are not to be trusted very far; they may betray or trick you and it is best to act alone. The United States, on the other hand, is a "joining" society, with thousands of organizations of all kinds, including informal political groups. Nigerians also seem to be "joiners," and new societies are constantly springing up there, while the Scots appear to share some of the Mexican attitude toward those who are neither kith nor kin.

Finally, there is a very important question that affects not only internal political life but relations between communities as well: the preference for compromise or for confrontation, and the role of violence— physical or mental—in relationships with family or neighbors or outsiders. Some political cultures clearly prefer nonviolence—persuasion and compromise—regardless of its effect on other goals. Other cultures quickly resort to violence, which may permeate life from infancy to old age, affecting all individual and collective experiences. Within a plural society various groups may have their own distinctive clusters of attitudes and behaviors which can be distinguished from the whole even after many generations of association. Such subgroups also contribute to the whole. One observer has asserted that "violence is as American as apple pie." Groups within the American polity that value nonviolence, such as the Amish and the Quakers, would certainly not agree. However, it may be argued that the majority of the groups that make up the American polity do have at least a tendency to permit, if not prefer, violence. The dueling Southerner, the aggressively macho Southwesterner, and gunslingers everywhere, are as familiar in American history as the "Fighting Irish."

Most plural societies present similar problems of characterization. Like the United States, Nigeria, Malaysia, India, Yugoslavia, Burma, and the Soviet Union are all composite polities, among whose many peoples we can find a wide range of preferences about violence as about other things. If the Yorubas of western Nigeria have a history of intracommunal fighting, does this make violence "as Nigerian as pepper stew"? If Tatars are warlike in their history, can we describe the USSR as militaristic? If modern India is characterized by riots, severe clashes between Hindus and Muslims, and violence based upon caste, religion, and language, does this mean that violence is inherent in the Indian character? To some extent the answers must be a matter of personal judgment. We put together an impression of our own or another culture from all the fragments of information we have—but it will be shaped also by what we look for and expect to find.

Political culture as we have described it is the product of many individual acts and ideas, past and present. In addition to these general patterns, there is a special form of belief about politics which we refer to as an *ideology*: communism, capitalism, liberalism, and Pan-Africanism are some examples. An ideology is a pattern of ideas that is often carefully constructed in intellectual terms, perhaps even proposed by a single person. Sometimes the political system itself may adopt a set of ideas and attempt to forbid others, enacting an *official* political culture. What distinguishes ideologies is that they are systematic, providing basic assumptions from which hypotheses and judgments about politics are derived. For example, political events may be said to originate in the ownership of the means of production, or the covenant with God, or the sanctity and centrality of property. Ideologies often incorporate programs for action— eradication of the bourgeoisie, state support of religion, or exclusion of all but property owners from the polity. It is not surprising that ideologies play a very powerful role in political affairs.

Ideologies are forces of change in many political systems. But whether or not we can discern an ideology at work, no political culture is completely static, although some appear to undergo more rapid and more extensive alteration than others. The rate and nature of change is an important element of a community's political life. Knowing how and why change occurs, and what its consequences are, constitutes a large part of our understanding of the political process. These complex questions merit a chapter of their own.

SELECTED READINGS

Almond, Gabriel, and G. Bingham Powell, Jr. *Comparative Politics: System, Process, and Policy.* 2nd ed. Boston: Little, Brown, 1978.*

Almond, Gabriel, and Sidney Verba. *The Civic Culture.* Princeton, N.J.: Princeton University Press, 1963.*

Davies, James C. *Human Nature in Politics.* New York: Wiley, 1963.

Dawson, Richard, and Kenneth Prewitt. *Political Socialization.* Boston: Little, Brown, 1968.

Eisenstadt, S. N. *From Generation to Generation.* New York: Free Press, 1964.*

_____. *Tradition, Change and Modernity.* New York: Wiley, 1973.

Erikson, Erik. *Young Man Luther.* New York: Norton, 1958.

_____, ed. *Identity, Youth and Crisis.* New York: Norton, 1968.

Greenstein, Fred I. *Children and Politics.* New Haven: Yale University Press, 1965.

Gunn, John. *Violence.* New York: Praeger, 1973.

Gurr, Ted Robert. *Why Men Rebel.* Princeton, N.J.: Princeton University Press, 1971.*

Hess, Robert, and Judith Torney. *The Development of Political Attitudes in Children.* Chicago: Aldine, 1967.

Inglehart, Ronald. *The Silent Revolution: Changing Values and Political Styles Among Western Publics.* Princeton, N.J.: Princeton University Press, 1977.

Lasch, Christopher. *Haven in a Heartless World: The Family Besieged.* New York: Basic Books, 1977.

Lerner, Daniel. *The Passing of Traditional Society.* Glencoe, Ill.: The Free Press, 1958.

Lichtheim, George. *The Concept of Ideology.* New York: Random House, 1967.

Lipset, Seymour Martin. *Political Man: The Social Basis of Politics.* Garden City, N.Y.: Doubleday, 1963.*

McCelland, Charles. *The Achieving Society.* Princeton, N.J.: Van Nostrand, 1961.

Montagu, Ashley, ed. *Learning Non-aggression: The Experience of Non-literate Societies.* New York: Oxford University Press, 1978.

*Indicates a paperback edition is available.

Pye, Lucian W., and Sidney Verba, eds. *Political Culture and Political Development*. Princeton, N.J.: Princeton University Press, 1965.*

Schwartz, David C. *Political Alienation and Political Behavior*. Chicago: Aldine, 1973.

Sklar, Judith N. *Men and Citizens*. Cambridge, England: Cambridge University Press, 1969.

4

Political Change: Growth and Decay of Communities

There is nothing permanent except change.
> —*Heraclitus*

Stability is not immobility.
> —*Prince Klemens von Metternich*

No government can remain stable in an unstable society and unstable world.
> —*Léon Blum*

Change is universal. Like the old joke that nothing is certain except that nothing is certain, the only thing about human life that stays the same is that it is always changing. These changes may be as basic as those of population size or physical space, or variations in climate from Ice Ages to droughts. Societies discover new resources, deplete their existing resources or find new ways to use them. They also change their ideas and institutions in the process. We can make some sense of this continuous flux if we ask some basic questions that suggest possible destinations and probable political consequences of change. Essentially we need to know certain *dimensions* of change.

The Anatomy of Change

We can look for the *source* of change, its *rate* or *speed,* its *direction, scope,* and the *means* or *agents* that bring it about. All these character-istics can be discussed as pairs of extremes, if we remember that there are gradations in between, and that the extremes are rarely found.

The source of change may be internal or external to the society. An example of the first kind is a new development in beliefs about gods or nature; an example of the second is the encroachment of the Sahara Desert on the states of West Africa. Both kinds of change may require a political response, but in different ways. A drought will force a political system to deal with hungry people. A shift in beliefs may alter the ability of society to respond to the natural disaster. Of course prolonged drought may also alter what a people believes about gods and nature, as well as how it organizes its food supply. Another way of thinking about this is to consider the impact on farming of a local invention of a better plow. This may be easier to incorporate than objects brought by colonizers or foreign aid experts. People's reaction to change will be influenced by its origin, and by whether it is imposed or voluntary.

Change may be slow and incremental, "one step at a time," or it may come very rapidly. The rate tends to reflect how much is changing, the scope of change. Is just one part of life affected, followed later by some change in another aspect of society, or is the society being "turned upside down," with everything happening all together? England, for example, altered little by little over a long period of time. The government did not have to plan for education, industrialization, and urbanization all at once, as many societies in this century—including Turkey and Cuba—have chosen or been forced to do. We can distinguish revolutionary governments from reform models, reactionary governments from conservative ones, by the element of scope plus the factor of direction.

Revolutionary governments are essentially forward-looking, rejecting the past; *reactionary governments* venerate the past and try to restore it. Both may embark on extensive programs to alter as much of society as possible, by force if necessary. In a revolution this may even mean a demand for a new kind of human being; both the Soviet Union and the People's Republic of China have claimed to be creating a "new socialist man." The resurgence of Islam in Iran, Pakistan, and other Muslim societies is in part a reaction to recent social change, an attempt to eradicate that change and return to the theocracy of old. In contrast, *reformist* or *conserving* governments are not so ambitious. They tend to reaffirm old values while suggesting new ways to maintain them. At most they assert a desire to change behavior. For example, the U.S. Supreme Court has outlawed public segregation by race, which may eventually lead to changes in beliefs about race in society. The court did not order mandatory indoctrination sessions to eliminate race prejudice, and in the key area of education some time was allowed for this reform to become legally required.

The difference between unconditional and moderate programs of change is also seen in the choice of methods—violence or nonviolence, if we use the terms of extremes. Political theorists and activists have debated for centuries over which type is more effective. They argue as well about the moral limits to violence and to pacifism, which can be a cover for support of existing wrongs. Violence has often been the vehicle of revolution, as in France, Russia, Mexico, China, Algeria, and Ethiopia. Peaceful revolutions are proudly called "bloodless revolutions" to distinguish them from the ordinary kind, as when the English refer to the overthrow of the last absolute monarch in 1688 as the "Glorious Revolution." Nonviolent change is generally a gradual evolution, moderate or reformist in character. Either pattern may be a result of deliberate choice or historical chance, although political violence is ordinarily a conscious strategy.

If you combine all these dimensions of change for a particular country, you will have a fairly good snapshot of what is happening today in that society and what it will *probably* look like tomorrow. Nigeria, for instance, has generally favored nonviolent change when possible, change that is slow, reform-oriented, and limited in scope. There are even efforts to turn back the clock by reintroducing institutions suppressed under colonial rule. At the same time change has been comprehensive, caused by both internal and external factors. While people are leaving rural areas at an accelerating rate, the government is trying to establish universal primary education, build steel mills, and construct thousands of miles of roads and railways, and private businessmen announce new ventures daily. It is very hard to deal with such massive change using gradual, limited programs. Without its enormous revenues from oil in the past decade, Nigeria probably could not have done it. In contrast, Angola and Mozambique arrived at independence by violence. Both are following a strategy of comprehensive, revolutionary change reaching throughout the society. Their approaches are different, but all three countries share the same problem, the problem of *modernization.*

Modernization and Political Development

Modernization, which is usually talked about as a problem for the developing nations, is in fact a part of every society's past and present. Modernization is not the same thing as Westernization, although many people think of it this way because Western nations were generally the first to undergo the process. Simply put, modernization is a set of changes in three basic orientations to the world, which produce corresponding changes in institutions. The three are *time, nature,* and *other people.*

In the first change there is a shift in the idea of what time *is.* In the most traditional societies time is a cycle measured by natural events—

sunrise, harvest and dry seasons, births and deaths. The present and the future will simply repeat the past. Such factors as one's ancestors and the community's history are the most important elements in decision making. By contrast, modern time is viewed as a straight line, moving forward—and ruling our lives as we "punch the clock." Measurement itself becomes very elaborate. The U.S. government has a Time and Frequency Division that spends $3.5 million yearly to keep Americans accurate to thousandths of a second. France has *Le Bureau International de l'Heure*, set up in 1910. The whole world takes its Universal Earth Time from Greenwich Observatory in England. In this perspective the past is insignificant and the present is important because it leads to the future. Ancestors and history lose some of their meaning. Of course if this process goes too far, there may be a reaction. People may take a new or renewed interest in long-ago events, or embark on quests for their ancestors, their "roots."

The second change is in the society's view of nature. In traditional life people are generally submissive to the forces of nature. These are thought of as given elements that cannot be altered very much nor controlled. A modern orientation to nature, on the other hand, will see it simply as a physical setting to be studied and then changed. If this process goes too far, there may also be a reaction. Some people refuse to use certain technologies. Others have brought suit for damages; for example, in the United States weather modification agents have been (unsuccessfully) sued. There may even be discussion of the "rights" of natural objects, such as trees or rivers, to be left alone. Perhaps the most crucial of such challenges today is the battle over the use of nuclear energy.

Finally, there is a change in the ways we see ourselves and our relation to other people. In a traditional society people generally define themselves primarily by their *ascribed* relations to other people—the family, including ancestors, the job and status one expects to have as a result of birth. As modernization occurs, the emphasis shifts to the importance and uniqueness of individuals. The network of relationships expands and becomes less personal. Traditional villagers determine their food supply by their own work and that of a small group of others, most of whom know each other. In Detroit or Paris or Mexico City, food comes from commercial shops, which get it from wholesalers relying on truck or rail transport. If part of this network breaks down, or goes on strike, there is no food. In the past few years the British have had to spend long hours in queues as a result of such sudden and artificial stoppages of supply. This is the paradox of modern life. As the possibility of individuals being independent, different, or simply private begins to grow, so does their dependence on other individuals whom they never see and know only as clerks, traders, manufacturers, truckers. The reaction to this often takes the form of trying to reintroduce some form of simpler, communal living, either as a retreat from modern life or as an improvement in it.

As these changes in the three orientations occur, the overall character of social patterns alters too. Among the major changes are *differentiation* and *diversification*, the specialization of many social roles. There will probably be *urbanization* and *industrialization*. There may be *secularization; information* disseminated through education and mass communications; *technological* change; and greater *participation* in decision making. These social changes can occur independently—a society does not have to become less religious in order to become urbanized—but they are generally linked. Industrialization depends partly upon the existence of cities and literate populations. Both industrialization and urbanization are linked to improved transport. Because of this linkage it is said that modernization cannot occur simply by transfer of an institution or a technology from one society to another. The imported structure will not fit in its new setting.

Political modernization is a special kind of social change. Social mobilization disturbs old ways of life and literally moves people around. Comfortable routines are disrupted. Feelings of dissatisfaction and a desire for some influence in shaping the new social system may translate into demands for increased participation. The people now have some of the education and communications networks necessary for greater participation, and their view of the kinds of power they will accept as legitimate begins to change. Authority becomes more constitutional and technical, and it encompasses an entire nation-state rather than the small traditional communities. Paradoxically, as the demand for greater voice increases, the potential influence of each person decreases in large-scale, technocratic politics. The impact of this change may be moderated by the fact that traditional forms do not entirely disappear, no matter how modern a transitional society eventually becomes. The important question in assessing political modernization is the mix of old and new.

Many people assume that political modernization will bring about *democratization.* It is true that demands for participation and changes in authority seem to imply democracy, but it is not true that they must produce democracy. The elite may expand to include university graduates or wealthy beer distributors or army officers. In only a very limited sense do these new tickets for admission to social and political status represent democratization. This is not really what we mean by government that is accountable to the majority, the basic concept of democracy. In fact such elite-oriented regimes are often quite authoritarian.

Another road to increased participation is a heightened competition among ethnic or religious groups, often with no intention by any group of allowing the others to share equally once it gets to the top. This is not really what we mean by democracy either. Even societies that try to create systems of majority rule based on frequent elections may find that they do not get democracy. Demands for participation, and for quick returns in greater benefits to particular communities, may simply outstrip the ability of the new institutions to cope with them. Old elites may find new ways to subvert the electoral systems. Some transitional societies therefore deliberately choose some form of indirect elections, or they may restrict elections to local government. In most places the elected leadership is very small in any case. The United States is one of the minority of nations in which authority over the police, public health, judicial, or educational systems may be elective.

Democracy may be abandoned or simply rejected when modernization seems to constitute a threat to the existing political or social structures. Perhaps there has been a cycle of civilian rule, anarchy, and authoritarian—probably military—rule. The leadership may announce that modernization itself amounts to a national emergency, requiring a strong government which is skilled, efficient, and isolated from public ignorance and private greed. The results can be seen in the dozens of life presidencies, uncontested elections, and powerful, long-standing monarchies. Many nations that have such governments—Ivory Coast, Morocco, Cuba, Saudi Arabia—appear to be economically and politically stable. However, when events such as a death or overthrow force a change of power, we do not know how secure they will be. Most have had no change of power at all since independence (or revolution); some of the others have had no peaceful transfer of power. The People's Republic of China is one exception. The leadership was able to hand over some power after Mao Tse-tung died, and even to begin democratizing some of that power. Kenya and Algeria appeared to have joined this small group of exceptions after the death of Kenyatta and Boumedienne. The United States escaped the dilemma very early, when George Washington—ignoring calls for his elevation to life president or even king—stepped down after two terms. National power soon passed to the opposition party, which held it for thirty years. Thus the right to vote or otherwise participate was expanded under informal one-party rule, which gave stability while allowing legal opposition to form.

Corruption and the Decay of Politics

The disorder that accompanies modernization, and may prevent or destroy democratic constitutions, is often visible in widespread corruption. Corruption is a sign of the disintegration of systems. Even well-established political systems may be rocked by revelations of bribery and other abuses of power. Thus we have had the Watergate and Koreagate scandals in the United States, the Lockheed scandals in Japan, charges of high-level involvement in drug running in Panama, a purge of corrupt officials in Mexico, and almost continuous disclosures of corruption in countries such as Zaire and Indonesia—to pick two from a nearly endless list. The possible extent of corruption and abuse of office can be seen in the purges carried out by the Nigerian government in 1975, in which nearly ten thousand people were swept out of their jobs by the military "new broom." Similarly, we can grasp the universality of corruption and political decay by noting the worldwide admiration for nations that do not seem to have such problems, such as China—to pick one from a regrettably short list.

Corruption is universal in two ways. It has occurred almost everywhere throughout history, and almost everyone, everywhere, agrees that it is bad. However, not everyone means the same thing by that. In some discussions "bad" simply means imperfect behavior, and everything the particular writer dislikes about a particular society is described as corruption. It is much more useful to narrow the definition to *abuses of public power for private ends,* whether it involves keeping one's own power, enriching personal bank accounts, or misdirecting government resources to one's own ethnic, religious, regional, or linguistic group. The targets of, and methods for, corrupt behavior will vary with circumstances, but this central characteristic of misusing public power remains constant.

The association of corruption with modernization is not surprising. Transitional societies contain imperfectly integrated sets of old and new values. For example, government officials may have to decide whether to favor job applicants from their own villages or to follow impersonal civil service requirements and thereby alienate families and neighbors who probably helped pay their school fees. What is moral in one world is immoral in the other.

Modernization also means that there are new "public goods," such as admission to universities, government contracts, free medicines, permits to sell beer, or licenses to cut hair. At the same time these are probably insufficient, perhaps by artificial restriction. The government may have decided that there are too many university students or beer sellers. It may not have enough money to import adequate medical supplies. There is a temptation to get these benefits by money or "connections," temptation which poorly paid clerks, under pressure from their own friends and family, may not be able to resist. The greater centralization of responsibility for distribution and development of economic resources that now marks government everywhere, as compared to earlier centuries, helps to create this market for influence. Governments today try to direct activities such as industrial development that were subject to private direction in the past, and they try to regulate activities such as street vending that were formerly left uncontrolled. The market for influence expands along with this expansion of government activity.

Governments everywhere are also held to different, perhaps "higher," standards than their predecessors. The sale of offices, or employment by patronage, was not seen as corrupt in Stuart England or Jacksonian America. Twentieth-century morality tends to condemn these practices, which means that they must be hidden or denied even if they serve some function of political development. Revolutionary governments are often particularly puritan in their views of politics and create unrealistic expectations about the behavior of the new regime. Nations that were subject to colonial rule may suffer from a habit of regarding the government as something alien which can be honorably manipulated as a form of protest. This attitude does not disappear automatically when independence arrives.

Corruption that results from colonial rule is an example of a broader pattern of corruption in governments that are not accountable to the people. Regimes that try to close trade routes, force changes in farming practices, or forbid traditional institutions such as secret societies, may be confronted by resistance through means that appear to be corrupt. The trader will bribe the customs officer; the farmer will conspire with the agricultural extension worker to report that cocoa bushes have been burned when they have not. If there is no channel for participation, or at least consultation, in policy making, then the bribe replaces the ballot and becomes a kind of voting. This sort of corruption is an indicator of political trouble as well as a means of informal solution to government failure in shaping policies or in explaining them.

Besides providing a means for grass-roots democracy by affecting the output channel of government when the input is closed to most people, corruption helps to ease the transition from the old to the new social order. We can say that corruption is sometimes functional: bribes are better than bullets. Yet the existence of widespread and seemingly permanent corruption is not a preferred state of affairs for most regimes and peoples; it would be better to replace bribes with ballots. The solution—responsive and secure governments, and public support for them even at personal cost—remains frustratingly elusive in much of the world.

Change and Stability

The acceleration of change in the twentieth century seems to imply the "inevitability of instability" for most peoples. Social patterns have moved within this century from villages dependent upon sunlight or

*"If political ferment bugs you, you might be happier with
our All-Dictatorship Cruise Itinerary."*

Drawing by Donald Reilly; © 1970 The New Yorker Magazine, Inc.

wood fires for illumination to swollen cities permanently lit by artificial light. If we notice the moon at all, we are more likely to think of it as a landing strip than a goddess. The hereditary elites that dominated past politics in many village societies also give way, often to regimes that may be elite-based but that take on at least the form of participatory democracy. Rulers face populations that are increasingly aware of how things are for their counterparts around the world. People expect to get a fair share of what their nation—and the world—can provide. If this is not forthcoming, they demand a change.

Fair shares are not yet the norm, and so instability plagues most societies. This is not always bad. Stability may be another name for immobility, for indecision and inaction or the preservation of privileges for the few. But at its best stability is not the opposite of change. True stability refers to a balance, an underlying order that is able to cope with political and social change. In political terms this means a flexible, efficient, and equitable political system that can meet the contending demands for both continuity and change. The art of politics thus becomes a kind of high-wire performance, balancing between too much and too little change—and there are no safety nets.

SELECTED READINGS

Ake, Claude. *A Theory of Political Integration*. Homewood, Ill.: Dorsey Press, 1967.

Almond, Gabriel, and G. Bingham Powell, Jr. *Comparative Politics: System, Process, and Policy*. 2nd ed. Boston: Little, Brown, 1978.* One of the basics in this field.

Almond, Gabriel A., ed. *Comparative Politics Today: A World View*. Boston: Little, Brown, 1974.

Bendix, Richard. *Nation Building and Citizenship: Studies of Our Changing Social Order*. Garden City, N.Y.: Doubleday, 1969.

Berger, Peter, Brigitte Berger, and Hansfried Kellner. *The Homeless Mind: Modernization and Consciousness*. New York: Random House, 1974.*

Brinton, Crane. *The Anatomy of Revolution*. rev. ed. New York: Random House, 1965. A classic comparison of the English, American, French, and Russian revolutions.*

Chailand, Gerard. *Revolution in the Third World: Myths and Prospects*. New York: Viking, 1977. Baltimore: Penguin, 1978.*

Coleman, James S., ed. *Education and Political Development*. Princeton, N.J.: Princeton University Press, 1965.

Connery, Robert H., ed. *Urban Riots: Violence and Social Change*. New York: Random House, 1979.*

Dwyer, Denis John, ed. *The City in the Third World*. New York: Barnes and Noble, 1974.

Eisenstadt, S. N. *Modernization: Protest and Change*. Englewood Cliffs, N.J.: Prentice-Hall, 1966.

_____. *Tradition, Change and Modernity*. New York: Wiley, 1973.

Enloe, Cynthia H. *Ethnic Conflict and Political Development*. Boston: Little, Brown, 1973.*

Freyre, Gilberto. *Masters and Slaves*. New York: Knopf, 1964.

Galbraith, J. K. *The Nature of Mass Poverty*. Cambridge, Mass.: Harvard University Press, 1979.

Gamer, Robert E. *The Developing Nations: A Comparative Perspective*. Boston: Allyn and Bacon, 1976.* An interesting critique of standard theories of change and development.

Geertz, Clifford, ed. *Old Societies and New States*. New York: Free Press, 1963. Despite its age, still one of the most provocative collections on this subject.

Gilbert, Alan. *Latin American Development*. Baltimore: Penguin, 1975.*

Goulet, Denis. *The Cruel Choice: A New Concept in the Theory of Development*. New York: Atheneum, 1971.

Gunn, John. *Violence*. New York: Praeger, 1973.

Gurr, Ted Robert. *Why Men Rebel*. Princeton, N.J.: Princeton University Press, 1971.*

*Indicates a paperback edition is available.

Heeger, Gerald A. *The Politics of Under-Development.* New York: St. Martin's, 1974.*

Hirschman, Albert O. *A Bias for Hope: Essays on Development and Latin America.* New Haven: Yale University Press, 1971.

Huntington, Samuel. *Political Order in Changing Societies.* New Haven: Yale University Press, 1968.

Janowitz, Morris. *The Last Half-Century: Societal Change and Politics in America.* Chicago: University of Chicago Press, 1979.

Johnson, Chalmers. *Revolutionary Change.* Boston: Little, Brown, 1966.

Kautsky, John H. *The Political Consequences of Modernization.* New York: Wiley, 1972.

Leys, Colin, ed. *Politics and Change in Developing Countries.* Cambridge, England: Cambridge University Press, 1969.

Little, Kenneth. *Urbanization as a Social Process.* London: Routledge and Kegan Paul, 1974.

Lloyd, Peter C. *Classes, Crises and Coups.* New York: Praeger, 1972.

Lofchie, Michael F. *The State of the Nations: Constraints on Development in Independent Africa.* Berkeley: University of California Press, 1971.*

Markovitz, Irving Leonard. *Power and Class in Africa: An Introduction to Change and Conflict in African Politics.* Englewood Cliffs, N.J.: Prentice-Hall, 1977.*

McCord, William. *The Springtime of Freedom: The Evolution of Developing Societies.* New York: Oxford University Press, 1965.* An interesting presentation of the positive outlook of the 1960s.

Pye, Lucian W., and Sidney Verba, eds. *Political Culture and Political Development.* Princeton, N.J.: Princeton University Press, 1965.*

Rudolph, Lloyd I., and Susanne Hoeber Rudolph. *The Modernity of Tradition.* Chicago: University of Chicago Press, 1967.

Scott, James C. *Comparative Political Corruption.* Englewood Cliffs, N.J.: Prentice-Hall, 1972.*

Wolf, Eric R., and Edward C. Hansen. *The Human Condition in Latin America.* London: Oxford University Press, 1972.

5

Communal Bonds: Power, Authority, and Legitimacy

Political power grows out of the barrel of a gun.
—Mao Tse-tung

The measure of man is what he does with power.
—Pittacus

Justice without force is powerless; force without
justice is tyrannical.
—Blaise Pascal

Despite the persistence of change, a political community may be said to depend upon the existence of some regularities of conduct, expectations, and relationships. In most cases these in turn presuppose substantial agreement about the presence of *authority*. This is another of those words, like "politics," that we readily use but cannot easily define. One way of putting it is to say that authority is "right rule," or more fully, "right rulers, ruling rightly." Authority is determined by the permissible exercises of power, and by which persons or agencies may wield it, under what conditions.

As we consider this we can see that authority, which binds the political process together, is composed of two elements: *power* to rule and the *legitimacy* or propriety of that power. Power is found throughout the relationships of a society. Armed robbers and tax collectors both have power to take money from citizens. Yet we know there is a difference between these two, and the difference lies in the acceptance (even if not happily) of the tax collector's right to take our money. Thus the question of legitimacy becomes central to the functioning of any political community. Different communities define legitimacy in widely different ways, but legitimacy must characterize the exercise of power if the community is to be cohesive enough to continue to exist and develop. Power itself is necessary too. Somewhere in the society there must be the capacity or ability to use resources, make decisions, and obtain compliance. Otherwise the society will collapse into disorder and immobility.

Power

In political life, power is a *relationship* in which resources are used by one or more persons to obtain the agreement and cooperation of others. Another way of thinking about this is to imagine power as a special kind of *influence*, as the ability to influence or manipulate others, to change them in some way, to point them in a certain direction and persuade them that this is the right way for them, for the community, for future generations. We may say that someone "has" power, as though it were a material thing, but we really mean that this person is able to bring others to alter their behavior, to take the action the person advocates.

Political power means that this influence is being used in the decision-making process of the whole community. The exact nature of power will depend on a number of factors: individual and community goals, individual values and community norms, external pressures, tactics used, resources now or potentially available. These are related to each other, since particular purposes may require or forbid certain tactics and resources. For example, the pacifist would not threaten others with physical violence to influence their opinion, even if they were much weaker. The decision to build a nuclear power plant will be presented in terms of scientific evidence for its feasibility and safety. It may be challenged by demonstrations and marches indicating that some community norms are opposed to this kind of energy, but an even more powerful counterargument will present technical evidence indicating that the favorable testimony is wrong.

The goals, values, and norms of a community and its members are ordinarily bound up together. A community that prizes martial qualities or believes that any method is permissible to convert others to the right way of living is not likely to accord nonviolence or "permanent peace" a high priority. A community that believes all people have the ability to use reason will probably support programs of education and communication, and will use persuasion as a tactic. Goals may be expansionist or conserving, radical or conservative, individual or collective, material or "spiritual" in orientation. Values and norms are even more difficult to classify in any simple way, since virtually every human trait and kind of behavior has been held in esteem by some community somewhere. This complex of goals, values, and norms will affect the kinds of resources that are available or possible. Certain ways of thinking promote, or prohibit, certain kinds of resources. For example, some American Indians have resisted, on spiritual grounds, the destruction of forests and mountains to get at energy resources which other segments of American society are eager to exploit.

These connections are suggested when we look at the basic types of resources for power, and the reasons why they "work."

Category	Example	Reason
Physical	Fists; weapons	Fear of injury
Economic	Wealth; petroleum; factories	Desire for gain
Moral or normative	Royal birth; religious position	Tradition or recognition of status or right
Individual or group "personality"	Charisma; honor; suffering	Attraction, loyalty
Skill or knowledge	Technology; special training	Recognition of need for expertise

The reaction to some of these kinds of resources is not always easy to understand or predict. One person may find someone very compelling on personal grounds, while another perceives that person with repugnance and is ready to reject anything he or she favors. Skill or knowledge may be ineffectual if it is inconsistent with moral values. Threats of physical violence intimidate some people and rouse others to fury, perhaps even enabling them to overcome objectively greater strength. Economic power can change overnight if workers strike or the value of the dollar shifts or blight strikes coffee plantations. Sometimes apparent weakness becomes strength. A small or insignificant state may get away with an attack on its neighbor that would provoke instant reaction from other states if launched by a powerful government. The very powerful may find themselves actually weakened by their status, burdened by expectations and demands from others that reduce their range of options. Strength may become weakness.

The exercise of power can be further characterized by what we might call *style*, which also affects the nature of the whole political process. There are four dimensions of style, or four pairs of opposites: *potential* or *actual* power; *personal* or *official* power; *coercive* or *consensual* power; and *positive* or *negative* power. First, we may recognize that some person is potentially quite powerful but for some reason does not choose to exercise this potential—perhaps from lack of interest or inability to recognize the potential. Similar comments are made about groups, including nation-states. Second, political offices are traditionally or structurally endowed with varying degrees of power. The occupant of the presidency, the holder of the premiership, the chief, and the senator acquire a certain amount of power by virtue of holding those positions. Their personalities will then help to determine how much actual power they can wield during their tenure—either expanding, maintaining, or contracting the power resources for the next incumbent. In some circumstances officials themselves may be powerful for reasons of personality when their office itself does not give them any advantage—perhaps among their peers (as in a meeting of heads of state). People with no official position at all may be quite powerful too. Consider the impact of Alexander Solzhenitsyn upon both the United States and the Soviet Union; the worldwide effect of Steve Biko's life and death in South Africa; or the force of pronouncements by private international groups such as Amnesty International.

A third distinction opposes a consensual style of power, using resources and tactics based primarily on reason or persuasion, against coercive power, based on force or on tradition that cannot be questioned. The implications of this distinction will be considered more fully in the chapter that follows, when we look at limited government as opposed to absolute government. Fourth, power may be negative or positive. It may be predominantly a capacity to prevent or a capacity to innovate, to move, to create. It is perhaps easier to exercise a veto than to get others to consider and agree upon changes in behavior or structures.

Beneath the various styles of exercising power there is the question of its *distribution*, in both empirical and normative terms. There are two basic models, often described as *elitist* and *pluralist*. In the first, power is held by one exclusive and homogenous group, and the rest constitute the masses, whose only role is the granting of the minimal consent we discussed earlier as essential for survival of rule. Change will be nearly impossible, exceedingly slow, and infinitesimal. If the masses finally revolt against this there will be chaos, often followed by some other ruling elite.

The second model has a broader view of distribution. The idea of pluralism, or polyarchy, is predicated on the existence of several partly opposed subgroups, each with its own dominant figures. These elites must bargain and compromise with each other. They will compromise, in part because they share a common interest in protecting their elite status by keeping the system going. But they will not form a united elite because they also share the differing interests of their subgroups. Change comes slowly here, but it comes, as the bargaining process goes on. The majority of the people again have a minimal but somewhat more active role, supporting their group elites in their representation of group interests "at the top." A third, less common model, sometimes referred to as egalitarian rule, assigns power more or less equally to all, and denies that power is or must be restricted to a few. For practical reasons leaders may be chosen, but the style is "every man a king," as the Igbo people of Nigeria say. The leadership must be accountable and responsible, open to its supporters, and it is readily changed if it is not satisfactory to them.

We may prefer any one of these models as the best kind of power distribution. At the same time, each claims to be a statement about reality. The validity of these claims must be tested by looking at the actual operations of our own community or others we are interested in. And it is possible that the one we think best will not fit the evidence of what actually occurs.

Authority

Those who have power, whoever they are, will find their power more stable and useful if it is established as *authority*, rightful power. This means that power has a source or claim to justification, which is accepted by those who are affected by it. These *justifications* may be generally classed as *personal, sacred, inherited, legal,* and *achieved.* Max Weber, the German sociologist, suggested three types: charismatic, traditional, and rational-legal. The five given here vary and expand this scheme somewhat.

The first, personal claims, we might also call charisma, following Weber. This word, from the Greek for "gift," reflects the fact that some individuals, but not others, win recognition by virtue of personal magnetism, heroic behavior, or "image." Sacred sources constitute religious bases for rule, perhaps even endowing the ruler himself with divinity—the Roman caesars, the emperors and sun kings of the Inca and Maya civilizations, the Egyptian pharaohs. Until quite late in Western history kings in Europe rested their claim on a "divine right to rule." This was supplemented by the correct "accidents of birth," the inherited bases of authority. This may mean being of the correct family, sex, age, position within the family (the firstborn). Depending upon the society, all may be needed or only one considered critical. Some societies today still rely heavily upon these measures of fitness, perhaps adding or substituting racial or ethnic background as inherited, ascribed elements of authority.

© Sidney Harris

"I HAD THE MANDATE OF MY FATHER, AND THAT'S GOOD ENOUGH FOR ME."

Together these sacred or inherited factors constitute the second Weberian type, the traditional.

Legal claims, which Weber called rational-legal, refer to the possession of power by lawfully prescribed means, whether election, proper appointment, rotation, lottery, or victory by combat. Rules and procedures governing election, appointment, or seniority are generally spelled out in statutes or constitutions. Other claims exist in unwritten or customary law. Finally, there is individual achievement—such as educational qualifications, often seen as fitting a person to claim some offices but not others. This kind of authority fits what some have described as technocracy, or rule by experts, in which the twentieth-century mystique of science is joined to bureaucracy. (Perhaps winning office through the patronage of some other powerful person may also be said to be a kind of individual achievement.)

There is probably a mix of these justifications in all systems. For example, in the United States legally based authority is important, but personal and achieved qualifications may be added, and there are both formal and informal expectations about ascribed or inherited characteristics. The President, who must be at least thirty-five and native-born, is put into office by prescribed election procedures. Yet the office is gained and used by virtue of personal and achieved advantages. Legally neither race, sex, nor religion should play a part; in fact they do. On the other hand, the traditional Islamic rulers (emirs) of the northern states of Nigeria must meet primarily traditional requirements that are sacred and ascribed. These requirements exclude females and usually young men. Certain families provide the candidates and traditional leaders choose among them by long-established procedures. Skills and educational achievements may influence this choice. In contemporary Nigeria an emir's appointment must also be confirmed by the state governments. Finally, this office is part of a religiously based political system, in which the ruler is expected to adhere to and promote the Islamic faith, and this in turn justifies his possession of power.

These sources of authority constitute the argument for the *legitimacy* of power. Legitimacy is important to governors and governed. It implies a relationship, a judgment about power and a reaction to it. Legitimacy is a major aspect of any political system, and it operates worldwide, as we realize by listening to the news and the comments individuals and governments make about other individuals' and governments' right to rule.

Legitimacy

Legitimacy has two forms—subjective and objective—and two locations or sources—internal and external. In exploring the *form*, we can distinguish two lines of argument about what legitimacy is and what it should be. According to the first, people's *attitudes* are determining. The members of a system judge it (on any of the grounds discussed above) and their expression of opinion is the empirical evidence of its legitimacy. Thus the important thing is subjective, responsive acceptance. In the second approach the view is that *performance*, what the system does and what kind of system (socialist, democratic, constitutional) it is, constitutes legitimacy. Both kind and performance can be objectively determined, or so the argument goes, and if the people have the "wrong" opinion, it can be corrected by education.

Turning to *source*, the second distinction, we can see that the judgment may be given by *outsiders* or *insiders*, and these views need not coincide. Members of a system may consider it legitimate while outside forces characterize it as illegitimate, or vice versa. Not all outside forces may agree on the matter either; from such disagreements alliances and wars are born. A rigid adherence to only one of these two measures of legitimacy is not useful. In the modern world both considerations are important to a political system's stability and capacity to develop. Acceptance of the present South African system by those within the country who are allowed to have a voice does not prevent outside forces from holding it to be illegitimate and attacking it. In some instances such a dilemma cannot be resolved, but the successful political system will pay some attention to both the acceptance and performance dimensions of legitimacy, and to external judgments as well as internal ones. The Communist regime of China, for example, was undoubtedly accorded legitimacy internally long before some external observers in the West agreed to recognize the regime. The Chinese government won further recognition through adroit diplomacy aided by changes in world politics. Much of world politics revolves around struggles to achieve external acceptance without making radical changes that would threaten internal legitimacy.

Legitimacy is not a constant. When a new state or government is formed, it is in a "prelegitimate" condition—newly established, not yet rejected nor accepted, although if its stated purposes are known, judgments about them may be offered immediately. As it matures, if its people are lucky the system will acquire legitimacy and validate its objective claims; if not, it will be judged illegitimate. Of course both things may happen. A regime that has had general acceptance may find that because circumstances have changed and it has not responded adequately, its legitimacy has disintegrated or simply turned to sullen apathy. It becomes postlegitimate, ripe for challenge internally or externally.

Legitimacy confers the necessary "grace" that turns power into authority; power is also important for without it legitimacy can do nothing and authority vanishes. Together these allow the system to govern with less coercion and to provide whatever benefits are available. Difficult decisions are easier, since there is a base of support that does not have to be created anew with every policy. Peaceful social change becomes at least possible. To maintain authority, both legitimacy and power must be conserved—if not increased. This means attention to their sources; increasingly, in the twentieth century, it has meant attention to legal, constitutional bases and to consensual power.

Constitutional Authority

Authority can and does derive from nondemocratic, nonconstitutional sources. Governments that are neither democratic nor constitutional have been accorded both internal and external legitimacy in the past—for examples we need only think of the long history of monarchies around the world, many of which still survive. Most of those accorded external legitimacy—Great Britain, the Netherlands, Lesotho, and so on—are now constitutional rather than absolute, with defined, perhaps written, limits to their powers.

The notion of constitutional government is still new as a factor in world politics and it is not universally applied. Governments that are firmly established and apparently accepted by their people are accorded recognition even by countries that find them objectively repugnant—or merely insignificant. The worst offenders, such as Equatorial Guinea and Haiti, may escape outside attention by virtue of their strategic insignificance. If the aristocratic ruler of Liechtenstein were a tyrant, probably few outside the principality would care. Despite the mounting cruelty of Hitler's regime in the 1930s, most of the nations of Europe accorded it recognition and were prepared to live with it. There was criticism, but the nations did not unite to confront the Third Reich until it had swallowed some and attacked others. The states of Africa similarly did not withdraw recognition from Ethiopia under Haile Selassie, nor under the military government that overthrew him, as they did not—with a few notable and noble exceptions—openly declare Idi Amin's dictatorship in Uganda to be illegitimate.

Nonetheless, international conventions and agreements, backed by dissident national groups and such worldwide organizations as Amnesty International, have begun to publicize the excesses of many nations. Such international action is still in its infancy, and is honored more often by form than true substance, but the demand for substance is growing. Within nations everywhere a movement to democratize and limit power is visible—from the smallest local group to the national governments. Some governments under military rule, such as Nigeria and Ghana, have recently prepared for a return to civilian power by first establishing accountable local governments. The argument is that these governments are of most importance to most of the people, since they have the most immediate impact on daily life. Here as elsewhere, the rising force of concern and demand for human rights in political life will at least give moral support to the primacy of democratic and constitutional forms of government, if those governments can also show some ability to improve the material standards of life for their people.

It is possible that both the national governments of the world and the myriad local governments will be increasingly pushed toward constitutional democracy in form and substance. One motif of the late twentieth century is participation, access to the decision making that affects so much of our ordinary lives. We will have more to say about this in chapter 9. At the same time, the vast forces of change that are sweeping over the globe, bringing so many new states to the world stage, make the need for order ever more compelling. The power of local and international elites for manipulating these conditions is also very great. Authoritarian rule and mass misery are other motifs of this century, and they may increase along with gross national incomes. The ensuing struggle between freedom and limits—between the desperate need to reduce chaos to stability so that economic development is possible, and the parallel need for human rights, including economic freedoms, as a condition of stability—will be a dominant feature of international, national, and local political processes in the coming decades. We will return to this argument in the final chapter.

SELECTED READINGS

Agger, Robert E., Daniel Goldrich, and Bert Swanson. *The Rulers and the Ruled: Political Power and Impotence in American Communities.* New York: Wiley, 1964.

Barber, James David. *Presidential Character: Predicting Performance in the White House.* Englewood Cliffs, N.J.: Prentice-Hall, 1972.

Dahl, Robert A. *After the Revolution: Authority in a Good Society.* New Haven: Yale University Press, 1970.

Friedrich, Carl J. *Limited Government: A Comparison.* Englewood Cliffs, N.J.: Prentice-Hall, 1974.*

Green, Philip, and Sanford Levinson, eds. *Power and Community: Dissenting Essays in Political Science.* New York: Random House, 1969.*

Greenstein, Fred I. *Personality and Politics.* Chicago: Markham, 1969.

Gurr, Ted Robert. *Why Men Rebel.* Princeton, N.J.: Princeton University Press, 1971.*

Hunter, Floyd. *Community Power Structure.* Chapel Hill: University of North Carolina Press, 1953.

Huntington, Samuel. *Political Order in Changing Societies.* New Haven: Yale University Press, 1968.

_____, and Clement H. Moore, eds. *Authoritarian Politics in Modern Society.* New York: Basic Books, 1970.

Inglehart, Ronald. *The Silent Revolution: Changing Values and Political Styles Among Western Publics.* Princeton, N.J.: Princeton University Press, 1977.

Kornhauser, William. *The Politics of Mass Society.* New York: Free Press, 1959.

Lasswell, Harold D., and Abraham Kaplan. *Power and Society.* New Haven: Yale University Press, 1963.*

Nisbet, Robert. *The Twilight of Authority.* New York: Oxford University Press, 1975.*

*Indicates a paperback edition is available.

Parenti, Michael. *Power and the Powerless.* New York: St. Martin's, 1978.*

Polsby, Nelson. *Community Power and Political Theory.* New Haven: Yale University Press, 1963.

Rogowski, Ronald. *Rational Legitimacy: A Theory of Political Support.* Princeton, N.J.: Princeton University Press, 1974.

Weber, Max. *The Theory of Social and Economic Organization.* Trans. A. M. Henderson. Talcott Parsons, ed. New York: Free Press, 1964.

Wolfe, Alan. *The Limits of Legitimacy: Political Contradictions of Contemporary Capitalism.* New York: Free Press, 1978.

6

Principles in Governing a Community: Rights and Restrictions

To no one will we sell, to no one will we deny, or delay, right or justice.

—Magna Carta

The dispensing of injustice is always in the right hands.

—Stanislaw Lec

Freedom of the press belongs to the man who owns one.

—A. J. Liebling

The man dies in all who keep silent in the face of tyranny.

— Wole Soyinka

The specific functions and institutions of politics which will be discussed in the chapters that follow occur in the context of broad general patterns of rule. In turn these patterns reflect some very simple and basic choices. We agree with Madison that if human beings were angels there would be no need for government, but as they are not, governments arise to help establish order. Yet, because human beings are less than angelic, the institutions they create are always flawed. It is necessary both to have government and to check it in some way. There are two basic principles at work here, which overlap but which are not the same. Their intersections create certain basic types of political systems and governments, which we may choose among by our assessment of how well they actually carry out the jobs we think are important.

The first of these issues is the question of sovereignty. Who rules? Is the preference for the people—democracy—or for some kind of minority rule—oligarchy, however defined? And perhaps just as important, how can we tell?

Who Rules?

Distinguishing *popular sovereignty* from *minority sovereignty* in action is not easy, in part because the definition of democracy is not clear-cut. The word literally means "rule by the people," a lofty but vague idea. Who are the people? How do they rule? To determine whether a state that calls itself democratic is at least attempting to let the people rule, some questions can be asked about its structure and operation. Perhaps most important is the simple matter of what "the people" means in political terms. How many of those who live within the boundaries of the system are actually granted the right and means of participating—voting, running for office, and so forth? Although the franchise (the right to vote) has been greatly expanded in this century, the size of the electorate as compared to the population in particular systems still ranges from a tiny percentage to as much as two-thirds, or even all adults. Locating a particular system within this range will tell you something about its claim to democracy.

Second, no matter how small an exclusion is, the way it is made is important. Excluding those below a certain age is generally accepted as less arbitrary than limiting by sex, race, or religion. The more of the latter, the more questionable the democratic principle. In addition, the methods adopted to enforce such exclusions, whether legal or informal, may be extremely damaging to both majority and minority. Finally, one can examine figures of actual participation. How many of those who *can* participate actually do? It is sometimes tricky to rely only on figures. A nation may have a turnout of 95 percent because it is not safe not to vote, or because there is a fine if you do not. A low turnout does not of itself indicate oppression, although exceptionally low figures indicate that something may be wrong. For example, the United States has had very low participation in some recent elections, even national ones, and many friends and critics of its system find this troubling. No one is exactly sure what the figures mean, although many explanations are advanced, including the supposition that many people do not vote even though they could, because they are so contented with the way things are!

The other half of the definition of democracy deals with the *mechanism of popular sovereignty*. Relatively few communities can be direct democracies. The simple problem of numbers makes this impossible in mass society—or at least it has until recently. The development of computer and telecommunications technology may well allow a "national town meeting" in which millions of people discuss and vote on a proposal without ever having to leave their homes. Even if this were to come about, however, there must still be leadership, to formulate issues and policies and to direct the implementation of decisions. The leadership itself in any case is not incidental to democracy. We can examine its composition to see if it reflects the whole society or has been drawn only from some small part of the community. Even those countries which have made the greatest strides in expanding their electorates have not generally been as successful in diversifying the leadership. Many factors account for this. Some subgroups have greater access to the money needed to run for office, or greater access to the qualifications considered important. Social norms that make it difficult for members of some sections of the community to be accepted or chosen as leaders by other sections are difficult to eradicate quickly, despite the end of legal restrictions. Nonetheless, the limited presence in many elected leaderships of women, minority ethnic and racial groups, and some religious groups is a cause for concern and continuing effort for change.

The organizing principle of a democratic mechanism, whether direct or representative, must be *majority rule* determined on a basis of *equality*. In representative democracies we may confront a mixed picture. The institution of *majority representation* and *control* will probably be the legislature. Executives may also reflect majority choice, but large parts of the executive agency of government are not elective or otherwise representative except by informal practice. With rare exceptions, the judiciaries are generally not established by majority rule either. The reasons for these arrangements, and their details, will be discussed in the chapters that focus on those particular aspects of government. Here we can note that it is still possible to identify some of these systems with mixed institutions as essentially democratic. First, the institutions based on popular consultation and majority rule have a prominent, if not controlling, position in the political process. Little, if anything, can be done without their consent. Second, these institutions have increased their powers over the years, while those of minority-constituency institutions (such as the British House of Lords) may have been reduced.

There are other avenues of popular representation and control. Special elections such as the referendum or initiative, for example, allow a direct vote on an issue rather than on a particular politician, thus opening policy questions for clearer public choice. Institutions such as factories, hospitals, and schools, if under public rather than private control, may be operated by majority rule. Those who work or are otherwise involved in their operation may be given some role in running these institutions, either directly or through boards that govern entire sections of the economy, such as energy or health care. A number of such experiments are under way in both Western social democracies and developing nations, and in socialist states such as Yugoslavia as well. Not all these systems are clearly political democracies, but even so, popular participation in the new ways is of great interest.

Institutional experiments with localized majority representation in societies in which some entrenched minority rules over the whole illustrate a mixed system with a balance that is not democratic. The basis for such overall minority rule reflects the history and culture of particular communities. The minority may be a traditional elite or aristocracy, entitled by birth to rule. Religious leaders may have a claim to rule or to choose rulers. A single party—whether Communist or Fascist or nationalist—may claim sole access to power, excluding all who are not members. In other cases the military may seize power and establish its own minority rule.

The distinction between majority and minority rule is not absolute—as we find so often in political questions. Most systems show some mixture. Few do not have some sign of minority or elite influence or control, and fewer have no channel for popular consultation at all, no matter how little used. It is possible to take various measures, however, and estimate what the balance is. The judgment that one then makes about it must reflect a personal perception of what is both right and effective.

Democracy has been compared to life on a raft; you manage to stay afloat but your feet are always wet. The British statesman Winston Churchill said that it is "the worst form of government . . . except for all the others." These remarks capture the ambivalence about democracy that even its friends may share. Is it possible, is it wise, to give control to the people, who may be uneducated, gripped by ancient prejudices, unaccustomed to rule and so irresponsible with power? Distrust of the ability of ordinary people to make decisions about complex or sensitive issues, as well as traditional or religious beliefs about authority, have led many people to conclude that the answer is no, that government is best entrusted to a minority that is better qualified to rule. Whatever we may prefer, however, the course of world history seems to be running in favor of majority rule, or at least its outward façade.

Restrictions on Rule

This distinction between *minority* and *majority rule* is often confused with the distinction between *limited* and *absolute rule*. They are similar, and often associated, but are not the same thing. The crucial feature in the second demarcation is the extent to which government itself is under law, with specific and enforceable limits upon its power, or is unrestricted except by its ability to mobilize goods and people in sufficient mass to carry out its purposes.

Like minority-rule governments, unlimited governments are not always so identified. A government may have a constitution with an extensive list of rights that belong to the people, including various participatory rights such as voting; in practice, however, it may pay no attention at all to these rights, economic or political. There are also governments which openly proclaim their right and intention to rule unchecked, although they are fewer than at some points in the past. Possibly the most obvious and infamous are the totalitarian systems, such as Nazi Germany. The principle of such rule is an argument for total control of all aspects of individual and communal life, including the interior life of thought and feeling. The greatest glory of the individual is to be submerged in the destiny of the nation, under the total sway of the "supermen" at the top. Such systems are essentially a twentieth-century phenomenon, the result of both mass politics and the technology that makes total control, total terror, at least possible. None of these regimes has entirely succeeded in realizing such control, but they have certainly attempted it. Some regimes in the more remote past are said to have had similar aims which their technological limitations obstructed—for example, some of the revolutionary regimes of France, or the late stages of Egypt under the pharaohs, or the Aztecs.

The human cost of such rule has been very great. Millions of people have perished under totalitarian rule, many without ever having made any effort to resist it or otherwise threaten the regime. During the worst years of Stalinist power, some twenty million people are said to have been killed in the Soviet Union, and many more millions died in Nazi Germany, Fascist Italy, and similar states. Many people think the present regimes of the USSR and China adhere to totalitarian principles. Whatever one thinks about that, it is certainly possible for totalitarian rule to appear in any country whose technology makes it possible. A new wave of totalitarian systems might assume a more benign appearance and be controlled by less brutal technology, as suggested by Aldous Huxley in his novel *Brave New World.*

Authoritarian, unlimited rule can exist in many forms. Uganda, Equatorial Guinea, Nicaragua, Paraguay, Argentina, North and South Korea have now, or in the recent past, fallen victim to one man or small group who ruled with deliberate cruelty. But authoritarian rule without mass violence is also possible. Absolute monarchies are still found—although some, such as that of Ethiopia, have been overthrown, and others, as in Saudi Arabia, are not entirely secure. Perhaps the most common of all forms is *military rule*, and no matter how benign, military rule, by definition, does not recognize constitutional limits. In fact this kind of system is so widespread that it warrants special attention.

Nearly half the nations in the United Nations are ruled by regimes that originated in military coups. What is more, the military has become the single most influential group in many other political systems. Almost all nations maintain standing armies regardless of real or apparent need; the exceptions, such as The Gambia and Costa Rica, are very small and often quite poor. For the rest, the military is a great expense. *World spending on arms outweighs all other categories of public expenditure,* outstripping spending on education, for example, by nearly three to one.

Such military dominance is not a new problem. Writers in all times have commented on the tendency of the sword to rule the plow. In some places military rule seems to be the permanent government; very few of the 115 changes of government in the past hundred and twenty-five years in Honduras, for example, failed to involve the military . What is new in this century is the expansion of military rule to vast new areas of the globe. In SubSaharan Africa, for instance, the first military coup occurred in 1963 in Togo, barely six years after the first independence celebration marked the beginning of the end of colonial rule on the continent. The bulk of the land, people, and power of Africa is now under military rule (although in 1979 Nigeria and Ghana returned the balance to civil rule). Much the same tale could be told of Latin America, the Middle East, and Southeast Asia. We might say that military rule has become the world norm. Only a handful of states—Canada, Great Britain, the United States, India, Australia, Kenya, for example—have never experienced such rule. How can we account for this?

There are two general sets of factors that help to explain the intrusion of the military into political life. The first factors are *internal*: the special role of the armed forces; their cohesion; and their political awareness. In the second set are *external* aspects of community life, the social and political circumstances that facilitate military entry into politics.

The most important internal motive is the unique role of the armed forces as the *protector of the state.* If civilian disorder appears to threat-

"In fulfilment of my promise . . .

. . . the time has now come . . .

. . . for me to hand over to civilian rule!"

en the integrity of the nation, intervention as a responsibility of this protector's role may result. Thus the soldiers and police who seized power in Ghana in 1966 called the resulting government the National Redemption Council. Significant differences between civilian government and the military about political programs—perhaps over a reduction in the arms budget—may also lead the military to take action, interpreting the protection of the nation to include protecting it from dangerous ideas. Such moves are commonly against left-wing, socialist, or communist policies, for the military is generally a conservative body. Peru, Portugal, and Ethiopia, however, illustrate in varying degrees military intervention against right-wing governments.

The propensity for military intervention is heightened by the cohesion of the armed forces, which may be far more unified than such social groups as labor. This solidarity may be spoken of as a justification for assumption of power, but the pressures of rule often reveal within the military the same ethnic, religious, or regional divisions that made civilian rule so fragile. Countercoups reflect the resulting struggle for supremacy in the military government. Despite this, the military leadership's autonomy and sense of professional identity are likely to serve as continuing bases for intervention. The fact that the military is increasingly an educated group increases its confidence that it can rule. When there are links with civilian intellectuals, as well as general exposure to political life, the political sympathies of the army may be quite strong. And links through family and friends will support awareness of civilian grievances against the government.

External social factors may either counteract these features of the military or support them. Where social cohesion and political legitimacy are both under strain, and scarcity makes conflict ever more bitter, the probability of a coup rises. If civilian politics has come to mean disorder and dictatorial but ineffectual rulers hanging on to power to enrich themselves, the opposition to a coup may be minimal—at least at first. Statues of deposed rulers are knocked down; there may be literally "dancing in the streets."

Once installed, military regimes take on the same distinctions as civilian ones; they will be reactionary or radical, activist or passive. Many have no particular program, other than ending disorder and providing some basis for national stability. These are "guardian" regimes, or caretakers, intending to restore civilian rule as soon as possible. Sometimes the assumption of power leads the military to forget the original intention, or the difficulties of national integration force it to postpone returning to the barracks. Other regimes clearly never intended to be temporary. In either case dislodging such regimes is not easy. Internal discontent must reach great heights, as it did in Ghana in 1978, to challenge military rule. Outside support at that point may help, as the condemnation of the Greek colonels in the European community did. Defeat in battle has ended the life of other regimes, such as that of Field Marshal Amin, or brought caretaker factions to power in a countercoup, notably in Mauritania in 1978 and Ghana in 1979.

We began this discussion with a note about the extent of military influence even under civilian regimes that firmly restrict the military to a service role. Some of the states that have never had direct military government are among those with the highest levels of military spending and employment. Some writers call such systems *garrison states,* civilian in form but devoting much political energy and much national wealth to military demands. For example, Israel and South Africa (and formerly Rhodesia) invest substantial portions of gross national product and labor force in arms. The United States and the Soviet Union are also in this category. Both devote a third or more of government revenue to the military establishments with which they confront each other; both allocate half or more of their public employees to military matters. The distorting effects of these concentrations are no less harmful domestically than they are dangerous internationally. For another pernicious consequence is the extension of military influence by the sale or donation of arms to real or supposed allies, which often leads to superpower combat through proxies. Despite all these adverse effects of the garrison state, it is unlikely to disappear. As long as the world remains divided into nation-states, separated by past enmities and present fears, holding on to irreconcilable visions of the future, the garrison state will probably be the major alternative to military rule itself.

The dominant political form in the world today is *one-party rule,* and the garrison state is often such a regime. Indeed, military rule is essentially a special form of one-party rule, in which the party is the armed services. In most instances one-party rule fits into the category of authoritarian systems. Often it is also a minority rule. Membership in the party, probably the key to attaining high status in many areas of life, may not be open to all. For example, in the Soviet Union only about 10 percent of the people are actually members of the Communist Party.

These general characteristics of one-party rule would seem to make supporters of popular sovereignty despair, but not all one-party political systems are hostile to democracy or to constitutional government. Some states have one-party-competitive systems which not only intend to support these two principles, but consider that in their circumstances multiparty rule might well detract from them. What has happened in these cases is a movement of competition from interparty to intraparty locations. In the newer and poorer nation-states, this is justified on grounds of the overwhelming primacy of deemphasizing social and political divisions and eliminating the waste and violence that has accompanied party competition. These systems are sometimes said to resemble what was called *machine government* in American city politics. They are based on careful organization of the population at the grass-roots and on the delivery of social services and economic benefits in exchange for political loyalty, much as the Democratic Party machine under Mayor Richard Daley in Chicago exchanged jobs for votes. The party itself provides a means of integrating the diverse peoples of the nation by eliminating divisive and sometimes artificial choosing of sides and mandated opposition even when there may be consensus, both inherent in multiparty systems. At the same time discussion and change can occur within the party, and upset victories by challengers are possible. In one election in Tanzania, for example, a number of parliamentarians who were also junior ministers lost their bids for renomination. In light of the all too real economic and political fragmentation of some new states, it is important not to dismiss these one-party options. For some developing nations, and also for some deeply divided older nation-states such as Yugoslavia, they may well be the best alternatives to cycles of disorder and military rule.

At the same time multiparty government under constitutional limits is not impossible in the Third World or in plural societies elsewhere. Both Nigeria and Ghana have reinstituted such systems, and others— Costa Rica, The Gambia, Switzerland—have had long experience with this form. Sometimes multiparty government is a reflection of the divisions of society. This may be called *consociational democracy*, in which government and party institutions are shaped around ethnic or other groups. Certain portions or positions of power are guaranteed to each group so that order can be maintained and social and political cohesion thus established. Consociational democracy is one solution to the difficulty of governing where there are deep cleavages in society. Other multiparty systems, even in plural societies, are built around national organizations that make appeals across communal divisions and propose to eradicate division rather than provide for it. Neither is absolutely right nor absolutely perfect. A key element in each, however, must be the presence of limits—restrictions on what government can do—so that minorities are assured of fair treatment while they remain minorities, and the parties that do not win office are assured that they can continue to compete for office.

The provision of limits to power, then, is a major consideration. What is a limited or constitutional government? How does it work? How is it compatible with democratic rule, if it is? In recent years, limiting state power, conceived of in terms of human rights, has become one of the most important debates in the world. We will take a rather detailed look at constitutionalism and its implications, because it is so important a problem. It is not always easy to separate the general issue from the charges and countercharges that specific states make about each other. Human rights issues thus become instruments of diplomacy and foreign policy. But they are more fundamental and far-reaching than that, no matter how often governments try to appropriate them for their own advantage.

Constitutionalism and Human Rights

Contemporary political communities, especially the nation-state, are established by a set of fundamental organizing principles, a constitution. This lays down the basic purposes of the community and the powers and responsibilities of its government. This is usually, although not always, a written document. A constitution in itself is necessary but not sufficient for constitutionalism. Some constitutions include guarantees of rights and freedoms, as either negative restrictions on government or positive commands to it. Where these are present, and there is some way to enforce them, then we can speak of a constitutional government, or constitutionalism.

The problem of application and enforcement of such rights is a thorny one. If the rules are to mean anything, some agency must apply them to the government. Often this job is given to the courts, although in some countries (Italy, Austria, West Germany, France) a special Council of State may be chosen. When the courts have the right to review the constitution, interpret it, and declare the actions and decisions of other parts of government to be constitutional or not, this is known as *judicial review*. It is an important political power, and often a determining element of constitutionalism.

Cases for judicial review may involve disputes between parts of the government or between government and citizen. How these are resolved depends upon the extent of judicial review. It may be granted to all courts or restricted to the highest. Certain issues, such as emergency regulations, may be excluded, or all aspects of government may be subject to it. There may be only a few categories of persons who can bring such suits—perhaps even a special official—or it may be extended to anyone who is harmed by the action being challenged. In much of Latin America a suit known as the *writ of amparo* makes it possible for anyone to sue, whether personally affected or not. The larger the grant of judicial review, the greater the power of the courts and their capacity to hold the government to its promises. In the United States, often said to be the originator of judicial review as a result of having the oldest written constitution, the review is very broad. Many American political problems wind up in the courts as constitutional arguments.

The function of judicial review is to uphold the constitution, even against a majority—unless the majority is at some point strong enough to change the constitution itself. Yet to be effective, judicial review requires both an independent judiciary and a supportive public. The first means that the judiciary must be willing and able to rule against the wishes or interests of the other branches of government if necessary, and even against a large part of the public. For example, the U.S. Supreme Court ruled against the practice of religious observances in the public schools, although it was clear that this decision angered a large section of the public. Guarantees of judicial independence can be enacted in statutes or constitutions. They can be easily manipulated, as many governments have proved, unless there is support from both public and politicians. This requires that the political culture be compatible with the principles of the rule of law. Courts themselves can help to build this support by speaking to these principles through their decisions in terms that can be understood, thus serving as "the conscience of the nation."

Judicial review has been attacked for its potentially undemocratic character, and in fact it may be sometimes used in support of a minority against the majority. This is inherent in the meaning of constitutionalism, part of the paradox of constitutional democracy. Combining popular sovereignty with protection for the rights of minorities must sometimes mean limiting the power of the majority. Those who framed the American Constitution knew well that majorities were not always right, that they might combine to oppress minorities, perhaps not even intentionally. Later, in the nineteenth century, the acute observer Alexis de Tocqueville remarked in his *Democracy in America* that such tyranny of the majority was perhaps the most difficult of authoritarian governments to dislodge, because it had so many heads. Unfortunately, unlimited or arbitrary government combines as well with majority as with minority rule. Limited government, on the other hand, is not incompatible with minority rule. The greatest difficulties seem to arise with the effort to combine majority rule and limited government. It was to this problem that judicial review was partly addressed.

Diversity Versus Conformity in Constitutional Democracy

The central problem in a constitutional democracy is the rights of the citizen as opposed to the power of the community. To what extent does the citizen have the right to conduct himself as he wishes without interference by the state? What are the citizen's obligations to the community? What are the rights of the community? What are the obligations of the community to the citizen? Too great a degree of diversity may lead to an atomism that destroys the cement binding the community together. The question of diversity versus conformity in a political community is the core issue dominating the history of constitutional democracy, the form of government in which such an issue is most vital.

Diversity is essential if there is ever to be change. Otherwise there is stagnation. To have diversity there must be a certain measure of freedom, freedom to be somewhat different from the majority. This utilitarian justification for freedom asserts that freedom is better because it produces a better society; it encourages a healthy diversity.

The radicals of the American Revolution would not have objected to this, but they went much further. The American Declaration of Independence justified human freedom by resorting to radical individualism, asserting that it is "self-evident" that freedom is an essential component of human nature without which human potential cannot be realized. Human beings had a right to be free because no agency had a right to take their freedom from them. On the other hand, as the great conservative writer Edmund Burke pointed out, the heritage of the past is of value to citizens in the present. Some measure of stable tradition is probably essential for a sense of security and dignity, as many who live in times of tumultuous change can testify. In a society in which free institutions have evolved, continuity and tradition should be preserved and protected.

Each of these justifications presents some difficulties. The conservative position can easily support restrictions on freedom when institutions that have evolved do not reflect principles of individual liberty. The utilitarian position also emphasizes society rather than rights themselves. If there is a situation in which society would be made stronger by restricting individual freedom, then the utilitarian doctrine would favor restrictions. The radical position, by contrast, is based upon the assertion of absolutes that many find it hard to consider self-evident. Nevertheless, it is the only justification that centers upon freedom as an end in itself and not as a means to another goal. It is the only justification that cannot be turned around and used as an argument against freedom. And however uncomfortable it may make the modern social scientist, it cannot be rejected without implying the ultimate rejection of human freedom itself.

If we follow this approach, and say that no human agency has the right to restrict individual liberty, what are the implications for democracy? With its majority rule basis, democracy presupposes some coercion of those who disagree with the majority. Although some argue that participation in the democratic process implies that the losers have consented to the outcome and are therefore as much a party to the victory as the winners, there are no completely satisfactory answers to the question of minorities as opposed to majorities. In the United States, John C. Calhoun's nineteenth-century formulations proposing a minority veto—effectively a unanimity principle—will not do in an era that emphasizes the importance of democratic principles. There are numerous theories of individual rights, and the same holds true for theories of the rights of the group. What is needed is a clearer statement of the relationship between the rights of each.

It is tempting to speak of the community as something with its own organic existence, but actually it is nothing other than a collection of people. It functions as the people who comprise it make it function, and its purposes are the purposes of human beings. The community exists to enable human beings to achieve something that would be impossible without it. Whether that something is security, public works, scientific advancement, or national glory, the political community is the tool of the human beings who produce it. As such, its "rights" are only those of the human group. It is a dangerous abstraction to speak of the rights of the community or the government as opposed to those of the people. They are the same. Governments, of course, may interpret their role to be that of the community and act as if they had rights that are separate from those of the people, but governments, like communities, are human creations and have no justification other than to serve the community, which is to say the people.

The question for democracy, then, is to what degree individuals have rights that should not be infringed, and to what degree they have obligations to the group or community, that is, social obligations. The form of government called constitutional democracy explicitly recognizes that human beings are endowed with rights as individuals, and that a certain measure of conformity is necessary to enable human beings collectively to form and to direct a political community, but always within established limits. It recognizes a place for both independently functioning citizens and a civic responsibility that demands of each citizen certain things that are necessary for the political community to exist.

Constitutional democracy emphasizes the similarities that unite, so that differences may exist but not divide. It attempts to obtain only the degree of conformity that is necessary to ensure the cohesiveness of the community, no more. Such a conformity must not be imposed upon the people, or the very basis for constitutional democracy crumbles. Cohesiveness must, instead, arise from the character of the people themselves as expressed by their democratic actions. The constitutional side of the formulation prevents democracy from overstepping the limits of government imposition. Social cohesiveness does not demand that every person conform to every practice of the community, or even that every person conform at all, except in some most basic respects. Constitutional democracy is designed to keep government what logic would have it, the tool of the people—the community—and yet to provide enough power to permit collective action while protecting the right of each person to differ from the group. It tries to draw the line only as a last resort, to prohibit only conduct that clearly damages other persons or the social fabric, not to stamp out ideas or conduct that merely differ from, or disagree with, the norm.

Like every other human creation, constitutional democracy is far from perfect, and it often fails to achieve the goals of promoting both individual and community potential. No form of government can insure that these goals will be attained, but some may guarantee that they won't. Constitutional democracy seems the form most likely to encourage success, or at least discourage failure. As a general category it contains greatly different institutions and practices, and new ones will be devised. Which of them is best suited for a particular community is a decision for that community, if it is fortunate enough to have the choice.

SELECTED READINGS

Barber, Benjamin R. *The Death of Communal Liberty: A History of Freedom in a Swiss Mountain Canton.* Princeton, N.J.: Princeton University Press, 1974.*

Bayley, David H. *Public Liberties in the New States.* Chicago: Rand McNally, 1964.*

Benello, George C., and Dimitrios Roussopoulos, eds. *The Case for Participatory Democracy: Some Prospects for a Radical Society.* Baltimore: Penguin Books, 1972.*

Bezold, Clement, ed. *Anticipatory Democracy: People in the Politics of the Future.* New York: Random House, 1978.*

Cohen, Carl, ed. *Communism, Fascism, and Democracy.* New York: Random House, 1972.

Dahl, Robert A. *Polyarchy: Participation and Opposition.* New Haven: Yale University Press, 1971.*

_____. *A Preface to Democracy Theory.* Chicago: University of Chicago Press, 1962.*

Domínguez, Jorge I., et al. *Enhancing Global Human Rights.* New York: McGraw-Hill, 1979.*

Duchacek, Ivo D. *Rights and Liberties in the World Today.* Santa Barbara, Calif.: ABC Clio Press, 1973.*

*Indicates a paperback edition is available.

Finer, S. E. *The Man on Horseback: The Role of the Military in Politics.* Baltimore: Penguin Books, 1962.*

Friedrich, Carl J. *Limited Government: A Comparison.* Englewood Cliffs, N.J.: Prentice-Hall, 1974.* Constitutionalism; judicial review.

_____. *The Impact of American Constitutionalism Abroad.* Boston: Boston University Press, 1967.

Gotlieb, Allan E., ed. *Human Rights, Federalism and Minorities.* Toronto: Canadian Institute of International Affairs, 1970.

Huntington, Samuel P., and Clement H. Moore, eds. *Authoritarian Politics in Modern Society.* New York: Basic Books, 1970.

Jenkins, David. *Job Power: Blue and White Collar Democracy.* Baltimore: Penguin Books, 1974.* A comparative study of democracy in the workplace.

Lijphart, Arend. *Democracy in Plural Societies: A Comparative Exploration.* New Haven: Yale University Press, 1977.

Lucas, J. R. *Democracy and Participation.* Baltimore: Penguin Books, 1978.*

McConnell, Grant. *Private Power and American Democracy.* New York: Random House, 1970.*

Nordlinger, Eric A. *Soldiers in Politics: Military Coups and Governments.* Englewood Cliffs, N.J.: Prentice-Hall, 1976.*

Nwabueze, Benjamin O. *Constitutionalism in the Emergent States.* London: C. Hurst, 1973.

Perlmutter, Amos. *The Military and Politics in Modern Times.* New Haven: Yale University Press, 1977.

Pollis, Adamantia, and Peter Schwab, eds. *Human Rights: Cultural and Ideological Perspectives.* New York: Praeger, 1979.

Revel, Jean François. *The Totalitarian Temptation.* Baltimore: Penguin Books, 1978.*

Thorson, Thomas L. *The Logic of Democracy.* New York: Holt, Rinehart and Winston, 1962.

Welch, Claude, and Arthur K. Smith. *Military Role and Rule.* North Scituate, Mass.: Duxbury Press, 1974.*

Wolff, Robert Paul, ed. *The Rule of Law.* New York: Simon and Schuster, 1971.* A critique of the concept as a politically loaded idea, and a comparative examination of its function.

Part Two

THE PRACTICE OF POLITICS

Every man is the creature of the age in which he lives; very few are able to raise themselves above the ideas of the time.

—*Voltaire*

7

The Organization of Territory

Unless we emerge out of colonialism as one
political unit, separate independence will have
made us less united than we are at present and
will at the same time have reduced both the desire
for unity and the chances of bringing it about.

—Julius Nyerere

The coexistence of several nations under the same
state is a text as well as the best security of
freedom.

—Lord Acton

A Union of the States is a Union of the men
composing them, from whence a *national*
character results to the whole.

—Rufus King

It is in general a necessary condition of free
institutions that the boundaries of government
should coincide in the main with those of
nationality.

—John Stuart Mill

The simpler [centralized] forms of government
are fundamentally defective.

—Edmund Burke

Whether governments are democratic or authoritarian, their methods of institutionalizing territorial control have important consequences. The territorial dimension of contemporary politics is diverse and fascinating; it ranges from the deceptively simple sophistication of states with a long tradition of centralization to the complex experiments in governing vast territories of North and South America.

The rise of the nation-state in the eighteenth century coincided with an emerging political philosophy that asserted the "rights of man" and began the transformation of the medieval serf into the modern democratic citizen. The form of these new national states was a mixture of tradition and innovation, and in the case of federal states, a significant new form was created. We can classify these modern states as *unitary, federal,* and *confederal.* Each form reflects a very different history and approach to politics, and a careful analysis of its essential characteristics will tell us a great deal about politics in those systems.

Unitary Systems

Unitary states concentrate political power in a central (or national) government. There is a striking resemblance between modern unitary states and the monarchies they generally replaced. The exercise of political power may be constitutionally limited, but the central government has no constitutional rival for the allegiance and, to be sure, the taxes of its subjects. As in France and England, subdivisions abound, but they exist as conveniences for the national government and may not, legally at least, claim the total loyalty of the population. The essential quality of a unitary state is in the *exclusiveness of its territorial claim,* although the exercise of power within its borders may be limited in the name of "participation" or "devolution" or traditions of local autonomy. It is precisely the traditions of local involvement that offset the rigidities of unitary systems. The need to provide for local customs and expectations in the nominally uniform policies of the central government is an essential element of politics in unitary states.

The form and content of such flexibility vary widely. In France, for example, the prefects, who are the heads of the major administrative units, the departments, are representatives of the national government rather than the local population. A successful prefect, however, is one who involves individuals and groups within the department in the administrative process and in the interchange of ideas that routinely takes place in the communication between the prefect and the ministries in Paris. There is a very thin but critical line between routine involvement and indifference. If a government is to maintain the allegiance of its citizens, that critical difference has to be respected.

In the American experience, the practice of "home rule" acknowledges a similar reality. The American states, within their borders, are unitary systems. Home rule is simply a measured grant of autonomy from the state governments to the counties or municipalities, allowing the realization of the ideals of local democracy and self-government. Once given, such grants of authority to local communities are not easily reclaimed, and the political system must adjust to this reality. The advantage of this kind of flexibility is obvious: the local community responds as part of a larger whole, and its goals and energies both reflect the locality and strengthen the center. The disadvantages are also obvious: too much diversity or deviation from a central norm may be undesirable. Success depends upon a sophisticated sharing of functions and responsibilities, despite the constitutionally unitary format. The way in which this sharing occurs depends on the traditions and customs of the particular state or country. Certain critical functions, such as police protection, are sometimes retained by the central government, as in France and Spain, while in other systems they are vested in the local authorities, as in the American states, although perhaps with substantial coordination by the center, which is the British practice. Determination of how much power the central government will claim varies according to historical and ideological influences, as well as judgments of how much responsibility can be borne by local communities of differing areas and populations. These judgments may change with time, and whatever degree of home rule has been permitted by the center may be augmented or diminished.

As the heirs of centralized monarchical (and colonial) regimes, unitary states presume that allegiance is constitutionally directed toward the institutions of the central, national government; there can be only one king. Although certain manifestations of local diversity may be allowed, even welcomed, the ultimate determination of policy is made by people in the national government, without the formal restrictions on national action found in the constitutions of federal states—and without any formal need to take local wishes into account. The implications of this for cultural and ethnic diversity are important. A centralized state's ability to adjust to pressures for regional, ethnic, or linguistic autonomy in education, for example, would be less than that of a system in which the responsibility for education is vested in a constitutionally recognized territorial subunit, such as a state in the United States. (Perhaps for this reason there was great opposition in the United States to the recent establishment of a federal cabinet Department of Education, even though the states would not thereby lose their role in education.) Decentralizing pressures in unitary states go against the grain of the system, while they flow naturally from both the logic and practice of a federal form of government. A decision by a school district in one of the southwestern states

©Punch/Rothco

*"What we need is a strong,
authoritarian government with the
courage to bring in
compulsory laissez-faire."*

of the United States to teach Spanish as a first language would have no direct impact on students in other districts or other states, although implementation would certainly be watched with interest in other places where Spanish is widely spoken. In unitary systems such questions of cultural diversity are automatically of importance to, and referred to, policy makers at the national level. The point is not that deviation and diversity are never permitted. It is simply that in unitary states the psychological and political momentum is directed toward the center and the expectation of unity. Local variation is a privilege granted by the center insofar as the effect on unity is expected to be insignificant.

In recent years there has been a substantial amount of pressure in unitary states for more formal distribution of power to local communities. In the Sudan, Ghana, and the Philippines either ethnic or religious pressures have forced changes in the internal allocation of power. This pressure is also visible in the debates about devolution in Great Britain and the Basque separatist movement in Spain—one conducted by ballots and the other by bullets. Local discontent also simmers in countries riven by linguistic battles, such as Belgium, India, and Canada, and in France, where such groups as the Celtic Bretons have never been fully reconciled to rule from Paris. Many modern nation-states are the random result of war and the disintegration of empires. They show intricate patterns of ethnic, national, and linguistic group dispersion that reflect their histories as collections of peoples, joined together by needs and loyalties that erode or shift as the fortunes of the nation are influenced by world events. The fate of movements for more local autonomy lies in the depth and intensity of the separatist critique, the response of the political majority, and the reaction of outsiders. Similarly, the meaning of independence will vary with the particular circumstances. In the case of Scotland and Wales, each seeks more autonomy in its internal or domestic affairs. There is no demand to alter the common arrangements for national defense or to conduct separate and distinct foreign policies. Other separatist movements, from Brittany to Katanga (now Shaba), have made more concerted efforts to achieve truly "national" independence.

The organization of politics in unitary states reflects the omnipresent role of the national government in the daily lives of the people. Whether the issue is the draft, education, the price of peanuts or cocoa, or the decision to build a nuclear power plant, the responsibility for these subjects will be exercised in a distant national ministry. This means that the objectives of political parties and interest groups are necessarily defined and articulated in national terms, because the target of their actions must be the national capital and the corridors and chambers of the national government. Local politics in unitary states thus tend to be national politics in miniature, and local issues and personalities are often overwhelmed by the intrusion of national affairs into the local community. In some cases there are no truly "local issues" in unitary states. The weight of national issues simply displaces any other concerns. This is particularly true in developing areas, where the effort to build stable national governments is so intensive that there is little room for local concerns to emerge. At least this is the hope, and often the rationale, when countries adopt unitary systems where federal systems might seem more compatible with the plural societies that are ubiquitous in the Third World.

Federal Systems

In federal states, by contrast to unitary ones, political power is shared by a central national government and a number of constituent governments—regions, provinces, republics, states, cantons, länder. Canada, Australia, Mexico, and Malaysia all have federal systems. (See chart on

p. 89 for other federal systems.) Power is shared by a formal constitutional division of authority between the different and clearly distinct levels of government. Each political system allocates powers in its own fashion, which gives to each federal system a distinctly different character. The hallmark of all federal states, however, is the constitutional division of power, including finance, between central and territorial units.

Federal states have adopted this model for a number of reasons. The framers of the American Constitution, the first document of national federation, wanted a system in which a careful and deliberate fragmentation of power would inhibit its abuse by a tyrannical person or group. The division of duties and responsibilities between the national government and the states was part of a design for regional patterns of political activity. The great distances between parts of the country made it unlikely that national majorities would emerge overnight. Elites in the various states, assisted by the limited suffrage of that era, stood as barriers against change and the tyranny of numbers that so many delegates at the Philadelphia Convention feared. For the framers, especially James Madison, the states were psychological and political impediments placed in the path of "mischief." Each state had many decades of separate colonial existence and a distinctly different identity to preserve. Each would continue to have a life of its own, part of the pattern of decentralization that would offer a limited number of voters a variety of issues and personalities. National majorities would not form easily because popular attention would be drawn to many separate and divergent local or state issues.

Another appeal of federalism is that it allows a reconciliation of the conflicting forces of unity and diversity within the same political system. This is a particularly attractive idea in states with large territories to govern, and in those with a number of distinct and geographically separate ethnic or linguistic groups. Both the Soviet Union and Yugoslavia have federal constitutions that give the territorial republics autonomy in a number of areas (including a unique Soviet arrangement of UN membership for Byelorussia and the Ukraine). In both these countries, however, federalism is overwhelmed by the apparatus of the Communist Party and decision making is effectively "nationalized" or centralized (and neither the Byelorussian nor the Ukranian UN delegation is truly independent).

The state of Utah provides an interesting example of how federalism works in the United States. Heavily populated by communicants of the Mormon Church, Utah reflects the strong influence of the Mormon presence in its social institutions and government policies. Federalism provides a political structure in which such a group, if it has the size and the inclination, can influence or even control the way of life in that jurisdiction. The national government may, however, set limits to this diversity,

Federalism in the World

Federal Constitutions

The Americas: Canada, the United States, Mexico, Venezuela, Argentina, Brazil.

Europe: The Soviet Union, Yugoslavia, Czechoslovakia, Switzerland, Austria, West Germany.

Asia and the Pacific: India, Malaysia, Australia.

Africa: Nigeria, Tanzania.

Federal Experiments

Systems that utilize a federal element (some degree of autonomy for one or more provinces within a formally unitary structure): Belgium, Burma, People's Republic of China, Colombia, Denmark, Equatorial Guinea, Finland, Iraq, Israel, Italy, Japan, Lebanon, the Netherlands, South Africa, Sudan, Tanzania, United Kingdom

Abandoned federations: Pakistan (after secession of Bangladesh), Burma (after military coup), Indonesia, Uganda, Central Africa (Rhodesia-Nyasaland), East Africa, Mali (separation into Mali and Senegal), Camaroon, Union of South Africa, United Arab Republic, Federation of Arab Republics, West Indies, Saint Kitts-Nevis-Anguilla.

Proposed federations: Cyprus, South Africa, Israel-Palestine, Europe, Spain, Chad, Ethiopia, Africa, North America, United Kingdom and Ireland.

as the United States did in refusing to admit Utah as a state so long as the Mormons sanctioned the practice of polygamy.

Federal systems, like their unitary counterparts, create their own unique style of politics. Their territorial governments tend to duplicate national institutions. Each of the American states resembles the others, and the national government too, in its government structure (Nebraska, with its unicameral legislature, is the notable exception). Each state is expected to provide similar services such as education, mental health care, and police protection.

The fragmentation of power among these units also fragments political parties and interest groups. Political parties in the United States are basically state parties organized around local or regional issues and personalities. Although forced to coalesce by the electoral college method of electing a president, they retain much of their separate character on issues. This side of American politics is vividly displayed at the national party conventions when the delegates of the fifty states (and the territories) meet every four years to choose presidential and vice-presidential candidates.

The significance of fragmentation is not lost on those who wish to localize certain issues and preserve them for local disposition. In the United States, for example, one would expect the state of Oklahoma to be more indulgent with the interests of oil producers than the distant and more diversified national Congress would be. Observance of religious holidays, or prohibition, may be retained in a state dominated by Muslims or Baptists, such as Nigeria's Kano and the United States' Kansas, when the national systems disregard these claims.

The movement of issues and personalities from the state and local to the national level is as important in federal systems as fragmentation. Issues that begin at an isolated spot may take on regional or national importance, and as they move from one level to another they are subject to the influences of different interests. The composition of local majorities may be quite different from those at another level in the constitutional structure. The recurring conflict in Australia between the national government and the state of Queensland about the state's harsh treatment of Aborigines is a case in point. In trying to influence policy making, groups may find it advantageous to change the locale of the debate, or, as in the Queensland dispute, it may be strategically sound for local groups to claim the principle of "state's rights." There is a form of political appeal in federal systems that can provide an outlet for groups isolated at the local level. A local minority's claim may be treated favorably because the group is part of a state or national majority on other issues. This is not likely to happen in unitary states, where there is usually a convergence of local and minority positions; a minority posture is solely a minority posture.

Additionally, attitudes about public questions can vary significantly among the units of a federal union. Each unit may have a different yet constitutionally acceptable response. The principle of diversity admits this possibility, but it can be a source of conflict if state diversity seems to allow local denial of some people's national rights. The question is: When do the actions of state or local governments become a threat to the larger consensus required for national unity? The claim of diversity in the name of constitutional rights produced the U.S. Civil War. It is at the heart of the conflict in Canada about the rights of the francophone community, Quebec.

Various methods exist to negotiate or, if necessary, adjudicate the disputes that arise in federal states. Disputes may involve the central government and one of the territorial units, or they may represent conflicting claims among units about the rights of their respective citizens or even the location of their boundaries. In the United States the states administer legal systems that are structurally distinct and may produce strikingly different conclusions from state to state. It is common in the United States, for example, to find state criminal justice systems dispensing significantly different punishments for the same offenses, and giving radically different interpretations of the nature, causes, and treatment of antisocial behavior. Similarly, treatment of crimes in local courts in Nigeria is often very different between the Shari'a courts of the Muslim northern states and courts of the southern states. Major discrepancies that cannot be dealt with through bargaining between the units may require the intervention of the national legislature or some other national agency empowered to resolve disputes. Since it is not possible to anticipate all possible sources of conflict in political systems, some authoritative body must settle disputes in a politically acceptable manner. It may be the national high court, through its power of judicial review, as we have noted. Alternatively a specially appointed body, some sort of council of state, may take on this job. The role of either court or council is to resolve conflict, and thus reaffirm the consensus and purpose necessary for the survival of the federal union.

Because criminal law in the United States is primarily the domain of the states, the clash of unity with diversity takes on special meaning in the role of the Supreme Court in guaranteeing national constitutional rights. Recently the issue of capital punishment as related to the federal constitutional prohibition against "cruel and unusual punishment" has been a major question appealed from the states to the Supreme Court. Resolution may eventually require promulgation of a national standard, as the differences in land tenure among Nigerian states led to a federal decree on that question.

As in the political arena, the duality of the legal system creates the possibility of appeal from one level of the system to another. The national court or constitutional council may reverse the decision of a lower, locally controlled body. In addition to resolving a particular dispute, the court or council indirectly standardizes, or nationalizes, the legal system. As the territorial judicial and legislative bodies adjust to these decisions, changes in the law and its implementation gradually take place. In this way other injustices at the state or local level are remedied. Hostility and refusal to comply with a national decision may require the threat or use of force by the national government or a moderation of the demands of both parties in a politically acceptable fashion.

A continuing problem in federal systems is the distribution of rewards on an equitable basis to all members of the national state. The locus of responsibility for various social-welfare functions is a critical choice. The United States is one of the few federal systems in which an extensive range of responsibilities is placed either at the local level or in the private sector (theoretically free from the influences and concerns of public institutions). The states in the United States have important roles in the provision of public assistance, police protection, and education. Certain functions such as health care are still essentially private activities. Such a system of localized, or private, responsibilities can lead, as in the legal arena, to major variations in the quantity and quality of services. Certain states may have superior educational facilities, while others may be recognized for the excellent standard of care in their mental institutions. These variations are potential sources of conflict within a population that is highly mobile. As families move from state to state for occupational reasons, major discrepancies in the quality of public services, and the level of taxation required to support them, could become issues of constitutional significance.

In federations in developing countries, the national government does most of the jobs done by the private sector in older states such as the United States, so that this is not a major issue. In some of these new federations fears of communal differences in other parts of the country may keep most people from freely changing their place of residence. Each state may in fact erect barriers to movement by favoring its own indigenes in giving out scholarships or civil service posts. Such factors temporarily reduce mobility and its resultant pressures for greater uniformity. But development will probably encourage mobility, and economic development itself is part of the argument against too much local diversity and autonomy.

The degree of state autonomy in a federal system is a major factor in its economic activity. The need to attract business and industry to particular areas can lead to practices that are harmful to the individual interests of some local residents. Some states may discourage labor unions, offer special privileges to business and industry, even establish government agencies to recruit new establishments and investments from other states or foreign countries. This is not a reflection of overall national wealth, but rather of distribution of that wealth, as the extensive business promotion activities of states such as North and South Carolina, Georgia, and Texas indicate.

The result of this competition may be uneven corporate and individual taxation, and correspondingly uneven social services, that offer a basis for national intervention in the name of national equality in crucial aspects of life. Economic development is one of the most important challenges to federal systems. For developing countries authority over the allocation of resources and over the principles that govern allocation are vital to rapid and yet evenly distributed growth. The states in the United States federal system represent wide variations in economic development. Their influence in national decision making through elected representatives or by informal means is important for their economic well-being. Each state calculates how much it contributes to the federal government and how much is returned in the form of grants-in-aid, federal military bases, or other economic benefits. The redistribution of tax revenues is a basic issue in the internal politics of federal systems. Development projects undertaken for national purposes may have the incidental effect of preferential treatment for some states; we can see this at work in Mexico's border improvement programs and Brazil's plans for frontier development. If there are shifting patterns of population, along with variable state or regional political influence at the center, the potential is high for economic imbalances within federations. Similar imbalances may also occur within unitary states, but the dynamics of federation require that such systems give these discrepancies more attention.

In many ways relationships within federal systems resemble those among nation-states. There is the question of dual citizenship and the right to move from state to state, and there is a long-standing problem in the United States on the matter of extradition between states in criminal cases. There may be problems, such as the degree to which states may control the movement of goods and people across their borders. Do states have the right to forbid people from other states to take up residence? To what extent may states try to protect their resources and environments from depletion by uncontrolled immigration from other parts of the country? Should the national government undertake an overall settlement program? In developing countries central governments have on occasion tried to restrict movement—generally from rural to urban areas—but often without success. Efforts by state governments to discourage new arrivals—such as Oregon's welcome to tourists but not to new residents—are frequently challenged as discriminatory. Such problems are likely to increase rather than disappear as the pressures on resources rise in most societies.

Citizens in federal states must also contend with the problem of mobility and residence in voting. Establishing the requirements for voting in the United States, for example, is historically and constitutionally a prerogative of the states. Population mobility and differing requirements have combined to disfranchise a large number of people. The result is increasing demand for federal intervention or standardization. Other federations, such as Nigeria, have simply abandoned locally established electoral rolls and given this job to a national agency.

Given the logic of federal systems, there will always be discrepancies between the ideal and actual achievement. There are, in the nature of this form of government, implicit tendencies toward both parochialism and universality. The substance of politics will, at any given moment, reflect this paradox. If there are constitutional grants of power to two or more distinct levels of government, the possibility and even probability of inequities and inequalities among citizens of the various territorial units is virtually guaranteed.

The most consistent source of tension in federal states is a result of the centrifugal forces that develop within the system. In the United States, for example, the Civil War was fought to answer a very theoretical question: Does a group of states have the right to sever the agreement that created the union? The centrifugal forces were slavery, industrialization, capitalism, and the intoxicating doctrine of "states' rights." The victory of the North in the Civil War was fundamentally a victory for the political and economic goals of that region. Ironically, the weakness of the central Confederate government was a factor in the defeat of the southern states that challenged those goals.

In the contemporary example of Nigeria there are strong similarities to the experience of the United States in the mid-nineteenth century. Nigeria arose through British colonial artifice, combining many ethnic and religious groups in a large and geographically varied territory. Since independence in 1960, Nigeria has struggled with the pressures of unity and diversity; as in the United States, a civil war was fought as a result of the intense conflict between two major partners to the federal agreement. The federal victory that ended the Biafran secessionist effort did not put an end to the divisions, but the Nigerian communities and their elites are committed to reconciliation of these differences within the framework of a single federal system. The intervention of the Nigerian military in the course of the breakdown that led to civil war dramatically altered the balance of power between central and constituent governments, and will profoundly affect the shape of federal politics in the future, even though the military itself supported federalism as it prepared to return to the barracks.

The complexities of the "federal bargain" are clearly visible in Canada as well, in the efforts of the Parti Québécois and the French-speaking community of Québec Province to redefine their political, economic, and cultural relationship to anglophone Canada. Here the logic of federalism is being put to the ultimate test, allowing one province an extraordinary degree of political, economic, cultural, and diplomatic autonomy without actual separation from the federation. The effort to create a "sovereignty association" for Québec indicates the intensity of nationalist feelings, and the consequent strains, that can develop in multinational states. From the perspective of the francophone separatists, Canada is an English country. The predominant language, traditions, and institutions reflect the English heritage of the majority. The minority status of francophone Canadians then becomes a simple denial of the right of self-determination, and the federal structure a negation of group prerogatives rather than the means of their guarantee.

The practical aspects of the Québec problem are equally important. Will an independent Québec be economically and politically viable? Would anything beyond marginal economic and political life require massive doses of external assistance, a kind of "neofederalism" paralleling the "neocolonialism" that converts one kind of dependency to another? Or perhaps, in a final irony, might the separatist path lead inexorably to association with the neighboring federal giant, the United States? From these considerations we may learn a basic truth for the Canadian example and for federal states in general: the equilibrium of a system may depend upon a number of very sophisticated and fragile compromises among what may be the best of various unattractive choices.

Secession need not be the total dissolution of a federal system, of course. In some cases the secession of a truly unwilling and incompatible partner may be the key to the damping of communal conflict in the continuing federation, as well as to political integration in the newly independent segment. Malaysia and Singapore chose this alternative when it became apparent that continued union would bring with it uncontrollable communal bloodletting.

Unity and Diversity

We should not conclude that centrifugal forces, whirling states apart, are found only in federal systems. It is clear that they exist in both federal and unitary states. Theoretically one would expect more flexible responses from federal states to demands for greater communal autonomy, since federalism presumes the divisibility and fragmentation of power for the good of the national community. Unitary states, in theory, prefer to centralize power for that same purpose. By informally or formally delegating greater power to subordinate units than theory requires, however, unitary states can respond to communal pressures. The use of regional or functional bodies can easily provide a different perspective and configuration of support on a wide range of issues if the central government wishes to have them. Intention rather than structural arrangements may be the differentiating factor.

The pressure for decentralization in unitary states is matched by pressure for centralization in federal states. And both types are faced by external challenges to their national integration and autonomy. The major differences between the two systems are therefore often more imagined than real, a subject of more interest to interpreters and observers of constitutions than to the population. It is misleading to draw major conclusions about the characteristics of unitary and federal states from their constitutions alone. Both kinds have responded to a range of issues and problems that affect their constitutional differences and their functional similarities. France, for example, has created a system of regional economic councils in a country often cited as a classic example of the unitary model.

By the end of the 1970s the world was divided into more than a hundred and sixty nation-states, and almost all had unitary systems. This preference is partly explained by the addition of so many newly independent Third World states in the years since World War II. Only a handful of these states are now federal, and many of the "federal failures" have occurred among them. Given the imperatives of economic growth and development, plus national integration, the appeal of a unitary form is not surprising. Control over economic change is of major significance, and unitary government is thought to be an advantage in that area. Yet substantial numbers of the world's people live in federal systems. Most of the largest countries, by area and by population, are federal. Elements of federalism are found in a number of unitary states that have heterogeneous or "plural" societies, such as Belgium. And new "federal solutions" are constantly put forward, in addition to experiments with the looser forms of association sometimes called "confederal" arrangements.

The Confederal Union

The confederal form is sometimes a precursor to federation, although it may stand of itself for long periods. The West African Asante Confederacy, the North American Iroquois League, the old Swiss Confederation, the United States before 1789 and the subsequent secessionist Confederate States, are examples of this arrangement. The essence of confederalism is retention of power by the constituent units. The central government has minimal responsibilities; it can be thought of as a coordinating unit, without the vast array of duties and responsibilities usually assigned to central governments in federal states.

Confederal systems declined as the need for more centralized power and authority increased. International affairs, national and international economic activity, and the centralizing influences of urbanization and industrialization produced their demise. In the United States, the Civil War answered the immediate issue of secession and strengthened the powers of the center at the same time.

Confederation is important today as an influence in the relationships between independent nation-states. Many of the international organizations of the world are in essence confederal; the member-states relinquish little if any autonomy to a supranational agency. The post–World War II era has been one of multiplying numbers of such agencies and organizations. Political, economic, security, scientific, educational, cultural, and health interests have led to joint activity by both nations and functional groups through international organizations. The United Nations and its associated agencies; the North Atlantic Treaty Organization and the counterpart Warsaw Pact; the European Common Market and other regional economic associations—all are manifestations of the use of confederal principles to stabilize political and economic relationships in a volatile world.

It may be that some of these confederal relationships will lead to greater—that is, federal—union among the nation-states of the world. There are long-standing visions of a "United States of Europe" and a "United States of Africa" based on the premise that a federal relationship provides the best of both worlds, recognizing regional unity while giving the myriad individual expressions of identity within that region substantial autonomy. The European community in particular is trembling on the brink of federal integration, having elected a directly representative European Parliament in the summer of 1979; but it may yet draw back. Neither the Organization of African Unity nor the Organization of American States has moved beyond the first tentative stages of confederal association—national unity rather than continental unity is still primary. But in the commitment to peaceful association that they represent, even such minimal associations should not be dismissed as inconsequential.

The issue at the heart of all these structural considerations is the regulation of conflicting interests, which, as Madison pointed out in the *Federalist Papers* (No. 10), is a basic or even primary function of the political process. Unitary, federal, and confederal forms of organization are simply different expressions of this function. The form chosen and the way it operates depend on the judgment of the best distribution of power among particular political communities and the achievement of their purposes. Some important elements in the regulation of conflicting interests are the nature of leadership and the quality of representation, regardless of the territorial distribution of power, in decision making.

SELECTED READINGS

Bertelsen, Judy S., ed. *Non-State Nations in International Politics*. New York: Praeger, 1977.

Burrows, Bernard, Geoffrey Denton and Geoffrey Edwards, eds. *Federal Solutions to European Issues*. London: Macmillan for the Federal Trust, 1978.*

Currie, David P., ed. *Federalism and the New Nations of Africa*. Chicago: University of Chicago Press, 1964.

*Indicates a paperback edition is available.

Diop, Cheikh Anta. *Black Africa: The Economic and Cultural Basis for a Federated State.* Westport, Conn: Lawrence Hill, 1978.

Duchacek, Ivo D. *Comparative Federalism: The Territorial Dimensions of Politics.* New York: Holt, Rinehart and Winston, 1970.*

Elazar, Daniel J. *American Federalism: A View from the States.* 2nd ed. New York: T. Y. Crowell, 1972.

_____, et al., eds. *Cooperation and Conflict: A Reader in American Federalism.* Itasca, Ill.: Peacock, 1969.

Eleazu, Uma O. *Federalism and Nation-Building.* Ilfracombe, England: Arthur H. Stockwell, 1977.

The Federalist Papers, Clinton Rossiter, ed. New York: New American Library, 1961.*

Franck, Thomas M. *Why Federations Fail: An Inquiry Into the Requisites for Successful Federalism.* New York: New York University Press, 1968.

Friedrich, Carl J. *Trends of Federalism in Theory and Practice.* New York: Praeger, 1968.

Gotlieb, Allan E., ed. *Human Rights, Federalism and Minorities.* Toronto: Canadian Institute of International Affairs, 1970.

Hay, Peter. *Federalism and Supranational Organizations: Patterns for New Legal Structures.* Urbana: University of Illinois Press, 1966.

Jensen, Merrill, ed. *Regionalism in America.* Madison: University of Wisconsin Press, 1965.*

Johnston, Richard E. *The Effect of Judicial Review on Federal-State Relations in Australia, Canada and the United States.* Baton Rouge: Louisiana State University Press, 1969.

Leach, Richard H. *American Federalism.* New York: Norton, 1970.*

Lindberg, Leon, and Stuart Scheingold. *Regional Integration.* Cambridge, Mass.: Harvard University Press, 1971.

Macmahon, Arthur W. *Federalism: Mature and Emergent.* New York: Russell and Russell, 1962.

Marshall, Burke. *Federalism and Civil Rights.* New York: Columbia University Press, 1964.

Riker, William H. *Federalism: Origin, Operation, Significance.* Boston: Little, Brown, 1964.*

Smiley, Donald V. *Canada in Question: Federalism in the Seventies.* Toronto: McGraw-Hill Ryerson, 1972.*

Watts, R. L. *Administration in Federal Systems.* London: Hutchinson Educational, 1970.

_____. *New Federations: Experiments in the Commonwealth.* Oxford, England: Clarendon Press, 1966.

Wheare, K. C. *Federal Government.* 4th ed. London: Oxford University Press, 1961.*

Wildavsky, Aaron, ed. *American Federalism in Perspective.* Boston: Little, Brown, 1967.*

8

Representation and Leadership

There is nothing more difficult to take in hand . . .
than to take the lead in the introduction of a new
order of things.

—Niccolo Machiavelli

It is frequently a misfortune to have very brilliant
men in charge of affairs; they expect too much of
ordinary men.

— Thucydides

A leader is best
When people barely know he exists. . . .
When his work is done, his aim fulfilled,
They will say, "We did this ourselves."

—Lao-tse

Every community has some institutionalized process for arriving at agreements regarding what is or is not to be required or permitted, some method that leads to decisions about group goals, strategies, and tactics. The political process permits societies to reach some agreement about the attitudes, preferences, beliefs, and values of the community, and then transmits them to the controlling institutions.

In theory at least, decisions in a democratic system are made by the community, or at least by representatives the community selects. In non-democratic systems, of course, the process is considerably different in form and substance. Nevertheless, virtually every modern nation has incorporated into its political structure an institution that formally proclaims community decisions, the legislature. Before turning our attention to legislatures, however, we should consider some broader issues.

In the very rare instances of direct democracy—situations in which the people meet regularly and administer their affairs directly with no formal institution other than the group—there may be no need for representation or formal leadership. In any other circumstances, representation would be totally absent only if there were no organized society at all. Even the most brutal and self-serving dictatorships claim to represent the people, and even they must take care to retain at least passive support if they are to remain in power.

History records few instances of truly direct democracy except in small societies, usually isolated and pretechnological. Similarly there are few examples of human groups with no organized social and political institutions except in brief periods of chaos or catastrophe. Nor has the ideal of anarchy—order without rule—been realized beyond a few transient utopian groups. Everywhere else there are and have been political institutions of various sorts, most of which we classify as governments. Some others are not considered governmental but they assume a political character in carrying out the basic functions of governments. They too depend upon some form of both representation and leadership.

Representation and Leadership in Political Communities

To examine representation we need to determine just what or who is supposed to be represented. Although today we are inclined to assume that the individual human being is the basic unit of politics, and therefore is to be represented, this is by no means a universal assumption. In some societies, for example, the basic unit is the family. In patriarchal arrangements fathers might be considered to represent the interests of the whole family, and thus alone have the power of political participation. In fact this was essentially the situation in the United States until well into the twentieth century, when the Nineteenth Amendment opened the vote to women. The operative presumption until that time was that women and children need not participate politically because they were fully represented by their fathers if they were children (or, it may be noted, unmarried women) or by their husbands if they were wives. In matriarchal societies it would be the mothers who possessed the right of political participation, once more as representatives of the family. An example of a political power that was restricted to women may be seen in the case of certain American Indian tribes in early colonial New England. The mothers in these tribes chose the chiefs.

Today, of course, the overwhelming political entity is the nation-state, and most nations provide the vote, in some form, to all adult citizens. Local governments within those nations are sometimes allowed to deviate from this principle when the constraints of diversity seem to require it. On traditional and religious grounds, northern Nigeria did not grant women the right to vote at independence, although the rest of the country did. The principles of popular participation and representation have gained widespread acceptance in constitutions, even if we suspect that this is sometimes feigned rather than genuine. There are some common exceptions. Convicts, the insane, and those not considered capable of mature reflection are generally excluded. The largest such category of the latter is of course children (defined at varying ages by different societies). They are citizens, yet they may not vote or otherwise participate in political affairs. Residents who are not citizens are also excluded in most nations (Sweden is a rare exception), as are expatriates in some cases.

During the North American revolutionary period, the Tories in England argued that the colonies were "virtually" represented in Parliament, even though the colonists had no vote and no other way to influence the selection of M.P.s. This notion of virtual representation, or representation of those with no power of political participation, is now ostensibly dead. Woman suffrage is not universal, but the idea exists in most places and the practice is spreading. This suggests that fathers need no longer be considered the sole representatives of families, and that adult citizens, not families, are the units to be represented. But the idea of virtual representation has not been totally discarded. For those who are excluded from participation in political matters, it continues to exist.

There are suggestions, also, of other variations on the theme of representation. The Italian Fascists of Mussolini's day argued for what they called "corporate representation," or corporativism, which would represent classes and occupational groups and perhaps other important social institutions such as churches and universities. This kind of representation might be very appealing to inhabitants of mass polities who feel that their votes as individuals are lost in the shuffle and their group interests as members of, say, the middle class or a university are slighted. In many societies, including Belgium and Malaysia, there is in fact a form of corporate representation called consociationalism. This provides arrangements for linguistic, ethnic, or religious group representation to preserve the identity and interests of these entities. Many modern theorists of the pluralist school argue that industrial democracies tend to operate on a group basis, regardless of individual suffrage and individualistic rhetoric, since they respond much more satisfactorily to the demands of organized interest groups than to individual pressures. Many of these societies initially moved toward representative government on the assumption that certain interests would be collectively recognized, and this is reflected in the naming of various parts of the legislature, such as the Three Estates in France and the Commons and Lords in England.

Another kind of corporate representation is based upon territorial grouping. The most common form of this is in federalism, which generally has one house of its legislature reserved for representatives of the states, provinces, or regions of the nation. There are suggestions for representation of cities in national politics in a similar way. Proposals have been made in some third world nations, such as Ghana, for a division between armed forces and civilians, with representation of each as a corporate group, in a "union government," by which it is hoped that the cycle of military coups could be stopped. This is obviously not a simple issue, and the most reasonable solution to corporate vs. individual representation will vary from society to society. There is no clearly right or wrong choice.

Direct democracy is best known in the example of the Greek city-states, which actually applied it in a very limited way, excluding slaves, women, and foreigners, even naturalized ones. It is also found in the town meeting in some New England towns, used for purely local issues. Similar arrangements exist in other systems, such as the *ujamaa* villages in Tanzania, the neighborhood committees in Cuba, and work groups in Sweden. In many developing nations these innovations are based on a kind of traditional politics focused on the village, in which the entire community met together, discussed problems, and reached a consensus without a chief or other authority to direct the process. Such societies are called "acephalous," or headless, to indicate the absence of formal leadership. Moots in medieval England worked much the same way.

Revolutionary periods have often produced direct democracy in the early stages. In revolutionary France, for example, as in Hungary in 1956, small self-governing groups—committees—were rapidly formed. Unfortunately these autonomous groups are generally swallowed by the institutionalized revolution or destroyed when revolution fails. International politics also looks something like these direct democracies, with collective decisions by all the members of an international organization or informal grouping. The actors themselves of course are nations rather than individuals (another kind of corporate representation), and the unlikely assumption is that national members represent the interests of all their citizens.

The issue of representation is made much more complex if we acknowledge at this juncture the concept and role of leadership in political affairs. Simplistically we may want to believe that our thoughts and ideas about what we prefer become policy in some direct, equal, and undistorted way. In fact we know that other people affect the way we think and act, leading and shaping our opinions and thoughts about the world around us. A newspaper editor, a village elder, or an elected president may also, in this sense, perform a representational role. The leader may articulate goals or directions with a force or clarity unmatched by a collective deliberation. Leadership is a quality. It is also a role, assumed in most cases by individuals, in some by institutions—a political elite, a party, a church, or a collegial executive such as the one planned for post-Tito Yugoslavia. Whatever the form, the leader symbolizes aspirations and, in a political sense, represents the hopes or frustrations of a people. Leaders can capture a mood, or create it, and draw our attention to both themselves and what they are saying. While leadership without politics is a nightmare, politics without leadership is impossible. Idi Amin in Uganda might be said to represent the first. Those who opposed him were for a long time unable to act in the absence of leadership, and so illustrate the second. One of our concerns in this discussion will be to assess the manner in which leadership appears and is institutionalized.

Political Implications of Representation and Leadership in Nongovernmental Groups

In recent years increasing recognition has been given to the political implications of certain nongovernmental groups, and particularly to the impact of their internal procedures upon the wider community. The formal institutions of the political process are generally governmental, established by, if not in, the government. There are also many private and semiprivate institutions that nevertheless have profoundly political effects and implications. Various economic institutions are among them; the public and its leaders take an interest in the behavior of business corporations—and through the mechanism of the corporate charter may attempt to control such behavior to some extent, as well as regulating it by statute. For example, there are demands in the United States that large corporations be required to have "public representatives" on their boards of directors. Some corporations in South Africa have had some impact on politics there by their decision to follow the "Sullivan Principles" and change their internal policies about discrimination in hiring, promotion, and benefits.

The most obvious of the nongovernmental groups that affect politics may be the numerous pressure groups that exercise influence upon governments everywhere. Even more fundamental is the political party, a frustratingly ambiguous and almost unclassifiable institution which has made its way into almost all national systems. The introduction of elec-

"All power to the board of directors!"

Drawing by Koren; © 1971 The New Yorker Magazine, Inc.

tions into the European Economic Community will certainly induce the formation of regional parties there, and the Communist International has long played a role in world politics. The political party is in some sense a bridge between the governmental and the private, which is now coming under ever greater public control. In the United States and Great Britain, for example, the position of parties is quasipublic. A U.S. Supreme Court decision recognized this in the 1940s when civil rights groups challenged the exclusion of blacks from Democratic Party activities, including primary elections. The Court rejected the argument that such activities were purely private and not subject to regulation. Since then the constitutional role of the parties in the United States system has been more or less taken for granted, and much of their behavior is regulated although they remain outside the official apparatus of government. No statutes prescribe the number of parties, their membership, or other programmatic features, although certain things are forbidden—such as exclusionary practices—and a great deal of the financing is public or publicly regulated. Other states have gone further; Nigeria, for example, now specifies in the new constitution that all parties must have a national membership and program, and must be certified by a national electoral commission. There was considerable support in Nigeria for the idea of actually creating parties within the new constitution, spelling out names and programs, and permitting no others. In the end this was not done, but it has occurred—constitutionally or by statute—in other countries. Such a structured system is particularly attractive to developing nations which feel that uncontrolled proliferation of parties is destabilizing. Senegal, for example, identified three ideological positions, and permitted only one party for each in its 1978 national elections. Other parties were simply eliminated from the campaign and thus from the possibility of governing, although they were not abolished. Still other nations have taken complete control of parties by making them official agencies of government and prohibiting opposition parties. The long list of such nations includes Tanzania to Yugoslavia to Argentina. Even here, however, distinctions are usually made between party and government.

Whatever their degree of governmental control, the character of representation and leadership in political parties is important to the whole political process. Parties are almost universally oligarchical, with control in the hands of a few powerful leaders. This is as true of Western parties as it is of revolutionary and Marxist ones. Research indicates that this is true in practice for most organizations, regardless of how democratic they may be in principle. However, democratic organizations do have the potential of popular control, at least for brief periods. In the United States recent revisions of party governance have created for the first time a structure that could operate at a fairly democratic level given the proper conditions.

Each of the two major parties is governed formally by a national convention, with a substructure of national committees and chairmen. There are similar organizations at the state, county, and local level. If they choose to exercise it, party members have the power of strongly influencing party affairs. Selecting delegates to the national conventions now involves local meetings at the grass-roots level, with party members choosing delegates to represent them at higher levels. Moreover, most party nominees are now chosen by the direct party primary election, in which party members may select candidates not favored by party leaders. Note that there is a major exception here: it is the national convention, not a primary, that selects the party's presidential and vice-presidential candidates. Presidential primaries merely select delegates from some states to the convention, and some primaries do not even do this.

Delegate selection in practice, however, is not so democratic as it may appear, although to some extent this is not the fault of the parties themselves. There are local meetings, but party members often do not take advantage of them. In nearly all instances the members who participate represent only a minuscule portion of those eligible. This occasionally permits a small but organized faction to seize control in a certain district, but what usually happens is that only a few of the party faithful turn out to follow the wishes of the leaders, and are thus able to dominate the procedures. The practice of providing for a hierarchy of meetings, each of which chooses delegates from among its participants to attend the next higher level, greatly increases the likelihood of elite dominance. At every level the actual representation of grass-roots party members becomes less and less. Party leaders similarly tend to dominate many of the direct primaries by control of funds, access to media, formal endorsements of certain candidates, and other devices. In this instance, though, the people do have the final voice, and may be more fully represented than in many others. The quality of that representation is another matter.

In most nations parties are even more under the control of leaders. The British Labour Party, for example, has less direct individual participation or influence than the U.S. parties. Most nations have not attempted to legislate democratic control of their parties, although some have tried to require that they not exclude certain groups or sections. Nigeria has established such qualifications in the constitution for the return to civilian rule.

Private organizations usually represent their members' interests in ways similar to those of governments. The members elect officers who manage the affairs of the organization. The larger groups will have professional administrators and staff who answer to an elected board with its various officers. The frequent practice of putting forth a slate of candidates chosen by a nominating committee usually guarantees that the selection will represent the wishes of the leaders rather than those of the membership as a whole; this is especially true when the election is not contested, as is often the case. The election of company management by stockholders is managed in exactly the same way. It is rare, though not impossible, in either group to find a faction challenging and defeating this approved slate. Custom and tradition often discourage democracy and reduce the degree to which an organization actually represents its members. And as an organization gets larger, so too does the power of the leaders, particularly when buttressed by a professional staff.

In theory the membership of a typical organization determines policy through its elected representatives, whereas the executive director or hired administrator merely attends to administrative details of routine functions. Once again the reality is different. Whether we are considering the common structure of business or other private associations, or the similar arrangements that exist in many governmental bodies (such as the school districts in the United States with elected boards and professional administrators, or council-manager cities with elected councils and a hired city administrator), the pattern tends to be the same. It matters little whether we are looking at Sweden, the United States, South Africa, or

New Zealand. Because the controlling bodies tend to be part-time, with few resources of their own, they tend to defer to the permanent administrative staff, which in most cases wields the actual power with little control by the governing body except in unusual circumstances. This is likely to occur in any institution with a lay board and a professional administration, whether it is private or public. In executive ministries the elected or politically appointed heads are often outwitted or outlasted by the "PermSecs," the senior permanent civil service officials and staff who have real control. The preference for generalist over specialist may reduce this tendency. British or Kenyan academics, for example, participate more than many teachers in running their institutions. They believe they *can* instruct the administrators, who may actually be academics on rotation. But the pattern is there. Representation functions minimally, at best, in many such organizations.

The Political Implications of Informal Representation and Leadership

Occasionally certain patterns of unofficial leadership exert great influence by their representational character. A prominent spokesman for a profession or a labor group may arise; the role of the spokesman is not necessarily rooted in a formal institution such as a labor union (as the early career of César Chavez on behalf of migrant workers in California attests). There are many examples of leaders who come to represent one section of the community, even without any initial group identity. One of the most obvious in the United States is Ralph Nader and his colleagues who work on behalf of "consumers." Although there are no formal processes of collective decision, and many would protest that consumers have not in fact been consulted, there are nonetheless some elements of representation present. The support (financial and otherwise) that developed spontaneously for Nader is partial evidence of this curious informal representation. (It should be noted that in 1979 a federal judge denied Nader's right to sue on behalf of the public, on the grounds that he held no formally representative position.) Another, larger-scale example is that of Mohandas Ghandi, one of the most famous figures of the twentieth century. With no official position at all, he mobilized the forces of Indian nationalism and led the way to Indian independence. Unquestionably he was at least as fully representative of the Indian people as any government leader could have been, and his influence, at least as a symbol, has lasted long after his death. In the same way Charles de Gaulle was representative of a major segment of the French people after the

Germans overran France in World War II and ended the Third Republic. His role began by default and grew to the point where he was able to found a new republic, the Fifth, brought about by the near civil war in 1958 and the paralysis of the Fourth Republic when faced with the Algerian crisis. The success of Martin Luther King, Jr., who had no official position beyond one of the civil rights groups in America but nevertheless represented the interests of black citizens at a critical point in American history, is another excellent illustration.

Many other figures emerge to represent large but unorganized groups, sometimes regional, linguistic, or racial, and develop great impact. Religious movements often create such leaders (and vice versa), as the existence of numerous spokesmen for traditional beliefs, cults, and splinter groups clearly attests. Traditional leaders outside the pattern of formal political mechanisms often exert great influence, whether as leaders of secret societies in West Africa or Mafia dons in Sicily. The old-time American political bosses who represented the interests of newly arrived immigrants not yet comfortable in American society present still another instance of a kind of representation that is largely political but also informal. Their importance is indicated by the difficulties today's immigrants have—especially those whose first language is not English—in finding a personal, nonbureaucratic helping hand.

Despite the many different methods that communities devise to decide on their basic directions and policies, the formal procedures almost invariably culminate in some form of legislative body, coupled with an appropriate form of executive. Both institutions deserve careful examination.

Origins and Characteristics of the Legislature

Legislatures take on many different forms and functions. The one thing they have in common is that they have the constitutional authority to make the laws, which is also the power to repeal or change them. The degree to which a legislature exercises power varies from nation to nation, but regardless of its actual influence in the political system, the distinguishing feature of a legislature is that it is the formal lawmaking body.

Because legislatures differ so substantially, it is difficult to generalize about their real functions. Certainly it is true that much legislation originates elsewhere, even for the most powerful legislatures, and it is true that much of the activity of any legislature is merely a holding action pending developments elsewhere. Nevertheless, the legislature formally enacts the laws, and the formal enactment of laws accomplishes whatever conflict resolution or management the legislature performs. In this sense, therefore, lawmaking or the passage of laws is the key to virtually all activities of legislatures. Regardless of how we may interpret the "true" functions of legislatures, the power to adopt statutes is the central and most important power.

Legislatures are not recent inventions, and they really are not inventions at all. They are as much the product of historical accident and evolutionary development as they are a carefully devised institution of politics. The tendency today might be to assume that legislatures arose as a reflection of a newly developing democratic spirit, to provide a voice for the people and a means to counter the arbitrary power of kings. The truth, however, is less romantic.

The theory of modern legislatures does, in general, assume them to be the representatives of the people. Their origins, however, are much more clearly rooted in the struggles of various elites to gain power than in a democratic effort to provide representation for the masses. The most easily identifiable beginning was in 1215, when King John of England granted the Magna Carta (Great Charter) and so agreed to some restrictions upon his power. But the impetus for the Magna Carta was not a people's uprising; it was a group of nobles who banded together to force the King to recognize the rights of the aristocrats. This mild but highly significant first step led ultimately to the British Parliament, the first modern legislature, so widely copied throughout the world that it is called the "mother of parliaments."

There were, of course, some legislative predecessors long before 1215. Throughout history rulers have been called upon to share their power with certain groups or councils, and some societies in all parts of the globe have developed mechanisms for representation and deliberation, sometimes strikingly democratic ones. For example, kings in some parts of East Africa swore an oath to do justice, and there were officials and councils to insure that they did. The Magna Carta was not a sudden and wholly new idea, but it was a point from which contemporary legislative development can be traced in an unbroken line. (An even earlier event was the convening of the *Althing*, or Assembly, in Iceland in 930; this body was dissolved from 1800 to 1874, but otherwise stands as the oldest legislature in the world.)

Although not very democratic at the outset, the modern legislature did grow from efforts to check one-person rule. The step toward a truly democratic theory of representation was a logical one, and so great has the ideal of universal participation come to be that nearly all societies now pay at least lip service to this theory. In both democratic and non-democratic political systems the tendency is to incorporate a legislature that at least in theory speaks for the people. It proclaims the laws and legitimizes the acts of the government as being of and for, if not by, the people. Exceptions to this are very rare.

Legislative power varies considerably. Some legislatures are purely rubber stamps, totally dominated by the executive. Even here, though, the legislature may possess some influence. Perhaps individual legislators have some persuasive power because of their prestige, ethnic group, or region. Perhaps the legislature as a group may have some effect for similar reasons. The detention of parliamentarians in executive-controlled states—as in Kenya in the mid-1970s—is testimony to their power at least to publicize critical views of the government. Other legislatures are moderately powerful, with regular influence on the government (especially with regard to procedural issues as opposed to broad policy matters). Approaching the other end of the continuum is the powerful legislature, one that participates routinely in many governmental activities that the executive consults regularly. At the extreme end is the all-powerful legislature, which has been called "assembly government." In this situation the legislature overwhelms a weak executive, as in the French Third and Fourth Republics. In such a system the tendency is toward great instability and great ineffectiveness, which many argue must invariably produce a powerful executive, possibly even a dictator, as an escape from this turmoil. There have been some small-scale models that did not end that way; some American cities, for example, have governed themselves without an executive. The need for some kind of executive direction, however, is very strong, and such experiments were often shortlived, although local governments in many countries have survived and prospered in an approximation of this form.

Legislative-Executive Relations

The two broad categories of legislatures in the modern world are those found in *parliamentary* and those in *presidential* systems, sometimes thought of as British and American models. Some legislatures are difficult to classify. The system in the French Fifth Republic, for example, displays certain characteristics of both the presidential and the parliamentary forms, and there are many others like it among developing nations. Legislatures in Communist nations are parliamentary in form, but they do not operate the way Western parliamentary legislatures do, partly because they serve different purposes. The variants tend to be some combination of the two broad types, or a variation of one of them, rather than wholly different forms.

In parliamentary systems the executive is technically a part of the legislature. The members of parliament are the only officials elected directly by the people, and parliament in turn selects the prime minister and other ministers from its own ranks. In practice, the majority party in parliament (which may be the only party) selects its leaders as these ministers. If no party is strong enough to do this, coalitions may be formed, with the government posts divided by some agreed-upon formula. Even very tiny parties can be important in forming coalition majorities and holding them together. The Liberal Party in Britain, for example, has recently played this role.

A major characteristic of parliamentary government thus is that powers and institutions are not clearly separated. The executive and the legislative are parts of the same institution. Another characteristic is that elections do not occur at regular intervals, but may come at any time (although a maximum interval may be specified). If the leadership believes conditions are favorable, it may call a parliamentary election hoping to increase its majority or at least extend its time in office. If conditions are not favorable, elections will be avoided if possible. When the governing party loses a major bill, there *must* be general elections. Parliament will be dissolved, and the subsequent elections will determine whether the same party retains power or is replaced. Such parliamentary votes are called *motions of confidence.*

The typical parliamentary system separates the executive function into two parts. The prime minister is head of government, and the monarch—or president, in a republic—is head of state. In federal systems this is repeated in the subsystems; for example, the state-level titles in India are chief minister and governor. The position of head of state is primarily ceremonial, and the real power usually lies with the head of government, although the symbolic role of the head of state as the representative of the nation or people can be very important.

The presidential form of government is dominated by the notion of separation of powers, or institutions. The legislature is elected, but it does not in turn choose the chief executive and cabinet. The chief executive is elected separately, probably at the same time, and has independent status. He may not dissolve the legislature, and elections occur only at regularly specified intervals, regardless of the state of relations between executive and legislature. This form also typically incorporates both executive roles (head of government and head of state) into the presidency. In federal systems too the same format is followed at state level, with a governor rather than president. (The municipal form is usually called mayoral government.) Other members of the executive—the department heads—may be chosen by the chief executive, or they may be elected separately, as in some states of the United States. This latter method may mean a politically divided executive.

The parliamentary system has been widely preferred because it avoids the deadlock that may occur in the presidential form when the executive and the legislature disagree. Any such major disagreement in the parliamentary form provides the people with an immediate opportunity to settle the issue by casting their ballots, but in a presidential system a deadlock could continue until the next election. Even an election might not settle the issue, because the people may choose a president of one party and a legislature of another. This has routinely occurred in the United States during the past few decades whenever a Republican president has been in office, since the Congress has been almost always controlled by the Democrats. Of course split party government does not always mean disharmony; a Republican president and a Democratic Congress worked well together in the late 1950s. Nor does one-party control guarantee cooperation. Democratic presidents have found that Democratic Congresses can be quite obstructive, as shown by President Carter's inability to get an overwhelmingly Democratic Congress to support his energy policy in the late 1970s. Whatever the party situation, deadlock is possible in a presidential system, and some contend that it is probable.

There is also a danger in the parliamentary system, and that is the possibility of instability. In plural societies the issue of particularistic leadership must be added to this general problem. Since elections are irregular, it is possible to have them so often, with such frequent turnovers in governments, that little if anything can be accomplished. Although this is different from deadlock, the effect may be the same. And where the prime minister and other dominant executive posts are seen by the nation as representing only a part of the whole—perhaps as the result of imbalanced coalitions—the instability is heightened by the consequent diminution of legitimacy. The governments of postwar Italy and of postwar France before De Gaulle illustrate the first aspect of this instability, overly frequent elections. Italy has had over forty governments in this period, and France had nearly two dozen before turning to De Gaulle. The collapse of the Nigerian republic after six years of independence is an example of the second aspect, overly narrow leadership. This issue in part turns upon underlying political and social conditions. If they are inherently stable, parliamentary government will reflect that, and if not, it will reflect that too. The British parliamentary system, for example, is among the world's most stable and most efficient, and is a favorite of a great many political scientists.

Nevertheless, the presidential form is inherently more stable, both because it provides a means of choosing truly national leaders and because it is designed to respond to a governmental crisis with compromise rather than confrontation by immediate elections. (If compromise is badly lacking, the ensuing conflict may lead to disaster, as so often seen in Latin American presidential systems.) In presidential systems elections are artificial in that they are "programmed" in advance and may have no relevance to any burning issues of the day. During a time of national emergency, such as war, the parliamentary system may abandon elections altogether and set up a government of all parties for the duration, as the British did in World War II. In dramatic contrast, the United States system is so committed to scheduled elections that it holds them in wartime, even in the Civil War, with soldiers on active duty voting.

Like most political entities, each system has its advantages and its defects. The presidential system offers basic stability and the parliamentary system offers efficiency and responsiveness to the popular will. The disadvantages of the presidential system are the possibilities of inefficiency and deadlock, and those of the parliamentary system are the possibilities of instability and perhaps an executive not perceived as representative by a majority of the people. In either case, when the system is adapted to the social institutions and political culture of the nation, it can work well. Nations that are "in transition" are likely to have difficulties with either form and to experiment with several versions, possibly bringing on army intervention in these circumstances.

Whatever the form of a legislature, it may be organized into one chamber or two—unicameral or bicameral. In federal systems there are almost always two houses, one to represent the constituent units, and their powers may be equally balanced. Otherwise the "upper chamber" is often the weaker of the two, particularly in parliamentary systems. The British model has the House of Lords, once very strong but now much reduced in power compared to the House of Commons. This model was carried to most of the British colonial parliaments and generally retained after independence.

In the United States the Senate is fully equal to the House of Representatives and even has some powers in foreign affairs not given to the House. Forty-nine of the fifty states have two equal houses, despite the lack of any obvious need for the duplication. At the national level federalism provides one such reason for bicameralism. Developing nations may find others if they wish to represent certain groups. An upper chamber may be established if some other kind of corporate representation, perhaps a symbolic one, is thought useful. Otherwise a single house offers the advantage of being less expensive, simpler, and probably more efficient—although critics sometimes say that efficiency can lead to ill-considered action. Either system can work well, depending on the circumstances and the general outline of the whole political system.

Another important aspect of legislative structure is the division into committees. Most legislatures handle their work in this way, to permit some degree of specialization and to reduce the otherwise unmanageable press of business. Very few of them, however, permit their committees to exercise as much power as the American congressional committees have acquired. Despite some recent reforms, these committees, and especially their chairmen, often have more control over legislation than the House or Senate as a whole. Many state legislatures behave the same way. The parliamentary committees of Great Britain and similar legislatures have far less power. Committees of other legislatures, whether European, Third World, or socialist, do not receive much attention because they are relatively insignificant except for more efficient operation.

Roles and Functions of Legislatures and Executives

Although the primary function of a legislature is lawmaking, it is paradoxically necessary to explain that the legislature is not, and cannot be, the focal point of policy making. For a variety of reasons legislatures have failed to be the primary originators of policy. Except in the rare and generally short-lived examples of assembly government, executives everywhere are dominant. The tendency in all nations, even the most democratic, is the growth and predominance of executive power. Legislatures lack the cohesiveness, singleness of purpose, and efficient organization that are possible for executives. Even their greatest justification in democratic terms, the contention that they are the segment of government most representative of the people, has been challenged by the argument that the executive represents the people as well, and in a presidential system is the only representative of the whole people. No matter how powerful, legislatures are overshadowed by the highly visible presidents, premiers, chairmen, and other chief executives and their coteries of bodyguards, advisers, *chefs*, and other aides. Does this shift indicate a usurpation of the traditional and rightful powers of legislatures, or does it reflect a profound change in contemporary social, political, and economic relationships?

The growth of executive influence is clearly a part of the evolution of the modern state. Government has become more complex, and the perspectives of those engaged in politics have changed as the boundaries of politics expanded. In addition, the significance of international affairs weighs heavily on domestic concerns. Legislatures are, as compared to the hierarchically organized executive branches, often unwieldy bodies (some have hundreds or even thousands of members), divided internally by ideological, regional, ethnic, or religious cleavages, and unable to provide a sustained and vigorous leadership. It is the idea of leadership that is important. Its relationship to the expectations of community members about the purposes of politics is critical in modern political life. We should be concerned about this for at least two reasons. First, it may indicate overreliance on a symbol of communal aspirations, whatever the level or size of community; and second, leadership without institutionalized restraints (including legislative prerogatives) may degenerate into arrogance or tyranny.

In many parts of the world hereditary monarchies and military regimes are the established pattern. The hallmark of both is the monopolization of power in the person of monarch, military officer, or group (known as *junta* from the common Latin American term). These forms are the antithesis of constitutional or parliamentary democracy. Monarchies and military regimes rule in the name of tradition or order, perhaps ostensibly "for the people," but at base they are a denial of the concept of popular sovereignty. Constitutional monarchies (and the occasional military aberration that claims constitutional origins, such as the first military government of Nigeria) are an effort to combine monopolized power and shared power. They succeed largely to the extent that the monarch has lost any but symbolic functions and powers.

Most Communist regimes provide yet another pattern of executive dominance. While the form of government in such regimes is often parliamentary, the locus of real power, both legislative and executive, is in the executive of the party. The party and its leaders dominate the political institutions and control the other social institutions. Party leaders are the leaders of government and governmental institutions are simply the intermediary bodies through which they exercise power. Debate and differences of opinion take place within the structure of the party, and only to the extent that it allows. Leadership is a function of party, not electoral, support and the monopolization of power by the party characterizes the political process. In these countries executive leadership is synonymous with the person who is the major force within the party, and while the administration of policy may be accomplished by traditional government ministries, the division of duties and responsibilities should not be confused with the exercise of power itself.

Within the ranks of the party, the posts of secretary general or chairman—as in the Soviet Union and China—are the preeminent positions. In some cases the holder of this office may not have an official governmental position, but nonetheless is the real wielder of executive authority.

Despite the formal or constitutional differences that exist among nations or regimes, executives share a number of characteristics. Their power is based on a structure of relationships that creates a basis of authority, ranging from the traditional, family-derived authority of kings or sheikhs to the electoral, constitutional authority of prime ministers and presidents. In any of these cases, however, the nature of the specific basis of authority defines the character of the regime and gives substance to the style of politics in that regime. What distinguishes regimes from each other, then, is not just strength or weakness, concentration or sharing of power, but also the claim to authority and the source of support for that claim, its legitimacy. This in turn determines whether certain kinds of action will constitute dangerous violations of legitimate authority in one regime and not in another. For example, the abuses known as Watergate drove Richard Nixon from the presidency when they became known, but in many governments would hardly have been cause for alarm—if indeed they would have been uncovered at all.

It is true, perhaps, that one inevitable but potentially dangerous condition of human existence is the division of social groups into those who lead and those who follow. What may be more important than a debate about the universality of this condition is an examination of the relationship that exists between leader and follower, elite and mass. What are the limitations to arbitrary and capricious action by leaders and slavish compliance by followers? To make this assessment, one must necessarily ask philosophical and ideological questions about the organization of political, economic, and social life. The trains may have run on time under dictators such as Mussolini, but the sufferings of those imprisoned or executed for their political beliefs outweigh that alleged efficiency. Did the rapid street repairs and the profusion of new buildings on the Chicago skyline compensate for the absence of political diversity in the government of that city under Mayor Daley? Under what sociopolitical circumstances are certain modes of leadership possible? For what sociopolitical purposes are various modes preferable? The answers are grounded both in our understanding of reality in a particular system and in our moral judgment about what we see.

Though the need for leadership appears to be an inevitable dimension of human organization, the form or expression of leadership is endlessly varied. Still, we can discern certain core features. The basic and persisting question is how communities determine and achieve their goals. We make judgments about governments, the executive figures who dominate them, and the legislatures that represent their peoples, however feebly. We assess and judge on the basis of our understanding of what leaders can and should do, and what representatives can and should do. There is debate over these matters. Some say that leadership should do no more than give direction to the whole complex of community interests and values. Others think that leadership itself must create or even impose those interests and values. According to some, the p role of legislatures is active participation in policy making. For others th correct work of the legislature is simply to react to executive initiatives or to help educate the public about them. For still others it lies in service to constituents and supervision of the bureaucracies, without any policy role. There are real and obvious differences in the many hundreds of political systems that the world now has and will have in the future. Our support for particular systems—those of which each of us is a part, and those we observe from outside—will rest in the beliefs that each of us holds about the nature of human beings, the communities that they create, and the quality of participation that should exist.

SELECTED READINGS

Blondel, Jean. *Comparative Legislatures.* Englewood Cliffs, N.J.: Prentice-Hall, 1973.*

Boynton, G. R., and Chong Lim Kim. *Legislative Systems in Developing Countries.* Durham, N.C.: Duke University Press, 1975.

Burns, James MacGregor. *Leadership.* New York: Harper & Row, 1978.

Crick, Bernard. *Basic Forms of Government: A Sketch and a Model.* London: Macmillan, 1973.

Dodd, Lawrence C. *Coalitions in Parliamentary Government.* Princeton, N.J.: Princeton University Press, 1976.

Ehrmann, Henry W., ed. *Interest Groups on Four Continents.* Pittsburgh, Pa.: University of Pittsburgh Press, 1958.

Eisenstadt, S. N. *Essays on Comparative Institutions.* New York: Wiley, 1965.

Kern, Robert, ed. *The Caciques: Oligarchical Politics and the System of Caciquismo in the Luso-Hispanic World.* Albuquerque: University of New Mexico Press, 1973.

LeVine, Victor T. *Political Leadership in Africa.* Stanford, Calif.: Hoover Institution, 1967.

Loewenberg, Gerhard, and Samuel C. Patterson. *Comparing Legislatures.* Boston: Little, Brown, 1979.

Mazrui, Ali A. *On Heroes and Hero-Worship: Essays on Independent Africa.* London: Longmans, Green, 1967.

Nelson, Joan M. *Access to Power: Politics and the Urban Poor in Developing Nations.* Princeton, N.J.: Princeton University Press, 1979.*

Nwabueze, B. O. *Presidentialism in Africa.* London: C. Hurst, 1974.

Prewitt, Kenneth. *The Recruitment of Political Leaders.* Indianapolis: Bobbs-Merrill, 1970.

*Indicates a paperback edition is available.

Selassie, Bereket A. *The Executive in Africa.* New York: Humanities Press, 1975.*

Wilson, James Q. *Political Organizations.* New York: Basic Books, 1973.

Wriggins, W. Howard. *The Ruler's Imperative: Strategies for Political Survival in Asia and Africa.* New York: Columbia University Press, 1969.

Zeigler, L. Harmon, and Michael Baer. *Lobbying.* Belmont, Calif.: Wadsworth, 1969.

9

Participation in the Political Process

Seek ye first the political kingdom.
> —*Kwame Nkrumah*

Among freemen there can be no successful appeal
from the ballot to the bullet.
> —*Abraham Lincoln*

How can one conceive of a one-party system in a
country that has over 200 varieties of cheeses?
> —*Charles de Gaulle*

The meaning of community changed dramatically as the nation-state became the dominant political form, spreading throughout the world in the nineteenth and twentieth centuries. Loyalty to other kinds of communities weakened under the assault of nationalism and the demands of the state, which often tried to absorb or control other communal groups, leaving the individual to face the power of the state alone. The demand for access to the political process accordingly began to rise, particularly in states constructed as democracies. In this new setting one of the most puzzling and persistent problems is the role of the individual citizen. How does the citizen routinely and institutionally influence policy? What is the meaning of political participation and the democratic imperative that, as Abraham Lincoln put it, government should be of, by, and for the people? Moreover, what is the role of groups? Although the creation of nation-states expanded community horizons, the ties of religion, occupation, and ethnicity did not break as new allegiances were formed. We

119

have noted the efforts to take these groups into account in the political process through representation and leadership. Here we will look at their influence on individuals as they join in the policy-making process. Among these groups is an explicitly political one, the political party, which has a special place in the configuration of forces that shape individual preferences and actions in the political arena.

The question of participation is resolved, formally at least, by a commitment to the idea of voting as the most basic and fundamental mode of individual political expression. Although there has been a continuing controversy about eligibility—is voting a right of citizenship or a privilege extended by the state?—the idea of voting is synonymous with democratic politics. (It is not in itself a guarantee of democracy, however. Completely controlled and noncompetitive systems may conduct elections that extract from the citizens an affirmation of rule rather than offering them alternatives.) Various countries have developed complex, intricate procedures and requirements for the extension and exercise of the franchise, the right to vote, as they go about implementing this important principle of popular sovereignty.

The Right to Vote

The exclusion of groups from formal participation in the voting process has often been a major source of political conflict. Women, for example, could not vote in most jurisdictions in the United States until 1920. Frenchwomen were excluded from full political participation until 1945. Women in northern Nigeria had no vote throughout the first civilian government, which ended in 1966. In all these cases it was simply assumed that politics was a male vocation, that the formal participation of women would violate the notion that a woman's place was in the home, not the voting booth or the legislature. Women's suffrage came about, in England and the United States, as women organized and demonstrated against their exclusion. In France, the major factor in women's acquisition of the right to vote was their extensive participation in the Resistance movement during World War II, and the contradiction that this represented in the minds of many Frenchmen. World War II was, after all, an effort to preserve democracy. It was simply embarrassing to acknowledge the contributions of thousands of women during this period and continue to rationalize their nonparticipatory status. Similarly, the demands for a return to civilian democracy in Nigeria were not consistent with the continued exclusion of women, and both northern and southern women's groups made this point clear in the debates over the new constitution.

Ironically, black male Americans were granted the right to vote long before women, with the adoption of the Fifteenth Amendment in 1865.

Full participation of black Americans, however, was impeded by deliberate efforts in many southern states to minimize black political influence (paralleled in other areas by similar efforts against such minorities as Mexican-Americans). Physical intimidation and fear of economic reprisals, along with the use of techniques like the "white primary" and the abuse of literacy tests, were effective barriers to black voting. One of the major goals of the civil rights movement has been to eliminate these barriers to electoral involvement.

Generally, democratization in voting has come slowly. Such factors as sex, race, religion, and ethnicity have been periodic bases of conflict as different groups have confronted the biases of political systems. Although the formal exclusion of groups or individuals does not mean that they have no political influence, it does severely limit the range of political activity and raise serious questions about the nature of the commitment to democratic principles. At its extreme, as in South Africa, such exclusion will ultimately destroy a democratic structure for the few as well as denying it to the many.

Voting is the expression of a person's preference for a candidate, or group of candidates, and in some political systems it is also a means of determining policy on specific issues. The latter is accomplished by such devices as the initiative and the referendum, respectively offering proposed laws or passing judgment on existing laws. These have been used extensively in American state politics, particularly those of the western states such as California. Voters are routinely asked to approve or reject new taxes, to fluoridate municipal water supplies or support or repeal "gay rights" ordinances. Great Britain submitted the issue of membership in the European Economic Community to referendum, and many constitutions have been adopted this way, beginning with the American elections of state conventions to ratify the U.S. Constitution in 1789. To understand the results of these or any other specific elections, it is essential to know the basis for individual decisions, and how such factors as ideology, class, age, ethnicity, and religion affect these decisions. It is also important to understand the way institutional arrangements—electoral systems and registration practices, for example—themselves influence the quality of participation and the outcome of elections.

Voting Behavior

Voting is a complex act. Voters are often called upon to support candidates they know little about and to decide issues that are far from clearcut. Upon what bases do voters decide? How does a voter chart a course through the confusion and disorder of the typical political environment? In answering, it is helpful to think of the voter as a citizen with allegiances and perceptions that interact and converge to determine voting behavior.

The contemporary political world is a complex spectrum of perceptions and influences. National politics in Britain is profoundly influenced by perceptions of class, and Catholicism is a significant factor in French politics, as Islam is in Senegal, or Hinduism in India. In the formerly colonial countries of Asia and Africa one discovers the influence of European ideological formulations, at least among the westernized elites. Vestiges of colonialism, combined with indigenous interests and concerns, have produced such local variations as the Tanzanian philosophy of *ujamaa* (self-reliance), and Castroism in Cuba. Formulations such as Pan-Arabism or Negritude reflect the significance of ethnicity or race in political behavior and social organization.

As these examples suggest, any analysis of politics must acknowledge the role of ideologies as an influence on perceptions and voter behavior. As we noted in the chapter on culture, an ideology is a pattern of ideas. Ideologies provide us with a way of looking at events, interpreting them, and deciding what we wish to do about what we have seen and interpreted. An ideology, then, is a basis for judgment. It provides an intellectual context in which issues and personalities are comprehensible, events have meaning, and the confusion and turmoil of political debate acquire a degree of order and coherence.

In many Western countries the competition between "left" and "right" illustrates the range and complexity of the ideological spectrum. The left, usually understood as Socialist or Communist, perceives a need for extensive changes in the distribution of wealth and the pattern of ownership and control of major economic units. The French Communist Party, for example, has publicized an extensive list of private enterprises it intends to nationalize if it achieves a parliamentary majority. Parties of the right typically reflect a commitment to more traditional, hierarchically organized societies and are hostile to the egalitarian assumptions of their competitors.

The United States is often regarded as a significant exception to the ideological rule, a country whose pragmatic politics point the way to an "end of ideology." The implication is that in the United States perceptions based on mutually hostile class interests are of minimal influence in developing habits of political participation. In the same way most Third World citizens seem to have little concern about class. As ideological politics are likely to occur in rigidly structured societies, perhaps on the basis of caste, religion, or long-established status ordering, the more fluid social structure developed in the New World might predictably create a different political style which the transitional society of "new nations" would resemble.

Although in much of the world class is an important influence in political transactions, individual or group consciousness of class and identification with a class position is not always an automatic, predictable response. For this reason consciousness raising is a normal attribute of ideological politics. Lenin wrote, for example, that one of the roles of the "vanguard" Communist Party was to awaken the proletariat to its exploitation, and we find similar roles for other ideological parties.

Even in the United States recent studies of voters indicate a much higher correlation between social status and political behavior than in earlier years. Only a decade ago some studies indicated that the influence of social class on voting behavior was declining. It is interesting to speculate on the possible reasons for this apparent renaissance of class influences. Are the issues of the 1950s and 1960s—the Cold War, civil rights, Vietnam—giving way to a more "bread and butter" orientation in the inflationary 1970s? Or is it, as Marxists would say, that the internal contradictions of capitalism are becoming more apparent in the United States? Whatever the reason, explanations of the significance of class are a major dimension of the ideological debate between critics and supporters of the United States economic system.

Class plays different roles in different political systems. In Italy and France, religion, including anticlericalism, is a salient factor. In France, for example, it is quite clear that many supporters of left-wing parties are motivated more by their attitudes about the traditional involvement of the Catholic Church in French society than by a commitment to socialist principles. In these cases attachment to parties of the left is almost incidental; the motivating factor is that the French left is identified with an anticlerical stance.

In many Third World countries there is a lively debate about the relevance of class and status; many observers suggest that ethnic-cultural explanations—communal loyalties—outweigh the significance of class in the drawing of political lines. What may be the most accurate generalization is that the debate about class, with its important ideological overtones, will certainly continue. The subject is a controversial one. Class and class conflict are pivotal concepts in the Marxist critique of bourgeois democracy. That social class may have a bearing on political perceptions should not, however, come as a great shock or be viewed as a major setback to democratic aspirations. It is one of many influences, not necessarily predominant or overriding, but one of many factors that inform individual behavior.

Generally we find a constellation of influences converging on the voter. Most voters, for example, identify with a political party and take many of their political cues from this relationship. They often view issues and candidates through the filter of party affiliation, and "straight-tick-

© *1964 United Feature Syndicate, Inc.*

et'' voting can be a rational response to an irrational political environment. The recent decline of straight-ticket voting, along with the increase of "Independents," in United States politics may also be a rational response to a changing political scene.

Organizational membership, especially in conjunction with a party membership, may provide a basis for political action. The alliance of the trade unions in Britain with the Labour Party and of the *Confédération Générale du Travail* in France with the Communist Party illustrate this relationship. In these cases each allegiance strengthens the other and provides an intense commitment of voters to a political position.

Group allegiances are not always reinforcing. Sometimes counterpressures may be at work, and voters are neutralized or torn between conflicting loyalties. A union member's family may have different views; a Republican's discussions with Democratic workmates may have an effect. People change their perspectives for many reasons—intellectual assessment, a change in status, perceptions about new acquaintances—and find a new outlook on life and political events.

In recent years sex and age have received special attention as important influences on political behavior. The significance of feminist movements is apparent. The volatile issue of abortion and a broad range of concerns about women's rights have, particularly in Western countries, become yardsticks by which many women measure their support for candidates or inform themselves about party or organizational positions. In the United States the position of many state legislators on the Equal Rights Amendment has become a major criterion for women and women's organizations. In a completely different setting, Iranian women's demands for change in the new Islamic Republic are an indication of the growing importance of women's rights in contemporary politics. In fact, women in many developing countries have begun to protest what they perceive as a political position inferior even to the one they had in traditional life.

Similarly, the appearance of "Gray Power" in some Western countries reflects the concern of the aged about such issues as pensions, physical safety, and health care. And in this area there is probably a more profound and fundamental issue. It is the question of age itself, combined with the separation of family members from each other in modern society and with the feelings of helplessness and uselessness that distress many elderly persons. In the United States especially, with its emphasis on youth, the elderly are often unwanted and urged to seclude themselves in retirement villages or institutions which relieve the burden of family responsibility. Western countries might take lessons from many developing countries in which the elderly remain within kinship groups and have useful roles as members of the social unit. These issues are on the minds of many aging people and they are emerging as significant factors in the formation of political attitudes.

For the average voter anywhere, the influence of family is a critical factor in the development of political habits. Family influences should not, however, be viewed as absolute. Rebellion against parental authority leads many young people to take political positions markedly different from those of their families, as the counterculture values of the 1960s and 1970s showed. Yet in the aggregate, as voters and as partisans, families are quite clearly a determining influence in the development of a political outlook.

One can hardly conclude that voters are automatons whose judgments are easily predictable. Many voters do assess issues and evaluate candidates on the basis of their records. Yet we consistently reflect who we are in our political choices. Our ethnic and communal affiliations are important; our places of residence—urban, rural, suburban—weigh in our considerations about politics and what we think about the world around us. New Yorkers and Lagosians and Cariocas share some perspectives, and so do farmers in Mexico and France and Iowa. One's ultimate political identity is typically the result of an interplay of factors. Political habits are formed and we can observe patterns in the amalgam of these habits. It is also true that these patterns may change radically as the result of cataclysmic events—economic depression, civil war, or major shifts in national policy.

Nonparticipation

The other side of the participation coin is equally intellectually and politically challenging. In many political communities nonparticipation is a common condition. For a variety of reasons the bases for participation may not be present, or cross-cutting factors may immobilize individuals and groups to produce a response to politics that is essentially not to respond.

Nonparticipation in electoral politics is not an uncommon occurrence. To some extent it has been a kind of fallout from the process of electoral expansion. The older political systems of the West, for example, have all experienced a major increase in the proportionate size of their electorates in this century. In the United Kingdom, to take one illustrative case, the 1906 electorate was slightly over 7 million, 27 percent of the adult population (or 58 percent of adult males). By the election of 1929 this had increased to 29 million, and the registration of women exceeded that of men by 1.5 million. A similar expansion occurred in the United States, but there, for reasons that are not fully understood, the percentages of participation have recently fallen far more than those of the United Kingdom, Canada, West Germany, Sweden, France, and the Netherlands. One persuasive explanation is that the absence of a meaningful ideological alternative and the general acceptance of middle-class values by the United States working class might predictably produce low levels of political interest among many low-status persons. By the 1970s American voting turnouts rarely exceeded 40 percent in mid-term congressional elections, and even with the added excitement of a presidential contest were barely more than a majority of eligible voters. Local elections, though they sometimes produce higher turnouts, are more commonly the occasion for a quarter or less of the electorate to act. European turnouts are commonly in the 80 to 90 percent range, although the recent elections to the European Parliament drew barely 61 percent and in Great Britain the figure was not much over 30 percent.

In looking at electoral participation on a cross-national or comparative basis a number of correlations emerge. The highest pattern of voter turnout appears in the one-party Communist regimes of Eastern Europe. Albania, the Soviet Union, Rumania and Bulgaria typically report voting percentages exceeding 99 percent. They are also the countries in which interparty competition is notably absent. In many one-party states, voting is essentially a demonstration of national patriotism and support for a regime rather than an opportunity for voters to choose among candidates or ideological positions. The regime will wish to obtain a turnout as close to 100 percent as possible. Under such circumstances those who choose not to record their support may not be expressing a lack of interest. In this case, nonparticipation becomes a deliberate expression of discontent, possibly a dangerous one for those who do not appear at the polls. The electorate in Zimbabwe-Rhodesia found itself in a doubly dangerous position in the 1979 elections. The government of Ian Smith was determined to obtain as high a turnout as possible, while the guerrillas fighting this regime were determined to prevent voting.

In countries in which some degree of competition exists, it is much more difficult to assess the real meaning of electoral nonparticipation. The decision not to vote is often as complex as the basis on which voters cast their ballots. If we think about nonvoting and about nonparticipation in general, it becomes apparent that the explanation must be more than an indictment of individual behavior. Many people have opted out of political involvement as a result of despair and resentment about the futility of political activity. Such feelings can be found in all strata of the political community. Although it is the better-educated and more affluent of a society who are its most persistent participants, this group may also feel powerless, unable to sense or predict any meaningful result from personal involvement. The idea that things cannot be changed and the haunting notion that the "real" decisions are always made in the smoky inner sanctums of an elite are powerful influences on the individual and collective psyche. Such events as Watergate substantiate the predispositions of many who view politics and politicians with disfavor. Survey evidence from many sources indicates that in the United States the levels of basic trust and acceptance of the political system—which were declining noticeably by the mid-sixties—have dropped precipitously since Watergate began to dominate the front pages, and scandals in other nations have contributed to political disaffection there.

From this point of view, electoral nonparticipation is a protest and a challenge to a political system to give more attention to its deepest, most persistent problems. This is not simply a question of apathy. Complex societies are increasingly troubled by individuals and groups who are, as in contemporary Western Europe, the Middle East, and Japan, quite willing to explore nonconventional means to exert some control over political events. The spread of political violence may speak more to the absence of meaningful channels of expression and influence than to the disintegration of civility in political life. Politics is fascinating because so much is at stake. It is potentially dangerous for exactly the same reason.

Nonparticipation has a less volatile but equally difficult dimension. Formal and informal barriers to participation exist in many societies. Caste, race, and religion may preclude or impede participation and become sources of conflict as they are for the Jews of North Africa, "Untouchables" in India, and nonwhites in South Africa. Residence requirements in the United States plague millions of people in occupations that require frequent changes of residence. Corporate executives, salesmen, and migrant workers are consistently disfranchised because of their mobility.

A problem as perplexing as nonparticipation is the nature of participation itself. How can it be made effective? How can we have a voice in the decisions that govern our lives, and have confidence that this is so? The answer lies partly in the character of the communities that we have developed, in the limits of participation in large, complex social settings. Although participation at all levels of civic life remains possible and necessary, it is, perhaps inevitably, limited to a range of decisions that are themselves controlled by events and activities in an increasingly distant political center. As multinational corporations, for example, assume greater international significance, local influences wane. Decisions to close military bases or shift the locus of manufacturing to a different region or country are decisions that intimately affect many lives but are unlikely to involve substantial local participation. A smug sense of self-sufficiency in the West has been shattered by a growing awareness of the importance of OPEC, the Organization of Petroleum Exporting Countries, and a subsequent sense of helplessness and frustration. As nations emerge and become active participants in the international community, the power centers of decision making and participation shift. Such a loss of influence is an inevitable consequence of the growth of more complex and interdependent regional and global systems. Does this mean that expectations of involvement and participation are forlorn hopes? The tenacious revolts against rulers who do not allow participation—Iran, Nicaragua, Uganda, Equatorial Guinea, the Central African Republic, and Greece come to mind—are powerful evidence that these hopes continue to be a call to action.

The Institutional Setting: Party Systems

Voting and other political participation occur in an institutional or patterned environment. Voters express themselves for or against someone or something. They make decisions on personalities and issues presented to them. Ideally we are discussing choices, and we know that choices do not exist automatically. They are the functions of constitutional or institutional arrangements that determine the manner in which both the substance and the form of issues will be perceived and acted upon by the voter. What we need to assess, then, are the patterns of institutional arrangements that make choices available, and the meaning of choice in different political and ideological settings.

Political systems can be characterized in a number of ways. One can, for example, discuss the differences between democratic and totalitarian states and contrast these with other types—theocracies, absolute monarchies, and other absolutist forms—as we did in an earlier chapter. In discussing the contemporary significance of participation it is helpful to use another approach, distinguishing political systems on the basis of the number of political parties effectively sharing in the determination of public policy.

Many observers consider the number and role of political parties the most significant factor in democratic political life. Some assert that democracy is impossible without them. Their significance is that they organize, or aggregate, voters, and they are instrumental both in mobilizing the electorate and in shaping and controlling issues and personalities in the political debate. Voting behavior is considerably influenced by party allegiance, and (recalling our discussion of the bases for individual judgment) political party allegiance may be the most significant determinant of that behavior. In the racial politics of Malaysia, for example, political party alignment accurately reflects the three major forces—Indians, Chinese, and Malays. Parties both influence perceptions and reflect those perceptions in an organizational fashion.

Using the number of parties to distinguish political systems, we can describe them as *one-party, two-party,* or *multiparty* arrangements. The relationship among numbers, the consequent degree of choice, and the character of the system is an important one.

For many years the ideal democratic system has been depicted by many political scientists as a competitive two-party arrangement. In this view competition between two dominant parties representing different positions is considered the desirable format for raising issues and presenting aspiring officeholders to the public. Voters, aligning themselves with one or the other party, would be able to act upon their preferences by choosing between persons representing different clusters of opinion and programs. In this two-party model the emphasis is on the importance of *interparty competition* as the generator of choices, and part of the theory is that choices between candidates will be reflected in subsequent public policy. Majorities will become minorities, and vice versa, without attempting to destroy each other. The dynamics of this competition thus allow voters to play a decisive role in the governing process. The example most often cited as approximating this ideal form is the two-party system of Britain. National politics are dominated by the Labour and the Conservative parties, and since World War II each party has controlled the government roughly half the time. When in power the two have pursued rather different programs, presumably reflecting the winning electoral mandate.

This two-party model is not, however, the only choice for contemporary politics, even Western politics. One-party and multiparty systems raise important questions about the significance of competition and the meaning of choice.

One-party systems are those in which the political dialogue and the institutions of government are monopolized by a single political party, as in Mexico and Tanzania. Historically a one-party system has been equated with dictatorship, but this view of one-party states has lately been modified in light of the relationship between the demands of economic development and the idea of "guided democracy." This formulation of political leadership emerged during the post-colonial era and stimulated a vigorous debate about the meaning of democracy, the question of choice, and the needs of new nations. Sukarno of Indonesia and Nkrumah of Ghana were two major exponents of the view that the imperatives of economic growth and development precluded, at least temporarily, the establishment of a truly competitive system, just as party politics were set aside elsewhere during national emergencies. The determination of priorities and the allocation of resources were so important that the need to proceed rapidly but deliberately in these areas eliminated the luxury of opposition parties and the delays and hesitations inherent in party competition.

A competitive system that seemed to require an opposition point of view even where none existed was seen as contrary to the needs of nation building. Guided democracy was viewed as more appropriate for the conditions of newly independent countries such as Ghana and Indonesia (and earlier examples such as Kemal Ataturk's Turkey), where national communities had not yet been created. What existed were conglomerations of smaller communities not yet accustomed to living together, perhaps even with traditions of mutual hostility. The nation-state was an artificial, imposed idea. Here the leaders must preside over the establishment of a new, transcending loyalty by creating some consensus in which national consciousness could emerge. Competition and choice could then be introduced without irreparably damaging national unity. The challenge in this point of view is whether or not democracy can exist in circumstances where the basis for communal action is either nonexistent or so precarious that the realization of national goals seems unlikely. It

makes us aware that deeply rooted traditional loyalties can produce cleavages and schisms that challenge the most fundamental assumptions of
self-determination and self-government. When such deep feelings are re-
pressed, they may find expression in communal violence.

One should not conclude, however, that debate and choice are necessarily absent in one-party regimes. We remarked in Chapter Six on the
possibility of one-party systems in which there is controversy, debate,
and dialogue, but *within* the structure of the dominant party rather than
between competitive, separate organizations. This is, indeed, the justification cited in Communist states, another variation of the one-party
model. Dissidence and nonconformity are tolerated, but within narrowly
circumscribed limits. The Leninist idea of "democratic centralism"—the
principle that debate and challenge must cease once the party has reached
a decision—is the theoretical response to the criticism that Communist
regimes will not tolerate any deviation from established positions. Controlled debate within the apparatus of the party is acceptable; what is unacceptable is a challenge to the theoretical or philosophical foundations
of the system. The Russian justification for its invasion of Czechoslovakia was that socialist goals were being compromised by Czechoslovak
party leaders who held unacceptable, in fact fascistic, positions. The intellectual challenge in all this is to recognize that an impasse exists between these perspectives on participation and leadership, because they
represent very different conceptions of the citizen's role in formulating
public policy. For the individual the question may be simpler: Can I
question the foundations of the system without paying the price of exile,
imprisonment, or death?

One way to look at the range and complexity of one-party systems is
to think of them as being at different points on a spectrum of political
maturity. Or we might say that the substance and form of democratic
government may vary in different countries. Despite these variations,
however, we are always compelled to know whether choices can be made,
and whether the price of nonconformity is bearable. We may also, in
comparing one-party with two-party models, wish to know whether the
parties represent *real* choices or—as many claim about the United
States—are no better than Tweedledee and Tweedledum.

The U.S. system presents a curious hybrid of one- and two-party
systems. While both the Republican and Democratic parties compete
with each other in many parts of the country, a number of regions are
easily described as one-party areas. For a long time the most obvious of
these was the American South, with its tradition of Democratic Party allegiance developed after the Civil War. Only recently have candidates of
the Republican Party, which many southerners still perceive as the party
of Reconstruction and carpetbaggers, been able to offset the Democrats'

electoral monopoly. (The significant exception to this pattern is the frequent southern support in recent years for the Republican or third-party presidential candidate and growing Republican support in the "new South" and "sunbelt" areas.) In such settings competition, if it exists at all, occurs within the structure of the favored party.

We must conclude that competition is a relative phenomenon, even in two-party systems, and that a one-party arrangement can provide for institutionalized competition as successfully as a two-party one. For example, in both Zambia and Tanzania intraparty competition has been able to respond to public concerns about policy and public disaffection with particular officeholders. Even government ministers may lose their seats if they lose constituency support. Five decades of one-party rule in Mexico have seen many different factions struggling for dominance within the Party of the Institutionalized Revolution, the PRI. Competition reflects society and political intent as much as it does formal structure. The model of a duel is not the only one.

The third system is usually described as multiparty. In this arrangement at least three or more parties compete for electoral support, usually within the framework of a parliamentary system. The best-known multiparty states are the countries of Western Europe, and the system illustrates some interesting things about their political environments. The existence of a number of active, competing parties is a reflection of the historical cleavages of religion, class, and region that influence the public's perceptions of a wide range of issues. France, for example, is a country in which the historical influence of Catholicism conflicts with post-Enlightenment anticlerical attitudes. The present *Rallye pour la République (RPR)*, the "Gaullist" party, is the heir to a tradition of "Christian Democracy" found in a number of other national settings as well. Once released from dictatorship, Spain and Portugal quickly restored very similar patterns.

The alleged strength of multiparty systems is that they allow voters a wider range of choice than is found in one or two-party countries. In Italy one can choose among parties of the left—Socialists and Communists; those of the right—conservatives and even neo-Fascists; and a centrist range, which includes the Christian Democrats. If this seems complicated or confusing, it is. It can be argued, however, that such complexity is a virtue, allowing the diverse strata and interests of a modern society to find expression rather than forcing them into artificial uniformity. Nigeria chose the multiparty arrangement for its constitution of 1979 instead of trying to prescribe parties in advance. The only imposed requirement was that they be national in organization and program. Five parties eventually established themselves out of nearly fifty different groups of candidates and opinions.

The debate between multiparty proponents and opponents is not simply over whether there are choices but how meaningful they are, and how adequately they represent the complexities and nuances of a typical political system. In many cases only two choices may be an inadequate range of alternatives. The major criticism of multiparty systems is that they lead to governmental deadlock. The case most often cited is that of France during the Third and Fourth Republics, and Italy is a current example. In parliamentary systems, if no party or coalition is able to get or keep a stable majority, there is—according to critics—a strong possibility of *immobilisme*, executive paralysis. The participants expend their energy in creating legislative majorities, and programs and policies go unattended, or are left to civil servants with only a minimal understanding of the needs and wishes of the populace. A variation of this theme is that the bureaucracy, given its composition and interests, may be the only hope for stability in countries with a history of parliamentary or governmental instability.

Stability is the primary rationale of those who prefer the compromise and pragmatism of the two-party system. One additional factor should be mentioned in this context. It is the importance of the particular electoral system in shaping the pattern of party politics and the question of choice, pushing systems toward a two-party mode or pulling them toward multiple-party forms by the specific way in which votes translate as victory.

It seems to be the case, for example, that national two-party politics are strengthened by the use of pluralities and single-member legislative districts, districts in which only a single winner is possible. The effect is to induce the formation of majorities through combining or discarding minority options. There is no reward for second- or third-best. Multiparty systems often employ variations of proportional representation, allocating legislative representation in accordance with party strength in the electorate, so that several victors represent a constituency rather than only one. Parties that receive less than half the vote have no representation at all in single-member, winner-take-all arrangments, unless they distort or significantly modify their positions in order to become majorities. When proportional representation and multimember districts are used jointly, this problem is minimized. Some representation is possible even for small parties, provided they achieve some minimum support; they need not become perpetual losers. The politics of moderation and compromise that characterize two-party systems is not absent but operates on a reduced scale during the formation of executive coalitions.

Within these broad electoral and institutional structures voting and voting behavior acquire meaning. One votes *for* something. One casts a ballot to protect a privilege or to deny an office to someone with dramatically opposed views. How these possibilities are presented and how the voter chooses among alternatives are vital dimensions of voting behavior. Electoral systems and political parties are more than decorative. Without them, voting—and the idea of participation—would be meaningless.

Group and Elite Influences

A brief analysis of voting and electoral systems does not, however, reveal the total picture. These two aspects of political life refer to the purely formal processes of politics and do not explain the informal, extraconstitutional patterns of involvement that are fundamental in any political community. In fact most commentators argue that an analysis limited to the formal arrangements would tell us very little about a community's true political life.

In the past several decades a considerable amount of attention has been given to the *interest* or *pressure group*; more recently, studies of the disposition of community power, and the question of *elites*, have engaged the attention of sociologists and political scientists. What these analyses share is an interest in the apparent discrepancies between the formal constitutional assumptions about who governs and the actual wielding of political power and influence.

Interest groups, a major medium of nonelectoral participation, are organizations of people who share a common concern. Unlike political parties, they are not set up to contest elections but to influence public opinion and those who hold elective or appointive office—which may of course call for assisting parties and candidates in elections. The examples are many: Muslim brotherhoods in Senegal, market women in many West African countries, Chambers of Commerce in Nigeria or Nicaragua, Chinese traders in Malaysia. In the United States, these groups number in the hundreds of thousands, and include such disparate groups as the Texas Association of Taxpayers, The National Rifle Association, and The Flying Physicians. Their efforts to influence legislation or administrative decisions are important dimensions of the political process. In turn, political systems have attempted, not very successfully, to establish limits on the ways and means of this influence. Governments everywhere, even those that forbid such organizations, find themselves confronted by powerful interests which they must consider. A strike by government workers in India can disable the economy; a quiet appeal by wealthy landowners in Mexico may effectively repeal redistribution of land to peasants.

We may take two such groups in the United States to illustrate important differences among types of interest groups. The American Medical Association is an organization of medical practitioners. Some doctors may also belong to the Sierra Club, made up of people who share a concern about conserving the environment and protecting natural resources. A bus driver who is sympathetic to the Sierra Club's purposes can join this group, but, no matter how interested they are in the question of health care, bus drivers would not qualify for AMA membership. This difference simply indicates that we can distinguish between interest groups that are basically occupational—bar associations, labor unions— and organizations that represent an interest not defined by the member's occupational status. There are innumerable examples of both kinds. Anti-capital punishment groups, groups supporting the arts, fans of "real ale," ethnic associations are as familiar as the "bread and butter" organizations of working life that are concerned about salaries, working conditions, benefits, or professional advancement. Communal or ethnic associations in particular have been politically influential in plural societies, and they are on the increase in many nation-states which had convinced themselves that such differences did not matter or had disappeared in the "melting pot."

Whatever their nature, interest groups are pervasive in politics. Many are able to hire professional lobbyists to roam the chambers and corridors of government and spend sizable sums of money to influence legislative and administrative decisions. Their presence in the political arena raises questions from many quarters. Do wealthy, well-organized interest groups make a mockery of the representative system? Should efforts be made to limit the access of such groups to the processes of decision making? How do groups without access to large sums and professional lobbyists compete with the more powerful interests? If some groups disproportionately influence policy making, what is the meaning of majority rule? These and similar concerns have led to the minimal requirement in the United States, for example, that lobbyists must register with appropriate state and federal agencies, and hold their spending below a certain amount. Such requirements, of course, do not resolve the problem or fundamentally affect the more informal processes of influence in personal contacts, which are widespread in the United States and other industrialized nations as well as in developing areas. The latter face an even more difficult problem in the hordes of foreign businessmen who try to influence their decisions. Third World anger about such activity has led some countries to try to control the overseas activities of their nationals. The United States, for example, enacted stringent penalites against money inducements to other governments by its corporations after the Lockheed scandal in Japan, but such controls are not yet widely copied or respected.

These troubles should not obscure the fact that lobbying—expressing a position and attempting to persuade policy makers to share that position—is generally accepted as legitimate activity, another dimension of participation. It is justified as an important alternative for groups which may not be able to express themselves through the procedures and politics of elections. But concerns about undue influence, including the many forms of corruption, must be resolved if the public's faith in the effectiveness of participation is to be maintained.

A second, and even more complex, aspect of participation has been raised by recent explorations into the subject of *community power* to assess patterns of influence and participation in local communities. These investigations have brought a new awareness of the importance of a world of informal and extralegal patterns of influence. Who are the influentials? Who in a community actually determines the shape and substance of policy? These queries flow from the realization that influence is not equally distributed among everyone in a community, and that those who are influential do not always hold formal positions in government. Community power studies in a number of countries are efforts to probe beyond the formal structures of government and determine who, if anyone, pulls the political strings.

The issue of elite influence that underlies the question of community power is a troubling question for democratic theorists. While it is clear that the people do not rule themselves in a direct and uncomplicated fashion, the idea of an elite is discomforting. The notion that there is, apart from and perhaps in opposition to "the people," an elite of wealth or birth or some other attribute is one that strikes at the foundation of beliefs in self-government and popular sovereignty. Indeed, the Marxist critique of capitalist systems states that political institutions in capitalist countries are simply the intermediary structures through which an economic elite, the bourgeois class, exerts political and economic control. Other students have identified racial, ethnic, or religious elites whose control over societies thwarts the very notion of popular sovereignty. These are formidable challenges to the very idea of democracy and popular participation.

As the debate has developed in the past two decades it has not centered on the presence or absence of ruling elites, but on their nature. Is the elite structure closed, accessible only to a few, or is there a representative elite, perhaps even groups of elites, whose open and representative character makes their existence at least compatible with ideas about how democracies should work? It is within this framework of concerns that the notion of pluralism emerges, an idea that seeks to reconcile the presence of elites with the idea of popular sovereignty.

If it could be demonstrated that U.S. society, for example, was ruled by a relatively small, closed group of White Anglo-Saxon Protestant males, predominantly Ivy League graduates and members of the same few social clubs, this would pose serious questions about the meaning and meaningfulness of representative institutions and popular government. If, on the other hand, one could demonstrate that the elite was broadly based, or that in fact there were different elites or "influentials" in different issue areas, the apparent discrepancy between theory and practice might disappear, or at least pose less of a threat to traditional democratic concerns.

This rather sophisticated debate assumes that in complex modern societies elites are a fact of political life. The issue is then transformed into a different question: What are the characteristics of elites and what are the appropriate and efficient measures of popular control over elite behavior?

The questions posed by the idea of an elite are often confusing. If the term refers simply to leaders and the preeminent position assumed by some members of the political community, the problem may be one of *accountability* and the efficacy of *institutional control* over elite behavior. This point of view takes it for granted that power and influence will inevitably be distributed in a disproportionate fashion, and that through systems of elections, referenda, and popularly elected legislatures, the public can play an important, even though indirect, role in the governing process. The task, then, of the citizenry and their agents is constantly to enlarge the scope of participation, creating a condition in which the wishes of at least a majority of the people are the basis for making administrative and legislative decisions.

A second approach, one usually associated with the idea of socialism, is formally to enlarge the arena of public control, particularly over the institutions of economic activity, by *nationalization*. In some countries almost the entire economy has been nationalized, as in China and the Soviet Union, or nationalized in major industries or sectors—railways in Britain, the aircraft industry in France, oil production in Mexico, electricity in Ghana, and most major sectors in India. Partial nationalization is a common format in developing countries, many of which have also tried to practice *indigenization*, the exclusion of noncitizens from major economic roles so that the "commanding heights" are held by nationals. Theoretically, accountability is enhanced and the interests of the public coincide with the policies and activities of the nationalized firm. In the case of petroleum and other essential commodities, public, indigenous control may be critical for a program of national development.

Whatever the chosen solution among these quite different ideological approaches, the subject of influence is one that remains a puzzle for many political communities. The closing of one channel of influence does not prevent the powerful from finding or creating others.

The recent community power studies are both revealing and inconclusive. Undeniably they illuminate a world of influence and power that was only dimly seen before, although long assumed. We know, either instinctively or from local gossip, that family X—which owns the local bank or newspaper or Mercedes agency—wields an important influence on the affairs of "our town." We know that those in certain professions or with particular educational, family, or class backgrounds have a disproportionate influence. That some are more involved and effective than others has been demonstrated both by examining patterns of involvement in various issue areas and by seeking out the powerful by asking knowledgeable people to identify them. These two approaches are the major techniques researchers use in tracking the footsteps of the powerful. Their work has not always succeeded, however, in providing evidence beyond conventional wisdom or rumor. It is difficult to develop methods of inquiry that do not lead to self-fulfilling prophecies or questionable data. The question remains: Is there an elite, or a group of elites, or any elite at all exercising power in political affairs? The answer is a continuing controversy among the political analysts who represent the "elitist" and the "pluralist" schools of thought. Thomas Dye's recent analysis of elites at the national level in the United States is a provocative effort to discuss these issues in a broader setting.

In thinking about elites our more general concerns should be remembered. As societies become more complex and as the realities of daily existence exact their toll, participation is threatened and the goal of self-government remains distant. The individual's capacity for survival is well known; our capacity to maintain democracy is not as firmly established.

SELECTED READINGS

Agger, Robert E., Daniel Goldrich, and Bert E. Swanson. *The Rulers and the Ruled: Political Power and Impotence in American Communities.* New York: Wiley, 1964.

Albright, David E., ed. *Communism and Political Systems in Western Europe.* Boulder, Colo.: Westview Press, 1978.

Apter, David E., ed. *Ideology and Discontent.* New York: Free Press, 1964.

Bell, Daniel. *The End of Ideology.* New York: Free Press, 1960.* Essays that have become classics.

Bottomore, T. B. *Classes in Modern Society.* New York: Random House, 1968.* Emphasis on Marxist analysis.

———. *Elites and Society.* Baltimore: Penguin, 1966.*

Butler, David, and Austin Ranney, eds. *Referendums: A Comparative Study of*

*Indicates a paperback edition is available.

Practice and Theory. Washington, D.C.: American Enterprise Institute, 1978.

Christenson, Reo M., et al., eds. *Ideologies and Modern Politics*. New York: Dodd, Mead, 1971.

Connery, Robert H., ed. *Urban Riots: Violence and Social Change*. New York: Random House Vintage, 1979.*

Dahl, Robert A. *Who Governs?* New Haven: Yale University Press, 1961.

Dinka, Frank, and Max J. Skidmore, "The Functions of Communist One-Party Elections: The Case of Czechoslovakia, 1971," *Political Science Quarterly*, 83 (September 1973).

Duverger, Maurice. *Political Parties*. London: Methuen, 1967.

Dye, Thomas. *Who's Running America? The Carter Years*. Englewood Cliffs, N.J.: Prentice-Hall, 1978.*

Epstein, Leon. *Political Parties in Western Democracies*. New York: Praeger, 1967.

Gilison, Jerome M., "Soviet Elections as a Measure of Dissent: The Missing One Percent," *American Political Science Review*, LXII (September 1968).

Gould, James A., and Willis H. Truitt. *Political Ideologies*. New York: Macmillan, 1973.

Hadley, Arthur T. *The Empty Polling Booth*. Englewood Cliffs, N.J.: Prentice-Hall, 1978.

Hennessy, Bernard. *Public Opinion*. 3rd ed. North Scituate, Mass: Duxbury Press, 1975.

Hopkins, Nicholas. *Popular Government in an African Town*. Chicago: University of Chicago Press, 1972.

Hunter, Floyd. *Community Power Structure*. Chapel Hill: University of North Carolina Press, 1953.

Huntington, Samuel P., and Joan Nelson. *No Easy Choice: Political Participation in Developing Countries*. Cambridge, Mass.: Harvard University Press, 1976.

Kornhauser, William. *The Politics of Mass Society*. New York: Free Press, 1959.

Lipset, Seymour Martin. *Political Man: The Social Basis of Politics*. Garden City, N.Y.: Doubleday, 1963.* A now classic essay on participation, democracy, and authoritarian politics.

_____, and Stein Rokkan. *Party Systems and Voter Alignments*. New York: Free Press, 1967.

Lichtheim, George. *The Concept of Ideology*. New York: Random House, 1967.

Lloyd, Peter C. *Classes, Crises, and Coups*. New York: Praeger, 1972.

Lowi, Theodore. *The End of Liberalism*. 2nd ed. New York: Norton, 1979.

Lucas, J. R. *Democracy and Participation*. Baltimore: Penguin, 1976.*

Markovitz, Irving Leonard. *Power and Class in Africa*. Englewood Cliffs, N.J.: Prentice-Hall, 1977.*

Michels, Roberto. *Political Parties*. New York: Dover, 1959.* A classic formulation of the "iron law" of oligarchy.

Milbrath, Lester. *Political Participation: How and Why Do People Get Involved in Politics?* Chicago: Rand McNally, 1965.*

Mills, C. Wright. *The Power Elite*. New York: Oxford University Press, 1956. A classie.

Milnor, A. J. *Elections and Political Stability*. Boston: Little, Brown, 1969. Includes procedural aspects.

Mosca, Gaetano. *The Ruling Class*. New York: McGraw-Hill, 1939. Another classic.

Nelson, Joan M. *Access to Power: Politics and the Urban Poor in Developing Nations*. Princton, N.J.: Princeton University Press, 1979.*

Parenti, Michael. *Power and the Powerless*. New York: St. Martin's, 1978.*

Polsby, Nelson. *Community Power and Political Theory*. New Haven: Yale University Press, 1963.

Pomper, Gerald. *Elections in America*. New York: Harper & Row, 1968.*

_____. *Voters' Choice*. New York: Harper & Row, 1975.*

Putnam, Robert D. *The Comparative Study of Political Elites*. Englewood Cliffs, N.J.: Prentice-Hall, 1976.*

Rokkan, Stein. *Citizens, Elections, Parties*. New York: David McKay, 1970.

Rose, Richard, ed. *Electoral Behavior: A Comparative Handbook*. New York: Free Press, 1974.

Rotberg, Robert I., and Ali A. Mazrvi, eds. *Protest and Power in Black Africa*. New York: Oxford University Press, 1971.

Sargent, L. T. *Comtemporary Political Ideologies*. rev. ed. Homewood, Ill.: Dorsey Press, 1972.*

Sartori, Giovanni. *Parties and Party Systems*. Cambridge, England: Cambridge University Press, 1976.

Schattschneider, Elmer. *The Semi-Sovereign People*. New York: Holt, Rinehart and Winston, 1975.*

Schwartz, David C. *Political Alienation and Political Behavior*. Chicago: Aldine, 1973.

Shaw, L. Earl, ed. *Modern Competing Ideologies*. Lexington, Mass.: D.C. Heath, 1973.

Sigmund, Paul E., Jr., ed. *The Ideologies of the Developing Nations*. New York: Praeger, 1963.

Tilman, Robert O., ed. *Man, State and Society in Southeast Asia*. New York: Praeger, 1969.*

Verba, Sidney, and Norman H. Nie. *Participation in America*. New York: Harper & Row, 1972.

Verba, Sidney, and Lucien Pye, eds. *The Citizen and Politics*. Stamford, Conn.: Greylock, 1978.

von der Mehden, Fred R. *Comparative Political Violence*. Englewood Cliffs, N.J.: Prentice-Hall, 1972.*

10

Conflict and Order

Civilization is nothing else but the attempt to
reduce force to being the last resort.
—José Ortega y Gasset

A state is better governed which has but few laws,
and those laws strictly observed.
—René Descartes

Nobody has a more sacred obligation to obey the
law than those who make the law.
—Sophocles

That action alone is just that does not harm either
party to a dispute.
—Mohandas Gandhi

Political scientists have generally been concerned with law only as an outcome of the political process. Similarly, the judiciary is often regarded as
an apolitical institution with which politicians and students of politics
need not concern themselves—except perhaps for the highest courts. The
same neglect is applied to the police and other enforcers of executive and
judicial decisions. Very little attention is given to the way in which law
shapes politics, and to the impact of differing judicial forms and processes on political life. It is essential to consider these institutions from a
political perspective if we are to understand how any political system
works, including our own.

The Centrality of Dispute Settlement

Most species of animals seem to have certain ritualized behaviors that inhibit or control aggression. A dramatic exception to this general pattern
is the human animal, who seems to have little instinctive control over ag-

gressive actions. In the absence of such conditioning, we have been forced to develop other means of limiting violence. This has been done through a unique mechanism, culture, and its supporting medium, language. The impulse to fight can be deflected by talking about the problem, doing what makes us human. This is essential for a community; conflict must be reduced to at least the point that allows survival of the group. Better, a level can be reached that allows enough peace and order for productive pursuits, using the energy that would otherwise be drained by endless fighting. A bewildering variety of forms and procedures—institutionalized talking—for the control of disputes has appeared in different times and places. Together these are known as the *judicial process*. It is not always easy to identify institutions like courts, or law, in particular societies, and many academic battles have been fought over labels. The important thing is that all of these particular forms are solutions to the same problem: the need to establish alternatives to force and violence as a means of settling arguments. The political history of the human species can easily be seen in the struggle to create these mechanisms and to extend their jurisdiction over individuals, groups, and the special groups called nations.

The judicial process and those responsible for it are therefore very close to the heart of politics. First, successful control of disputes allows the survival and growth of a society and a political system. Second, settlement of disputes has generally been the cutting edge of political leadership and authority. The role of judging has been one of the main ways in which leadership and authority developed. It helps hold societies together as they become more complex and perhaps generate more conflict. As courts and police are created, they may represent the government itself to most people, who have little contact with other agencies of government except the tax collector. Legitimacy, or loyalty to the government, will depend heavily on the quality of these institutions. Finally, the legal and judicial systems of a society have a major, even dominant, role in structuring and distributing resources. The law is the result of social, economic, and political choices, and it sets the limits of choice in a society. What is called the Rule of Law represents a general ideal about both content and procedure in the law. What this ideal becomes in real life will be determined by the way in which law is made and the way in which it is applied and monitored by judicial institutions.

Systems of Dispute Settlement

The simplest way to settle an argument is for the two sides to talk, to bargain with each other until they reach an acceptable decision. Alternatively, or if no acceptable decision emerges, the injured parties may resort to self-help, or "revenge," perhaps with the aid of family or friends. Both of these are common in everyday life everywhere. Much of international politics works in these ways too, and in some very simply organized societies (such as the Bushmen, or the Nuer in East Africa) these may be the only choices. A related and slightly more complicated procedure is for the two parties involved to agree on a third person, perhaps a social "notable," to arbitrate the problem. Serving as arbitrator is for this person just a temporary, *ad hoc* role. This may also happen in international politics if the two nations can agree on a respected outside figure for judgment, as Chile and Argentina did in choosing the Vatican to arbitrate their recent territorial dispute.

As life becomes more complex, it is common to find regular, even mandatory, intervention by a third party. A family head, an organization such as a work group or an age group, or a chief may carry this responsibility. When there are fights, the injured party is expected to take the problem to these recognized authorities. If this is not done, then another offense has been committed. The political system gradually expands its influence in this way, and power probably becomes increasingly centralized. It may try to reserve certain questions for its exclusive control. Regular days for hearing cases may be set aside and certain people or groups designated to help, such as a councilor for judicial matters or a group of young men to enforce decisions. The apparatus of government is being constructed.

Eventually specialized institutions come into being. The courts get their own staff, the judges; the police become a full-time, career force; and professional arguers, or lawyers, appear to assist the people involved in cases. Most chiefdoms and kingdoms show at least the beginnings of these developments. As the state grows more powerful it insists that most cases be brought to it, especially if some violence or deprivation is part of the resolution. The state, in other words, tries to monopolize the use of force. Other forms of dispute settlement, however, may go on: families still deal with their problems, labor unions settle work disputes, and the individual is allowed to use self-help in emergencies. A modern political system such as the United States contains many levels of judicial process, from local union bargaining to the Supreme Court.

Contemporary Forms

The courts, judges, lawyers, and police that constitute today's complex systems, along with the laws they apply, take an amazing range of forms. These can be summarized very briefly, with the details safely left to specialists.

Courts

One of the most important questions about courts is their control; a second is their relationship to each other; and a third is their jurisdiction or specialization. In what we have called a unitary political system there may be one centrally controlled system of courts, with a simple hierarchy ending in a superior or supreme court. This is the situation in most of Latin America, in nations such as France, and in the states in the United States (although two of the fifty have *two* supreme courts). If the political system is a federal one, with power divided territorially, there are several choices. The component units may operate their own systems with only a few central courts coordinating major decisions. Australia uses this model, as most federations do. Where there is a very powerful single-party government, as in Mexico or the USSR, such courts may be effectively controlled by the center. No federation operates with *only* federal courts, however. A few, such as the United States, have a dual system, with both central and component governments operating complete sets of courts, linked only at the top by the review powers of the single national high court. The business of law becomes very complicated in such dual arrangements of courts.

The courts may form a hierarchy in which each level is subordinate to the next in powers and in decision making, so that a higher court can overturn the decision of a lower one, until the final court is reached. Sometimes, as in many state systems in the United States, the higher courts also have powers to discipline or even dismiss judges of lower courts. It is more common, however, for some other branch of government to have this power of removal. A special agency, such as the judicial service commission common in many countries of the British Commonwealth, or even the ruling party, may supervise the judges. In the former colonial countries there is often another division between the statutory courts and those modeled upon traditional precolonial institutions. These are called customary courts. Decisions and staffing in the customary courts will follow one hierarchy and those in the statutory courts another, with little connection between them. If there is any relationship, the customary courts are generally "inferior" in terms of appeals and other procedures. This reflects the complicated heritage of colonialism, in which one set of rules applied to the indigenous peoples and another to the colonial governors and their modernizing assistants. Other kinds of specialized courts may appear in both new and old states, including tax courts, customs courts, and labor tribunals. They are also limited by subject matter and generally are not part of the regular hierarchy. Sometimes they are called "legislative" or "administrative" courts.

Judges

The various kinds of courts are run by judges. They may be laymen, which simply means not trained professionally in law. (The American Supreme Court upheld the use of such untrained personnel for petty courts in a 1979 decision.) There are many examples around the world: the justice of the peace in the United States and Britain, the English magistrate, the neighborhood judge in Russia, Cuba, Angola; the customary court judge in Nigeria; the lay assessor in Tanzania. For the more important courts judges are usually required to have legal training, either training as a lawyer or special training as a judge, as is the French practice. The way judges are chosen will reflect and affect these requirements. There are four basic methods of choice: appointment, career, election, and inheritance. Appointment by some other branch of government is most common; the executive, the legislature, or both, selects the judges, perhaps with advice from the legal profession. A second method of recruitment is through professional training, just as doctors in many countries select themselves by going to medical school; like doctors, judges must pass examinations. Public participation in the selection is far less common. The United States is almost the only country that elects judges to courts above local ones. In the United States even state supreme court judges may be elected, while in most other cases, such as Cuba or the Soviet Union, only the very limited neighborhood courts get their judges this way. Finally, traditional patterns that are now dying out relied upon certain families to provide judicial candidates, or judgeships were automatically attached to certain offices, such as the traditional emirships in northern Nigeria.

Lawyers

Lawyers have assumed the status of a profession in most contemporary nations. They may be a "unified" or "fused" group, in which completing the necessary training and exams leads to a single occupation. A lawyer in the United States, for example, can conduct all kinds of legal business, from drawing up wills to arguing cases in court. In other systems he would join a division of the legal profession and might be restricted to certain activities. The English barrister can present cases in court, while the English solicitor, who deals with the public, cannot appear in court. Similar divisions are found in other European countries and in some of their former colonies. Most new states have adopted the unified model, even those that were British colonies, because they do not have enough lawyers for the luxury of division. In either case the lawyers may organize and supervise their profession, or the government itself may estab-

*"I'm a believer in equal justice, Mr. Bucknell . . .
let's say we give you three years, and your lawyer gets five!"*

lish standards and conditions. In revolutionary times, lawyers may suffer badly. They are seen as defenders of the old order, and the government will probably take over the profession and reorganize it, as many in the United States wanted to do after the War of Independence. In many other societies there is hostility to lawyers, as well as concern about "excessive litigation." No modern nation has succeeded in doing away with the legal profession entirely, however, although China came very close to completely destroying both the profession and the legal system. The changes in Chinese society and constitution after the death of Mao Tse-tung in 1976 will almost certainly require professional lawyers once again.

Police

The government itself provides the last important set of actors in the judicial process, the police and the prosecutors. These executive agencies have substantial impact on the operation of the judicial system. The character of police work in particular may be critical in shaping the entire process. Most countries have a national, more or less uniform system of police. Federal states such as Mexico and the United States (and formerly Nigeria) that have multiple police agencies are in the minority. The U.S. system, like its courts, is one of the most complex in the world, with many thousands of police agencies, most of them controlled by local governments. The United States is also unusual in having some elected police officials—the county sheriffs and some town police chiefs—rather than entirely appointive or career police leadership. Very few nations have followed these U.S. models, although some federal states permit duplication of police forces at some levels. Inefficiency, cost, or political divisiveness have led some federations, such as Nigeria, to eliminate the local forces.

Laws

All these institutions and personnel must work with a system of laws. National legal systems can be grouped into categories based on different legal traditions. One is the *common law*, which spread from its origins in England to North America, and to many other parts of the world, as a result of colonial rule. Common-law systems are based on the idea of the use of tradition and community custom, and on judicial obedience to precedent. The judges are given a large role in determining what the law is, what it means, and when its application should change. Another great tradition, the Romano-Germanic, includes the *civil law* of nations such as France. This is based on the use of comprehensive codes, without any deference to community standards and customs. Like the common law, civil law is now found far from its home as a result of colonialism. Elements of this law can still be found in parts of the United States that were French or Spanish colonies before they were joined to the United States. Many national systems show elements drawn from both traditions. Scandinavian and Scottish laws are examples.

In this century the spread of Marxist-based systems has created a third major category, *socialist law*, with the model in the Soviet Union. Many of the socialist states in Eastern Europe have adopted versions of the codes introduced in the USSR after 1917, although they have not always completely abolished preexisting (largely civil) law as the Soviet Union did. States such as Yugoslavia reflect differences with the Soviet model in their legal systems. The newer Communist regimes such as Cuba or China, which came to power in radically different circumstances, may also have legal systems that diverge in logic and operation from the Soviet parent. All socialist systems resemble the civil law family much more closely than they do common law.

Sacred or *religious law* includes a number of very different systems. Some are largely restricted to private affairs (Catholic canon law); others have national or international political significance. Of these *Islamic law* is the most important today. This law, sometimes called the Shari'a, is derived from the principles of the Koran and the commentaries on it. From its origin in the Middle East it too was spread by imperialism as well as conversion, and it is now found in many states of North Africa, the Indian subcontinent, and much of Southeast and East Asia. Contemporary religious nationalism has led many of these states, such as Libya and Pakistan, to revive or expand the role of this system.

The major systems of ancient Asia, Hindu, Confucian, Buddhist, and Shinto law, also had a religious basis. Although colonialism and wartime occupation, along with indigenous modernization, eliminated these as national systems, much daily village life is still governed by their precepts. Revolution also affected the legal culture of much of Asia. The Communist regime in China abolished the existing laws when it came to power, and the new codes that were promulgated were never really put into effect, as the government chose to rule by party decrees. Only after a generation of party rule is the Chinese leadership establishing legal codes and courts outside the party organs. When this process is completed, a remarkable experiment in politics without law will end.

Finally there is the very complicated family of *customary law*, which varies from place to place but is almost always unwritten. Such law is the product of tradition and incremental change over many generations. Some of this law is now being written down and incorporated into the other systems. For example, much traditional family law in Africa is now enacted as ordinances by local governments and used in courts that are part of common-law or civil-law systems; similarly, traditional law in Indonesia is incorporated into the Islamic system there.

What the Courts Do

Courts everywhere have the primary job of applying the laws. By so doing they help to shape policy as well. In some countries the courts have an additional job, that of upholding and preserving the fundamental law, the constitution. All modern states are established by this basic set of laws, which sets out—almost always in written form—the structure of government and the powers and responsibilities of its various agencies. These rules must be applied. Most often the courts are asked to do this job, although in some countries, France and Germany for example, there may be a special council to do it. When the courts interpret the constitution and apply it to public laws and actions, this is known as *judicial review*. It is an important political power, and it may be critical in establishing limits to government power. (Our discussion of constitutionalism, or limited government, considered this power in some detail.)

Policy Making

Judicial review is the most obviously political, or policy-making, role of the courts, but it is not the only one, or even the most frequent. Courts that do not have this power can also share in policy making. All judges are called upon to interpret statutes and assess claims in particular cases, and from this basic task they derive many opportunities to affect public policy. Legislatures may force this on the courts by writing vague laws, perhaps because they cannot agree on the details of a program or do not wish to challenge the executive's preferences. But even the most specific of laws may be applied to unanticipated situations and circumstances. One law may conflict with another, particularly in a federal system with its multiple levels of lawmaking. Laws inherited from a colonial past must be employed in the rapidly changing conditions of independence and modernization. Customary practices must be reconciled with statutes. These may sound like questions for lawyers to argue about in dusty offices, but the judicial reading of legislative intent and language—even the punctuation—may determine whether a whole group of people is eligible for a government program or how a company must treat its workers. In the new states judicial decisions have had great impact on the use of public power in industrialization, state planning, land use, and control of corruption, just as they affect the ever expanding government activity in the older states of Europe and the Americas. Political activists everywhere have not been blind to the possibilities of court action, and so the courts have been an arena for interest group contests. Even if political organizations such as parties, or interest groups such as labor unions, are forbidden, the courts will still hear cases of political and economic significance.

Judicial policy making is sometimes attacked as usurping a role that rightfully belongs to others. This is not the case. Even if the courts wished to remain absolutely aloof from the policy process, it would be impossible to decide all cases without in some way affecting public life. Such policy making is subject to a number of constraints. The professional schooling of judges in most traditions generally leads them to be conservative, reluctant to rule on controversial political issues unless there is a supporting community consensus. And even if judges are eager to declare a position, they must wait for cases that concern a given issue; they are not self-starting. Courts are also dependent on the rest of the government. The executive branch enforces—or ignores—their decisions. Legislative action is often required, since staffing, structure, and financial support of courts generally comes from the legislature. Lower courts may defy the opinions of higher courts with near impunity. Decisions can be evaded or resisted in many ways, by both private and public actors. Judicial dictatorship is thus an imaginary beast; no court can overthrow a government or seize control of public policy. At the same time the courts and judges *will* have some say in shaping this policy, and so their quality is of importance even for those who never take a case to court.

Norm Enforcement

The great bulk of the courts' work consists of *norm enforcement* through the daily application of general rules to particular situations. Such cases usually begin and end in the same court, without any appeal—often without going to trial at all—and without any published opinion other than the decision itself. The resolution of most cases in this way is not necessarily a failure for the courts. Negotiated settlements under judicial scrutiny make it possible for the courts to manage their huge workloads. More important, they help manage conflict by resolving it before it reaches the point where a trial must be held.

Even here there is some policy impact. The seemingly most trivial cases may conceal political struggles: for example, the power of landlords versus tenants, or management versus labor. Particular politicians may make their reputation in such cases—for instance, the prosecutor who "puts criminals behind bars," or "the champion of labor." Over the years the pattern of norm enforcement may show a strong pull in one direction or another as the judges slowly change the way a rule is used. The community concept of marriage rights or its attitude toward thieves will be reflected in the courts, and the courts in turn may lead community change in some areas by the way they apply and state the laws. The judge who never decides a constitutional question still influences community norms and their evolution.

Police and prosecution behavior also affects political life. In particular the police are "the front line of government" among the people, called on to perform a critical role by maintaining order for the system. Increasingly they are expected to perform social services as well, partly because the police are the only public agencies likely to be available twenty-four hours a day, seven days a week, and partly because successful maintenance of order and prevention or solution of crime is supported by preventing social crises that can quickly rise to flash point. Once the police have sifted out problems that seem to call for court action, the prosecutors (who may be part of the police or a separate group) must decide which to pursue. The way these two jobs are done, and who controls the necessary and increasing exercise of discretion in enforcement, can have important consequences for nation building and for general acceptance of a regime and its policies. These agencies may act for the executive or for themselves. In both cases they affect politics.

Finally, the people themselves participate. Most cases, whether civil or criminal, are initiated by private action—filing a claim or making a complaint to the police. The public determines what kind of work the courts and police will do. In some systems the citizens are also called upon to assist, by serving on juries or as lay assessors. The judicial process can thus be one of the most vital parts of the political system, providing a lively arena for general participation in governing the changing community.

Reforms

Judicial systems of both old and new states have been much criticized in the past decade. Revolution often requires radical change in the judicial system; reform or evolutionary change also needs supporting judicial changes. In turn it is difficult to reform the courts without considering the whole political system. Otherwise what results is likely to be just "tinkering with the machine."

Many courts in the United States, for example, have been in the forefront of political change since World War II. Much of the credit for expanding political participation and broadening distribution of government benefits belongs to them. They have also been under considerable attack from both left and right. In part this is only the latest stage in a long struggle over the role and control of courts that dates back to the founding of the country. At the beginning of the nineteenth century there was a great reform era, with changes such as an elective judiciary, intended to make the courts both accountable and useful to the ordinary person and neutral in partisan politics. Much of this reform has been lost under the pressure of workloads, the growth of government power, and the failure to use twentieth-century technology for twentieth-century courts. As a result, for redressing grievances, the courts are often of use only to the very poor, who are eligible for free legal help, and to the very rich, who can purchase the best legal advice.

Other Western societies have had similar experiences. In the developing nations such problems are complicated by the multiple legal and judicial systems dating from tribalism and colonialism, as well as by the modernization process. The courts have become a confusing and frightening place to be avoided at all costs. The problem of making courts accountable and useful in managing the complexities of life in this century is worldwide. Reforms are needed everywhere.

And indeed, experiments are under way in many parts of the globe. Some involve designing judicial systems to take advantage of technology—using computers, videotapes, television, new techniques of management—to make judicial operations more efficient. At the same time there are efforts to restore some elements of tradition to the system, perhaps drawing upon the examples of societies far removed in time or place. Nations as different as Mexico, Angola, Guinea-Bissau, the United States, and Cuba are incorporating "informal" courts into their array of mechanisms for conflict management. These are places where small problems can be dealt with quickly and fairly, by and in the community—as the name of the Cuban version, the Popular Tribunal, indicates. These courts try to deal with both criminal and civil cases before they enter the formal judicial process, by referral to community agencies or private bodies; for example, the U.S. Department of Justice has funded a number of experiments with such "diversion" schemes in which administrative agencies, boards, or courts take on specialized problems such as consumer complaints, worker-management issues, welfare disputes, pension problems, and so forth. The office of ombudsman (discussed in the chapter on administration) provides a means for investigating and resolving citizen complaints about government action, as do the growing numbers of human rights commissions such as the U.S. Equal Employment Opportunity Commission and Civil Rights Commission, and the Race Relations Office in Great Britain. Compensation and restitution schemes based on very old principles of the judicial promotion of social harmony have been tried and established in many countries. Community-based rehabilitation schemes, such as the barrio project in San Juan, Puerto Rico, have not only helped prevent repeat crimes but contributed to community improvement in general by generating a sense of local competence.

The demonstrated success of many of these ideas will encourage other experiments. Some will turn out to be unworkable or unacceptable in particular places. The extent to which reforms meet the needs, and other reforms are devised when they do not, will depend in part on how well the relationship of the judicial process to the entire political process, and to its basic values, is understood.

SELECTED READINGS

Abraham, Henry J. *The Judicial Process.* 3rd ed. New York: Oxford University Press, 1975. The United States, the United Kingdom, and France.*

Allen, Francis A. *The Crimes of Politics.* Cambridge, Mass.: Harvard University Press, 1974. Political justice.

Barkun, Michael. *Law Without Sanctions: Order in Primitive Societies.* New Haven: Yale University Press, 1968.

Bayley, David H. *The Police and Political Development in India.* Princeton, N.J.: Princeton University Press, 1969.

Becker, Theodore L. *Comparative Judicial Politics.* Chicago: Rand McNally, 1970.*

———, ed. *Political Trials.* Indianapolis: Bobbs-Merrill, 1970.*

Bohannon, Paul, ed. *Law and Warfare.* Garden City, N.Y.: Natural History Press, 1967.* Traditional approaches to conflict.

Buxbaum, D. C., ed. *Traditional and Modern Legal Institutions in Asia and Africa.* Leiden, Netherlands: E. J. Brill, 1968.

Clinard, Marshall B., and Daniel J. Abbott. *Crime in Developing Countries.* New York: Wiley-Interscience, 1974.

David, René, and John E. D. Brierley, *Major Legal Systems in the World Today.* London: Stevens, 1968.

Davis, Kenneth Culp. *Discretionary Justice.* Baton Rouge: Louisiana State University Press, 1969.

Ehrmann, Henry W. *Comparative Legal Cultures.* Englewood Cliffs, N.J.: Prentice-Hall, 1976.*

Eldridge, Albert F. *Images of Conflict.* New York: St. Martin's, 1979.*

Ellis, Richard E. *The Jeffersonian Crisis: Courts and Politics in the Young Republic.* New York: Oxford University Press, 1971.

Friedman, Lawrence M. *Law and Society: An Introduction.* Englewood Cliffs, N.J.: Prentice-Hall, 1977.*

*Indicates a paperback edition is available.

Gluckman, Max, ed. *Ideas and Procedure in African Customary Law.* Oxford, England: Oxford University Press, 1966.

Hazard, John C. *Communists and Their Law.* Chicago: University of Chicago Press, 1969.

Klonoski, James R., and Robert I. Mendelsohn. *The Politics of Local Justice.* Boston: Little, Brown, 1970.*

Merryman, John Henry. *The Civil Law Tradition.* Stanford: Stanford University Press, 1969.

Montagu, Ashley, ed. *Learning Non-Aggression: The Experience of Non-Literate Societies.* New York: Oxford University Press, 1978.

Mosse, George L., ed. *Police Forces in History.* Berkeley, Calif.: Sage, 1975.

Pospisil, Leopold. *Anthropology of Law.* New York: Harper & Row, 1971.

Quinney, Richard. *Class, State and Crime.* New York: David McKay, 1977.*

Roberts, Simon. *Order and Dispute: An Introduction to Legal Anthropology.* New York: Penguin, 1979.*

Schact, Joseph. *An Introduction to Islamic Law.* Oxford, England: Oxford University Press, 1964.

Schafter, Stephen. *The Political Criminal: The Problem of Morality and Crime.* New York: Free Press, 1974.

Scheingold, Stuart. *The Law in Political Integration.* Cambridge, Mass.: Harvard University Center for International Affairs, 1971.

Schubert, Glendon, and David J. Danelski, eds. *Comparative Judicial Behavior: Cross-Cultural Studies of Political Decision-Making in the East and West.* New York: Oxford University Press, 1969.

Wolff, Robert Paul, ed. *The Rule of Law.* New York: Simon and Schuster, 1971.* An examination of the impact of law on various societies, and a critique of the state.

11

The Implementation of Politics: Administration

I do not rule Russia; ten thousand clerks do.
—*Czar Nicholas I*

The nearest thing to immortality in this world is a government bureau.
—*General Hugh S. Johnson*

If the British ever come back—a possibility which is strengthened by the number of Beatles records sold in Nigeria—they will find that among the few institutions they left behind which have survived independence, is bureaucracy.
—*Peter Enahoro*

One key element of all these aspects of political decisions remains to be discussed: their *implementation*, or *administration*. In modern times, or at least since the time of the influential German sociologist Max Weber, one cannot consider administration fully without considering bureaucracy. Today "bureaucracy" and "bureaucrat" are often terms of derision, but they describe organizations that are nearly universal and the individuals who staff those organizations. In governmental terms, administration puts laws and policies into effect, and the bureaucracy is the organized group that accomplishes this.

It is through bureaucracy that modern governmental authority becomes actual practice—assuming that it does. Bureaucracy is characterized by strictly prescribed rules and regulations about function and performance. Highly detailed written codes of conduct, rights, and duties are one of the hallmarks of a modern bureaucracy. Another is a hierarchical structure with a chain of command. Promotion within the structure is governed by the written procedures, as are hirings and dismissals, both controlled rather tightly. The salaries and the technical requirements for various positions are matters of record and are usually consistent throughout the system. At least these are the characteristics of an "ideal" bureaucracy, in Weber's terms. Like the other aspects of politics we have discussed, bureaucracies reflect human imperfections. These norms may also be interfered with for what seem to be necessary political purposes.

The Rise of Bureaucracies and the Bureaucratic State

In the most rudimentary social settings there probably was no administrative apparatus. In many simple groups everyone participates in making decisions and in carrying them out. With the rise of separate and more formally structured governments came the need for administrations to put governmental decisions into effect. In some instances these grew into huge bureaucratic empires. Modern students and critics of bureaucracies often forget the highly developed systems that existed in ancient Egypt, in Rome, and in ancient and medieval China. (The Chinese bureaucracy had one characteristic generally thought of as recent: recruitment by examination. The examinations, however, were on classical and not technical knowledge.) The bureaucracies operated by slaves are also frequently ignored. Such systems grew up in the early Middle Ages in southwestern Asia, later under the Ottoman Empire, and in what is now India, in Delhi.

After the fall of Rome the independent bureaucracy disappeared from Western society for several centuries. In the emerging feudal jurisdictions the tasks of administration were likely to be performed by parts of the princely or royal households, by servants to the rulers. Some of the curious titles of today's officials, such as the British chamberlain, derive from that day. As territories grew and administrative needs became more complex, the positions gradually separated from the households of the rulers. For a time they were most often filled by the clergy, which had almost a monopoly on literacy and education. (Thus the 17th century provision in criminal law for "benefit of clergy," which meant that those who could read or write their names were assumed to be members of the clergy and so escaped execution.) But with the increasing conflicts between church and state, churchmen lost ground to a powerful new class, the lawyers.

The Western pattern, therefore, has been an evolution from the notion of public employment as the result of personal privilege or family right, or patronage or puchase from the monarch, to the idea of a nonpartisan, merit-based service entered by competitive exams. Public employment is now considered a public trust, and government an institution that exists to render service. Moreover, although the practice varies considerably from country to country, in theory the ideal civil service is neutral politically and will serve any government regardless of its politics.

However well or poorly the presumed ideals of a bureaucracy have been met, the professionalization of bureaucracies has laid the groundwork for the development of modern governments and the growth of governmental power. With the huge administrative structure of modern states, even liberal democracies today command power far in excess of most absolute rulers of the past. For one thing, technology has created powers hardly dreamed of before. For another, bureaucracy as an institution is capable of great and ruthless efficiency, however inefficient particular agencies may be. Technological resources combined with tight organization produce a capacity to translate government dictates into reality with heartening—or, depending upon one's point of view, chilling—efficiency. Perhaps first among technological resources is the computer, which has spread around the globe since mid-century. Because of computers and the systems that support them, governments can now process, store, and retrieve information in astronomically large quantities and amazingly small detail, and do it simply, inexpensively, and almost instantaneously. Forms of communication such as the teletype, telephone, radio, television, and numerous other devices (most of them much less than a century old) enable the system to transmit information quickly and also to transmit orders and commands from superiors to subordinates, no matter where they are. (This is the "Brave New World" we spoke of in discussing the future of constitutional government, or at least its potential.) Even the recent development of sophisticated copying machines, a seemingly minor invention, has revolutionized bureaucratic practice.

Truly the bureaucratic state exists. If it is not worldwide, it is only a matter of time. Change is constant, but never has it been so fast or so extreme, and never has it brought with it the promise, for good or ill, of such a radically different future.

Modern Bureaucracies

In England the separation from the royal household led ultimately to a highly sophisticated bureaucracy that serves the executive. The British Civil Service has become a model of administrative practice that is admired by political scientists and observers the world over. It seems actually to have achieved a neutrality that most other systems can only envy. Entrance to public employment is by examination, and there is no requirement for specific administrative training. Generalists are preferred over specialists in this system. Traditionally the top positions were available only to members of the elite, who entered at that level, but since World War II it has broadened its base considerably by emphasizing promotion from the lower positions to the highest levels.

The pattern on much of the European continent has been similar, but rarely has any nation achieved the United Kingdom's degree of success in patterning its bureaucracy. One distinction between the British arrangement and that of most of the Continent is the high degree of localism in Britain, considerably more than in nations such as France or Germany, or those of Latin America (which also follows the continental model). In France before World War II the bureaucracy seemed rigid, authoritarian, and openly antidemocratic in its attitudes. During the war many French civil servants welcomed the puppet Vichy government that collaborated with the occupying Germans.

When the war was over, the French criticized their bureaucracy very strongly, and it was reformed in an attempt to broaden the base of the civil service and produce a neutral system more in the British pattern. Although civil servants were selected by examination even before the war, the examinations, in contrast to those in Great Britain, had been technical and specialized, and were so constructed that only graduates of a particular kind of curriculum could hope to pass. The only school that provided this training was the Ecole Libre des Sciences Politiques, a bastion of rigidity and antidemocratic elitism. The French government nationalized the school and it became the National School of Administration (ENA). The new school selected students by merit, provided scholarships so that lack of wealth would presumably be no bar, established regional institutes of administrative studies, and made other efforts to democratize the ranks of the bureaucracy. Its graduates, the *enarques*, have become very important in French political life.

The degree to which these reforms have achieved their goals is questionable. The French bureaucracy in modern times has always provided a large measure of stability to the French system, even during the Third and Fourth Republics when elected governments came and went with alarming regularity. The governmental leadership had virtually no continuity, and the instability was so great that many wondered if France as a nation could survive. In fact this instability reached crisis proportions, which ended with the introduction of the much more powerful and stable, if more authoritarian, Fifth Republic. Through all these changes of government the bureaucracy persisted with virtually no change. The equal ability of other bureaucracies to disconnect themselves from government has concerned leaders in both Western and developing nations. This is true of the British system as well. The dramatic election of Margaret Thatcher, the first woman to be prime minister, in 1979 should not obscure the bureaucratic continuity—from permanent secretary to the clerks.

In the United States a system based first on membership in the elite and then on party patronage gave way to a merit-based Civil Service a century ago, at least at the national level. Many states continued to use a patronage system, but are changing now partly as a result of federal requirements. State programs increasingly have some direct or indirect federal money involved. The federal agencies that disburse money to the states require them to use merit systems in the selection of employees to administer federally assisted programs. At the national level, most public employment is under the jurisdiction of the Civil Service Commission. Personnel matters are thus separate from what are called "line" administrative activities in federal agencies, a situation that has been praised for impartiality and condemned for inefficiency. Selection is by examination, with requirements, both technical and general, rigidly prescribed for each position. The system has grown from the efforts of reformers in the late nineteenth and early twentieth centuries who were concerned with corruption in government and advocated merit systems for all public employment. Guarantees of job security against political interference may make it very difficult to fire incompetent employees. No really satisfactory solution for this dilemma has yet been found.

At municipal levels the formal pattern is different, partly because the problems and programs in cities are different from those of the states and the nation. Nevertheless, the basic motivations tend to be similar. Many cities have even tried to organize virtually an entire government under a merit system by adopting a council-manager form. Here there are no elected or politically appointed administrators at all; nothing corresponding to ministerial or presidential-cabinet officer, nothing resembling an elected state auditor, attorney general, or treasurer. Instead, the people elect only a nonpartisan council (and sometimes a mayor, who only presides over the council). The council then hires a professional manager as head of the city government. The manager is supposed to remain free from political interference except as the council supplies broad policy direction. The original idea was that administration is a neutral function, which should be and can be separated from policy making. Experience has demonstrated how unrealistic this notion was. Modern training in public administration recognizes that it is impossible to divorce policy from administration, that administration has enormous policy implications. The choice of *which* streets to repair, or clinics and dispensaries to close, is bound to have political consequences. Despite this, the council-manager form appears destined to be the overwhelming choice of small and medium-sized cities in the United States. Because most such cities have relatively few social divisions they can more easily ignore the political aspects of administration. This "nonpolitical administration," like the nonpartisan elections which even large cities have adopted, is symptomatic of a powerful element in American culture that considers open partisanship, or "politics," somehow corrupt and inefficient. The same attitude is found in many other countries, and the same effort to "depoliticize" administration goes on, with similar effects.

Many of the forces that led to the development of bureaucracies in the West were lacking or were radically different in the nations that today make up the Third World. In general, the developing nations lack the traditional middle class that is so characteristic of the West, and they often attempt to use a bureaucracy to perform the modernization that in the West grew from the middle class. Except for some Asian nations, and some of the great kingdoms and Islamic states of Africa, most of the Third World had no tradition of a state bureaucratic apparatus. Instead, the present bureaucracies are outgrowths of colonialism, left behind when the colonial power withdrew (although sometimes continuing to provide senior staff). This has led in many cases to conflicts with tradition and to great personal and social tensions. The bureaucracies are probably the most lasting aspect of colonial rule, but they are subject to great stress. In most of the Third World, government is expected to do, in a very short time, what both public and private agencies took centuries to do elsewhere. Even the most conservative of new states have relatively large bureaucracies. Business and industry offer few posts as yet, and there is great competition for bureaucratic positions.

In the Communist nations the picture is substantially different. There are extensive bureaucracies but they function in a manner considerably at variance with other styles, partly due to the great influence of the party. Public employees are explicitly chosen for political reliability (a practice that the United States seemed to echo in the McCarthy period of the 1950s), and political clearance for bureaucrats is an accepted and basic part of the system. There tend to be three separate bureaucracies, that of government, of the police, and of the party, all of which have a pervasive influence on political life. Other revolutionary nations may also show some of these aspects, especially in the overlap of party and administration. Much as the followers of Jefferson and Jackson argued in the early nineteenth century in the United States, these regimes believe that government programs will not be carried out by those who do not believe in them. In an ironic twist, some of these one-party states have carried the politicization of the bureaucracy to a point where the party itself is beginning to be bureaucratized. Party leaders are as likely to come from the bureaucracy as the other way around, as in Zambia.

Implications of the Bureaucratic State

The modern bureaucratic or administrative state is characterized by extensive record-keeping systems and by an enormous number of public employees organized into structures employing hundreds of thousands of persons. These giant agencies overlap and occasionally even compete with one another. Both the state's manpower resources and the availability of information to government officials have great implications for the average citizen. Openly authoritarian nations do not hesitate to control or try to control all aspects of their citizens' lives. Their ideologies justify such control, for various purposes transcending the individual.

In Western democracies, on the other hand, the lives of the citizens are presumed to be their own and not the concern of the government so long as they do not break the law. Protection of the individual is held to be a major concern. Yet the Paris prefect of police has detailed files on vast numbers of Parisians who have attracted police attention, even indirectly. In the United States revelations of questionable and even illegal activities by agencies such as the Internal Revenue Service or welfare departments, as well as state and local police, the Federal Bureau of Investigation, and the Central Intelligence Agency, suggest the dangers of the administrative state even when the government is designed to be strictly limited. Many people even distrust the Census Bureau, not believing that it will keep information private.

Just as it is normal for police to develop a mentality of suspicion because of their occupational concerns, tending to look for something wrong and to suspect the worst, so other bureaucrats tend to develop certain attitudes and mental habits as well. One of these is that if information exists, it should be collected, even if it is useless—which makes it expensive—or subject to misuse—which makes it dangerous. An application for a library card or a driver's license may call for information totally unrelated to these requests. Insurance companies have collected information about the personal habits of their customers. Such agencies may share their files with others, including police. Yet in the United States new laws have been required to force *public* disclosure of ordinary information. Telling the citizen what information has been gathered about him or her is resisted. Both kinds of abuse reflect a basic mistrust of the "common man."

Abuse of power for personal financial gain is a clear-cut example of corruption. Abuse of power to safeguard one's position or to achieve some psychological gain is equally corrupt. Both these excesses subvert the intended purpose of a government agency and its offices. Although it is not unusual for a grafter to try to justify his graft, it is much easier for other kinds of corruption to be ignored or not to be seen as constituting corruption. The Bombay official who steals shipped goods to sell on the black market, the Cuernavaca postal clerk who removes cash from mail passing through his hands, the San Antonio customs officer who delights in performing strip searches of young men returning to the United States, the Lagos policeman who routinely exacts bribes from drivers, are all guilty of official corruption. The inevitable consequence of such acts is diminished confidence in government in general, or even contempt for it, and this makes it easier for other officials to abuse their authority or cheat the government and the public.

Difficulties with accountability are also a feature of the administrative state. Although there are fairly clear-cut chains of command in most hierarchies, the structure is often so complicated that it is hard to find out who is responsible for a specific action. Much administrative decision making is haphazard, almost without control. It is easy to assume malevolent intent, but it may be even more frightening to realize that many irregularities occur simply because no one recognized what was happening, or took the responsibility of intervening. Then the pressure to justify rather than rectify may become overriding.

Even when it is possible to determine clear-cut responsibility for certain acts, there is another dimension to accountability. The purpose of the bureaucracy is to put political decisions into practice. A permanent bureaucracy, however, tends to have a life of its own regardless of the changing political forces above it. Inevitably, since administration cannot be separated from policy, the character of the bureaucracy will affect what is done. Even if the bureaucracy is fully efficient, it may carry out directives slowly, or sabotage programs that offend those who are supposed to carry them out, or implement them differently from what the political authorities intended. Any change in policy that is seen as a threat to the interests of the bureaucracy itself will certainly be resisted, as politicians from Angola to Paris to Washington have found to their despair. In this regard we may note President Carter's inability to accomplish the sweeping changes in the U.S. civil service which his 1976 campaign envisioned, and the resistance of Nigerian public employees to reorganization of their service in the mid-1970s.

At least in theory, the people in a democratic state affect public policies by voting officials out of office and replacing them with others. "Throw the rascals out," as they say in the United States. It is much more difficult to deal with unsatisfactory workings of a bureaucracy.

©Punch/Rothco

Even in theory the voters have no recourse over public employees who hold their positions by merit rather than by political means. The higher reaches of the administration are politically appointed, because these are "policy" positions, but other jobs are presumed to be *purely* technical or administrative, and therefore politically neutral. Unfortunately, it is not possible to separate policy from administration so neatly, but if newly elected officials intervene in the operations of the bureaucracies too rapidly or radically, many people will consider it improper, even if such intervention is intended to carry out a "mandate for change."

One of the greatest faults in a bureaucratic structure, and all too obvious to ordinary citizens as well as scholarly observers, is the tendency toward inflexibility. By definition the bureaucrat functions according to written rules and regulations. These are often unbending dicta that provoke conflict in specific applications. Officially the bureaucracy is powerless to change, and temperamentally the bureaucratic imperative is to adhere to the rules at all costs. The solution is not simply to do away with the rules and regulations. Arbitrary and unpredictable action is hardly to be preferred. The flaw seems to lie in the nature of mass society itself. The more people there are, the more difficult it is to deal with them individually, and the less likely it is that unusual or uncommon individual needs can be accommodated by uniform standards. The more people there are, the more necessary it is to have a bureaucracy to get anything done. Discretion is necessary, both to prevent injustices and to carry out administrative purposes in unforeseen situations, but flexibility is needed too.

It may be possible to provide for some kind of flexibility within a bureaucratic structure, tempering the impersonality inherent in the nature of the organization without destroying neutrality. Some innovations have brought limited improvements, but as yet there is nothing fully satisfactory. The most promising development is the office of ombudsman, developed in the Scandinavian countries and now widely adopted by nations as diverse as Venezuela, New Zealand, Canada, Tanzania, the Philippines, Israel, France, and Great Britain. An ombudsman is an official whose job it is to hear citizen complaints against the bureaucracy, and to determine whether the complaint is justified. If so, the episode is widely publicized, and the bureaucrat responsible is disgraced, if not subject to other penalties as well. The ideal ombudsman not only protects citizens from arbitrary and unjustified actions by the bureaucracy but protects the bureaucrat against unreasonable complaints. The only experiment with this office in the United States that attracted wide publicity was the police review boards established in some cities and made up of elected, or more often appointed, private citizens. Although some of these boards functioned effectively in the 1960s and 1970s, or perhaps *because* they did, police hostility toward them was so great that most have been eliminated. As in other bureaucracies, internal police review, has clearly been unsatisfactory, but police forces resented being singled out as the only offender. The office of ombudsman must be able to investigate *any* bureaucracy if it is to be successful. The substitute for this in many Western countries has been private legal action. Socioeconomic status, as well as government policy about suits against it, often determines who can seek redress in this way, and so there are pressures to expand publicly supported legal services. In this clumsy and expensive way a form of ombudsman protection is provided, but it is less effective than the real thing.

There are other problems to be solved in the modern administrative state. To what degree is it permissible to delegate authority from the legislature to the bureaucracy? Some delegation is inevitable, because it is impossible to put complicated legislation into effect without power to issue regulations. But where does legislation end and the power to issue detailed regulations begin? If an agency uses this power too freely, it is infringing upon legislative authority; if the agency is too cautious or restricted, it may not be able to carry out legislative intent even if that can be ascertained. Another question is: to what degree do public employees themselves have the basic rights of citizens? Can they participate in politics as individuals? Should they be restricted in some way? There are many such restrictions in operation; in most democracies the most rigid is placed on that special group of public employees, the military. Other restrictions are debatable. The prohibition against partisan activity by federal employees in the United States has been made less restrictive, but not to the satisfaction of all.

What is probably the most serious difficulty of the administrative state seems to be permanent and unavoidable. The bureaucrat is a professional; the legislature is an amateur body, at least so far as the bureaucrat's specialty is concerned. How does an amateur body, be it parliament, state legislature, or city council, deal with a group of technical experts with vast resources? One way is for the legislature to equip itself with its own resources and experts, but inertia and expense are realities that permit few if any examples of successful efforts to beat a bureaucracy at its own game.

The organizational pressures that encourage the attitudes and practices mentioned above are strong everywhere that bureaucracies are found. It is remarkable and worthy of note that in every country there are bureaucrats who perform their functions with courage, efficiency, integrity, an awareness of the fundamental principles of their political system, and a sense of humaneness despite the mechanistic imperatives of the organization. Moreover, a recognition of the various difficulties that bureaucratic structures and merit systems present does not require that one oppose administrative organizations or merit systems in themselves. In most nations there are at least a few efficient and fair agencies. Before attacking the others too harshly, we should consider the probable results of alternative schemes. Is it certain that, on balance, they would produce much improvement?

There is now greater concern for budget and finance, sound techniques of personnel management, data processing and statistics, information flow and communication, and some recognition that policy and administration are intermingled at the bottom as well as in the top ranks of bureaucracies. As a consequence there is a greater awareness in many countries of the need to understand both the interaction of bureaucracies with the political process and the internal politics of bureaucracies, to make them more effective agents of community decisions. This must be so, because administration has as its primary function the implementation of the collective decisions of the community it serves. If it begins to operate instead for the benefit of administrators, it becomes parasitic. It should be a subordinate function, existing not as an end in itself.

Alexander Pope once wrote, during a rather dull period of English political history, "For forms of government let fools contest—whatever is best administered is best." Perhaps he could say this because the great peaceful political revolution in English history had taken place already, in 1688, the year of his birth; in any case, he was wrong. A good system badly administered may well be bad, but a poor system efficiently administered—if this is possible—is hardly better; and a poor system is likely to be accompanied by a defective bureaucracy. What every political community seeks is effective administration of decisions taken by a "good" political process.

SELECTED READINGS

Altshuler, Alan A., and Norman C. Thomas. *The Politics of the Federal Bureaucracy.* 2nd ed. New York: Harper & Row, 1977.

Caiden, Naomi, and Aaron Wildavsky. *Planning and Budgeting in Poor Countries.* New York: Wiley, 1974.

Dvorin, Eugene P., and Robert H. Simmons. *From Amoral to Humane Bureaucracy.* San Francisco: Cornfield, 1972.*

Eisenstadt, S. N. *Essays on Comparative Institutions.* New York: Wiley, 1965.

_____. *The Political Systems of Empires.* New York: Free Press, 1963.

Etzioni, Amitai. *Modern Organizations.* Englewood Cliffs, N.J.: Prentice-Hall, 1964.*

Krisler, Samuel. *Representative Bureaucracy.* Englewood Cliffs, N.J.: Prentice-Hall, 1974.*

Landau, Martin. *Comparative Bureaucracy.* Englewood Cliffs, N.J.: Prentice-Hall, 1972.*

Mainzer, Lewis C. *Political Bureaucracy.* Glenview, Ill.: Scott-Foresman, 1973.*

Marx, Morstein. *The Administrative State.* Chicago: University of Chicago Press, 1969.

Peter, Lawrence, and Raymond Hull. *The Peter Principle.* New York: Morrow, 1969.*

Peters, Guy. *The Politics of Bureaucracy: A Comparative Perspective.* New York: Longmans, 1978.*

Presthus, Robert. *The Organizational Society.* rev. ed. New York: St. Martin's, 1978.*

Riggs, Fred W. *Administration in Developing Countries.* Boston: Houghton Mifflin, 1964.

Rourke, Francis E., ed. *Bureaucratic Power in National Politics.* 3rd ed. Boston: Little Brown, 1978.

Weber, Max. *The Theory of Social and Economic Organization.* Trans. A. M. Henderson. Talcott Parsons, ed. New York: Free Press, 1964.

Woll, Peter. *American Bureaucracy.* 2nd ed. New York: Norton, 1977.*

*Indicates a paperback edition is available.

12

The Global Community

With increasing well-being all people become
aware, sooner or later, that they have something
to protect.
                    —*J. K. Galbraith*

When two cultures collide is the only time when
true suffering exists.
                    —*Hermann Hesse*

All wars are civil wars, because all men are
brothers.
                    —*François Fénelon*

Human war has been the most successful of all
our cultural traditions.
                    —*Robert Ardrey*

If we believe absurdities we shall commit
atrocities.
                    —*Voltaire*

In the twentieth century international politics became truly world politics
for the first time in history. Not only are the leaders and elites of nation-
states in contact with one another, but the masses of people everywhere—though they may never go more than a few miles from home—
are becoming aware of what other people around the globe are doing,
what they think, what kinds of values and material possessions they have.

Some of this is of course highly selective information, shaped by national and international media for their own purposes. But it is supplemented by the ever greater number of people who see for themselves by traveling outside their own countries, or living abroad as tourists, students, business representatives, or other workers. Although we certainly cannot say that all people everywhere share equally—or wish to—in these exchanges, we can discern the outlines of a global, self-conscious community in formation. Peasants in China appeal to the American president in their wall posters; students in the United States issue pronouncements on South African affairs; taxi drivers in Tunisia comment about Mexican immigrant workers in the United States.

By contrast, international relationships in earlier centuries were much more limited and fragmentary. When people in eighteenth-century Europe spoke of world politics, they meant European politics. Vast areas of the globe were not known to them, or were of interest merely as appendages to Europe, targets of its energetic exploration and colonization. By the early twentieth century technological revolutions in transport and communications had laid the groundwork for much-expanded international linkages which would incorporate many new areas. The experiences of two great wars, increasingly worldwide in impact, helped to set these linkages in place. The wars also hastened the end of the great colonial empires, with the exceptions of the great land empires of the Soviet Union, China, and the United States. (The fact that these three are rarely thought of as imperial systems, although all three arose from colonial expansion through conquest, negotiation, or purchase, partly insulates them from the external anticolonial demands for self-determination that have been the hallmark of the post–World War II years.) Since the first waves of newly independent nations swept over the two camps of the Cold War, the scope and nature of international politics have become ever more complex. The emergence of Latin American states and of China as major role players rather than supporting cast has brought the remainder of the globe into this new system.

It is useful to think of this whole nascent global community and its political process as a kind of developing nation. There are many similarities, and we can use this idea as a framework in which to fit many isolated or odd events—as long as we remember that we are imposing an artificial order on human disorder.

Development of a World System

Like most developing nations, the world community is pluralist. Virtually all peoples are being pulled into the "global village." Certain cultures within this complex have been, by accident and by design, more successful than others in promoting their ways of life, languages, social structures, and attitudes. English and French are spoken everywhere, partly as a result of the long centuries of colonial rule. Spanish and Portuguese spread over large territories as well, but then lost the edge as world languages to the first two. American television programs are seen in most nations and far outweigh locally produced offerings in many. The artifacts of a few cultures—Beatles records, *Time* magazine, platform shoes, Kentucky Fried Chicken, Toyotas—litter the world. At some point resistance to this intrusive "Coca-Cola culture" may set in. Many people in the industrialized nations encourage this reaction, whether or not they know and appreciate the other cultures. They sympathize because they are attempting to revive their own local traditions against the onslaughts of commercialism. Throughout the world a surge of communal revival challenges the homogenizing influence of international trade, aid, and communications. These two countervailing trends provide confusion and tension. Where we are going is uncertain, but we are moving very rapidly. Different passengers see the journey from varying points of view, and as we noted at the very beginning of this book, identities are layers of perceptions, which may shift unpredictably as more layers are piled on.

Actors in World Politics

The political process of this world community is very complex, although it has not yet established much in the way of institutions. Few truly global political institutions have emerged from the experience of the twentieth century, although we might well be surprised at the existence of any, and pleasantly surprised by even partial success. The first such venture, the League of Nations—established after World War I—was little more than a European league. Despite President Woodrow Wilson's close connection with the founding of the League, the U.S. Senate rejected membership. The League collapsed at the onset of World War II, having failed ignominiously in efforts to deal with the civil war in Spain and the Italian invasion of Ethiopia (although the Emperor of Ethiopia made an unforgettable speech at the League, decrying the invasion and the imperialist mood of the world).

The weaknesses of the League led to a renewed determination to devise a workable system rather than abandon union. Immediately after the war ended an international meeting in San Francisco established the United Nations. The structure of the UN, more complex than that of the League, gave it six major components. The General Assembly contains delegates from all member states, each member voting equally. The Security Council, which has more substantive power, reflected postwar reality by making the five major powers of the time (the United States, the

USSR, the United Kingdom, France, and China) permanent members, with a veto power. Ten other members are elected by the Assembly for two-year terms. The executive agency, or Secretariat, is headed by a Secretary General elected by the Assembly. These three are combined with an Economic and Social Council, a Trusteeship Council (whose work supervising the decolonization of territories seized from the losing powers in two world wars is nearly done, with the exception of Namibia), and the International Court of Justice, composed of fifteen judges elected for staggered nine-year terms by the Security Council and Assembly together.

The UN's capacity to promote international peace, order, and progress is, to say the least, controversial. On the plus side is the fact that the UN is the most comprehensive world organization ever established. Only a few states (such as Switzerland) have chosen not to join, or have been prevented by veto (the two Koreas, Vietnam, and formerly the two Germanies and the People's Republic of China). Some of these participate in the specialized agencies. The UN provides a meeting place for the world, for debate and for informal contacts, friendly or not. Many of its specialized agencies, such as the World Health Organization (WHO), do invaluable work in their special fields. On the minus side, the UN has not affected the reality of territorial states and their claim to sovereignty, nor the inequalities of those states, despite the pretense to equality in the UN (except for the five veto powers). Very often these two features of international life are insurmountable obstacles to effective international action. This is particularly true in peacekeeping work, which has generally been possible only when the superpowers were not directly involved, or favored some solution that would keep them from becoming further involved—the Congo in the 1960s, the Middle East in the 1970s. Although there have been some limited successes, few believe that the UN has much of a role to play in controlling the central violent danger to the world: the escalating arms race under the shadow of a potential nuclear war. The UN has a disarmament and arms control agency, but the real work of arms control is carried on between the two giants, the United States and the USSR. Their Strategic Arms Limitation Talks (SALT) were not held at the UN, and they did not include European or other nuclear powers. In these matters the larger states jealously guard their sovereignty, even at the cost of possible destruction.

There are some specialized global institutions. Many are functional agencies associated with the UN, such as the International Labor Organization (ILO); the International Bank for Reconstruction and Development (IBRD), known as the World Bank; the International Monetary Fund (IMF); the Food and Agriculture Organization (FAO); the Atomic Energy Agency (AEA); the Universal Postal Union (UPU); the World

Meteorological Organization (WMO); and the UN High Commission for Refugees (UNHCR). Some of these, such as the International Monetary Fund, have come to play a very large part in domestic politics, even of the larger nation-states. Great Britain, for example, had to make some painful changes in its public expenditure plans to meet the IMF's requirements for a loan in 1976. The UN and its various agencies are far from constituting a world government, and proposals for powers such as international taxation to redistribute world income are still visionary. However, the UN is equally far from being simply the creature of any one state or group of states.

Below this global level, international organizations (meaning associations of nation-states, not individuals) range from two-party efforts to large multimember groups. There are many hundreds of these organizations, which we can classify to some extent by their *scale* and by their *purpose*. The simplest is the bilateral, or association between two states. When the pair expands even slightly—more than two but less than ten— these intermediate arrangements become much more complex. Large-scale groupings are even more difficult. These may consist of all states in a geographic region: sixteen in West Africa, twenty in Latin America, ten in Europe, and several dozen in the Caribbean and in all of Africa. Many of these regions, including continental ones, share common features of culture, language, or religion, and they have been the focus of supranational federal hopes for political visionaries such as Pan-Africanists or Europeanists. However, the practical difficulties of getting national states to surrender any of their autonomy—particularly if it is newly acquired, or if past relationships have been hostile—are very great. In addition there are multistate groupings which join members not geographically related, such as oil producing states.

These groups may have a specialized function, such as the promotion of international research on animal disease, or they may have a broader financial and trade coordination goal, or even the goal of eventual economic union, which will involve the coordination and cooperative planning of national economies. Others may intend broad *political* coordination, including military functions. The density of this network is suggested by West Africa, where there are some thirty organizations composed only or primarily of West African states, in addition to nearly a hundred larger groups with which these states are associated. In the chart on p. 172 the characteristics of scale and purpose are combined to produce twenty possible types of international organization—not all of which now exist. Examples, using West African states where relevant, are given of existing categories.

To this international cast of thousands must be added some other players. International, nongovernmental organizations (called NGOs),

Types of International Organization

Size	Purpose			
	Specialized	Finance/Trade	Economic Union	Political/Military
Bilateral	Mano River Union (Liberia, Sierra Leone) Electrical Community of Benin (Benin, Togo) International Boundary and Water Commission (United States/Mexico)	Singapore/Malaysia Morocco/Ceula & Melilla (free ports)	United States/Puerto Rico	Niger/Nigeria Commission Senegambia Permanent Secretariat
Intermediate	Lake Chad Basin Commission Niger River Commission West African Examinations Council	West African Customs Union West African Economic Community	East African Community (defunct)	Conseil d'Entente ANZUS (Australia, New Zealand, United States), military
Regional	West African Rice Development Association (WARDA) Committee of Sahelian States Against the Drought European Atomic Energy Community (EUR-ATOM)	Latin American Free Trade Area Caribbean Free Trade Area African Development Bank	Economic Community of West African States EEC; COMECON	WARSAW PACT Organization of African Unity Organization of American States
Multistate	International Olympic Committee International Air Transport Association (IATA)	OPEC General Agreement on Trade and Tariffs (GATT) Organization for Economic Cooperation and Development (OECD)		French Community NATO Arab League Common African & Mauritian Organization (OCAM)
World	FAO WHO Red Cross	World Bank IMF		UN ICJ

are composed of individuals who do not officially represent their countries. Perhaps the most famous of these is the International Red Cross. Another is Amnesty International, recipient of the 1977 Nobel Peace Prize for its work in promoting human rights. The multinational corporations (MNCs) with management, capital, and transactions in many countries, are also generally private although a few, such as Royal Dutch Shell, are owned in part or entirely by one or more governments. They have come to play a major, if not controlling, role in all sectors of the world economy in this century, especially since World War II. Often they are powerful enough to challenge the autonomy of governments themselves, even the largest. One of the troubling issues presented by these MNCs is their role in fostering economic dependency.

Finally, there are the people of the world, who have begun to form a kind of international public opinion on some occasions, through the linkages of the international media. Certain individuals, of course, stand out. Although there is no formal international leadership, except perhaps the Secretary General of the UN and the heads of a few other institutions such as the World Bank, there is clearly a set of international elites; national leaders; diplomats; international bureaucrats; well-known private individuals whose opinions carry beyond their own countries; owners and managers of multinational business; and the financiers who guide international economic life. This polyglot group shows some homogeneity. Many of its members know each other better than they do most of their countrymen, and it is sometimes said that a truly international class and culture is developing, supported by the cosmopolitan outlook of globe-trotting academics, students, and other travelers. Yet these elites and subelites are also deeply divided, for they are still products of, and attached to, particular nation-states. The divisions among nations are still far deeper than any intranational cleavages.

Nation-States and Their Contacts

Nation-states, then, are in a real sense the primary actors in the world. They divide the territory of the world among themselves. The nation-state itself, which was both a result and a cause of the end of medieval, feudal politics in Europe, stands as one of the most enduring political forms yet created by human communities. Its peculiar strengths and weaknesses are much the same throughout the world. Nonetheless, this form is superimposed upon vastly different economic and social bases. At the risk of oversimplifying, the resulting differences among nations can be grouped as several elementary families.

One commonly used distinction sets off the capitalist or socialist democracies of the West from the authoritarian Marxist-Leninist regimes of the East, reflecting the legacy of the Cold War between the United States and the USSR, as well as a much older distinction between the "rationalist" West and the "mystic" East. The developing nations are known as the Third World in this typology, and some even refer to a Fourth World, the weakest and probably least viable states. As the "rich poor countries" such as Mexico and Nigeria consolidate their systems, a gap develops between them and the "poor poor nations" like Haiti and Burundi, a gap as wide as that between all developing nations and the other two camps. A simpler division on grounds of wealth is North versus South, reflecting the general correspondence of those hemispheres with the richer and the poorer nations. These simple categories do no more than symbolize the enormous range of differences among nations in all aspects of social, economic, and political life. They do not take account of complexities such as the substantial discrepancies within nations, or anomalies such as the economic slippage that may put a nation like Italy within the income range of some developing nations. But they do mark the fundamental issues that form a large part of the international agenda, a few of which we will examine below. And they help to explain why international politics has been, and is, so disorderly—despite the growing interdependence of the world's peoples.

Although there are regular procedures in operation for the discussion—and, with luck, resolution—of some recurring general problems, we can see only the rudiments of a world dispute-management system. This system may eventually expand its jurisdiction and displace violence as the primary method of resolution, but that day is still a long time off. The world has few international judicial institutions, and most of them rely on voluntary reference of cases, by governments rather than individuals, and on voluntary compliance by the losers. The most inclusive is the International Court of Justice (ICJ), which has heard forty-four cases in its first thirty years. It is the successor to the unwisely named Permanent Court of International Justice, which decided fifty-one cases before it collapsed along with the League of Nations. Regional organizations such as the Organization of American States and the European Economic Community have associated courts, which are generally more active than the world body and which seem now to be the major source for new international law. This is a substantial body of rules, composed of treaties, judicial decisions, principles of international law and opinions of authorities, and international "custom." The Permanent Court of Arbitration (PCA), established in 1899 as the first modern international tribunal, is still in existence, although its limited jurisdiction and rules have meant only twenty cases in over seventy-five years of work. The Dutch city The Hague is the home of both the PCA and the ICJ; it is thus the center of gravity in international judicial work.

Systems of Relations

The maintenance of order is accomplished, when it is accomplished, mostly by the maneuvers of various nation-states, centering on those with the most power. There has been a sequence of such systems in world history. There may, for example, be a single dominant nation, as the United States was immediately after World War II, in a monopolar world. When the USSR acquired nuclear power the pattern began to shift to another classic type, the bipolar system, with the rest of the world's states attached to one of the two major powers (or uneasily trying to remain neutral). In past centuries a single nation-state might attempt to serve as a balancer, throwing its support first to one side and then the other, in an effort to keep either from overcoming the other. No state has been able to play this role in the nuclear age; only the United States and the Soviet Union acting in concert can serve as a balancer in today's world. More often the states compete with each for influence or control, selling or supplying arms around the globe, and often allowing localized wars, such as those of Africa, to serve as surrogate battles between themselves. The overwhelming nuclear arsenals of these two states will mean a dominant role for both in the foreseeable future, although the economic strength of the European Economic Community, and of Japan, gives these two areas an increasing significance in world affairs. The domestic politics and economics of the great powers, especially in regard to raw materials and energy supplies, also mean that other areas formerly thought to be quite weak have expanded their roles—for example Nigeria, Saudi Arabia, Mexico. Within the basic bipolar structure, the system has become much more fuzzy, and some now speak of trilateral, or pentagonal, or even multipolar lines of power in the world.

These power struggles among nations are carried out by innumerable kinds of contacts, friendly or hostile. Each nation has internal constraints of some kind, arising from institutions or from public demands. For example, the U.S. Senate plays a role in foreign affairs and has its own reasons for its decisions on foreign policy, reflecting public opinion or the constituencies of individual senators. Economic interests within each country make demands that may run contrary to a general national policy. Shoemakers in the United States want limits placed on imports, while national policy supports the reduction of international trade barriers. The personalities of those in power—and sometimes those of prominent private figures, or even overseas travelers—help shape contacts between states. Consider, for example, the personal impact of leaders such as Castro, Sadat, Kissinger, Khrushchev, Ian Smith, Idi·Amin, and John Kennedy, in contrast to their predecessors or successors. For all these reasons some problems in world order may occur partly as the result of

*"I used a standard obscure diplomatic code word, but
perhaps it wasn't obscure enough."*

Drawing by Ed Fisher; ©1978 The New Yorker Magazine, Inc.

poor fit between domestic priorities and international policies, or abrasive personalities or signals misread by nations that have not carefully studied the other's internal life. Successes may also arise from such unpredictable factors.

In addition to all these special encounters there is a regular series of contacts. Nations have sent emissaries—ambassadors, envoys, attachés, plenipotentiaries—to each other for many centuries, and a tradition of diplomacy (procedure, language, code words) has developed. Part of the furor generated by the seizure of diplomats as hostages in Iran was a response to the violation of the tradition of diplomatic immunity. In addition, myriad conferences on general or specialized subjects are held almost continuously now; the United States, for example, may attend 500 or 600 such events in a single year. (For example, the UN Conference on Trade and Development held its fifth meeting in 1979. During this period, Nigeria and the United States met to discuss technical cooperation, preparing for a meeting of 158 nations on the same subject. Meantime a Pan-African Conference on Refugees was going on in Tanzania.) Both private and public figures may be involved in such meetings. Many international agreements—treaties, protocols, proclamations—emerge from this endless round of meetings as well as from regular diplomatic channels. These pass into the body of international law.

World Issues: Violence

The observance of treaties and other agreements is almost entirely up to the nations concerned; there is no world policeman to enforce them (with the occasional exception of UN peacekeeping forces). Nor is it likely that any enforcement agent will soon emerge in a world so divided that it cannot agree upon any substantive definition of, or solution to, spreading terrorism—despite the stated intent of many terrorists to destroy the present nation-states, and the world system itself. One nation's terrorist is another nation's freedom fighter. After years of argument an agreement was reached in the early 1970s at the UN to refuse assistance to hijackers, largely as the result of pressure from the International Association of Airline Pilots. Otherwise there is little global action against disturbers of the peace, state or non-state. There is not even an agreed-upon definition of aggression or intervention. The Soviet move into Afghanistan in January 1980 provides an excellent example of the problems in defining and responding to aggression. It seems that for many of the players in world politics, international order has less value than its disturbance.

And so we find a complex web of organizations, states, and private individuals supporting campaigns of violence that in many places amount to states of war. Northern Ireland, for example, is the scene of near civil war as the official Royal Ulster Constabulary and the British Army combat the warring Catholic and Protestant factions of the Irish Republican Army and its splinters and the Ulster Volunteer Force. The Palestine Liberation Organization and the government of Colonel Gadaffi in Libya contribute money and arms; so do sympathizers in the United States and elsewhere. The British and Irish governments have been unable to find a solution for the ceaseless violence, which has spilled over into both England and Ireland. The pattern is repeated elsewhere—Germany, Italy, the Middle East—and many of the actors appear to be the same.

The control of violence, and the manufacture and spread of armaments from handguns to nuclear warheads, is therefore still the responsibility of the nation-state, acting alone or in concert if it can find allies. For many observers this is the indisputably preeminent issue in world politics. All other purposes—promotion of economic and political rights, trade, scientific exchange—must take second place if they appear to conflict with arms control. In the context of nuclear weapons, this is a difficult argument to answer. No matter how accustomed we have become to talk about the possibility of nuclear holocaust, nor how remote the possibility may seem, that does not mean that there will never be a Doomsday. Only the bizarre structure of nuclear politics, in which the gigantic arsenals of each superpower constitute a "balance of terror," makes it possible to keep postponing the day of reckoning. The internal politics of the nuclear powers, and their international relations, however, make arms control very difficult, and in early 1980 the prospects for reduction of nuclear arsenals or control of nuclear proliferation seemed very dim. Potential nuclear states such as Pakistan or South Africa were clearly moving to acquire nuclear capability in arms, while the SALT II treaty was postponed—in effect, indefinitely.

Whatever tomorrow brings, one thing is certain—the cost of such weapons, and the vast array of other means of destruction, is truly staggering. Given the terrible poverty of some three-quarters of the world's peoples, and the faltering economies of the wealthy states, such expenses form a crushing burden in the effort to raise or keep standards of living. Even the few states that have no armies cannot escape the worldwide effects of such massive concentration of resources in nonproductive goods and organizations. We noted in Chapter Six some consequences of military rule for internal economic life, and it is worth repeating here that world spending on the military outstrips all other categories. As long as the arms race remains essentially uncontrolled—even if it is merely kept at its present bloated level—expenditures for education and research, agriculture, arts, town and city renewal, and other social welfare will be doomed to inferior and insufficient rank. Thus the discussion of nearly all world issues must occur within the context of world violence and its control.

World Issues: Dependency

The first issue is the problem of economic dependence and its agents, the multinational corporations and banks that exercise so much power in the world economy—and which some think are beyond the control of even their parent nations, responsible and accountable only to themselves. The great gaps among nations in terms of economic sufficiency, autonomy, and prospects are clearly fact. The cause is the subject of much academic and political debate. For some, including most of the developing nations, the economic sufferings of those nations can be attributed only in part—if at all—to their lack of resources or low level of technology, poorly integrated societies, fragile political institutions, or any other domestic cause. Rather, the cause is inherent in the international economic system, which creates wealth for the few by establishing the rest (through colonialism and other, newer means of imperialism) as poor—relatively or absolutely—and therefore dependent upon the rich. Minuscule improvement may occur, but no development that would produce self-sufficient economies. Such development would eliminate the subordinate functions performed by the "have-not" nations for the "have" economies of the world, and these states and their multinational corporate offspring will not permit this to happen. In this perspective the relatively wealthy Soviet Union is more closely allied to the West than to the Third World, and the real division is between the wealthy Northern Hemisphere and the poverty-stricken southern one.

The issue of world resources—their control, conservation, and distribution—is closely connected to the dependency question. Those who fear that the world is squandering its finite mass of raw materials and energy supplies, or endangering the ecology of the planet, urge strict limits upon growth. The poor nations are also aware of environmental hazards, but are afraid that such limits are largely a device to stunt their own chances of development and entry into the world of the haves. Leaders of poor nations perceive that one means of establishing order without repression in their societies is the provision of material benefits; in this view, the ecologists threaten their access to the necessary resources. Many in the industrialized West also express concern about the possibility of internal unrest there if the growth of the economy ceases and there is a fixed or even shrinking national income. Under such circumstances, apparently stable and integrated societies can begin to crumble, for what one sector gains another part must lose. The continuing battles over pay scales that threatened to paralyze Great Britain as its economic position declined are but a hint of the future, according to these prophets. The violence that marked the 1974 oil shortages in the western countries reappeared in 1979. Few are willing to contemplate sacrifice of what they might have in the future, and even less so what they have now.

The political consequences of these situations are potentially very grave. If the pessimists of the world are right about the coming world scarcity and environmental destruction, the poor nations of the world are doomed to permanent poverty, and even the rich are in for a bad time. The prospects for constitutional democracy are particularly grim, because the measures that would be required to enforce order as resources ran out would hardly be tenderhearted. Similarly, if the dependency theorists are correct, the permanent poverty of the world's South will continue. The aid programs of the well-off will certainly not be allowed to break that dependency, and may well be structured to increase it by establishing a debt level sufficient to guarantee the submission of client states. Under such conditions, when more equitable distribution of goods by voluntary and peaceful means appears foreclosed, the only recourse is forcible change. War may be terrible to the comfortable, but to the crippled and starving it may seem less dreadful; the possibility of winning some greater share of the wealth may outweigh its anticipated costs. The image of the future world in these scenarios is fearsome.

These summaries of very complex arguments overstate them in a sense, by giving only the extreme versions of the problems and the solutions. The role of the multinational corporation, the power of cartels such as the Organization of Petroleum Exporting Countries, as well as the new economic entities of common markets such as those of Europe and West Africa, complicate the debate. Nonetheless, it is clear that the division of the planet into deluxe passengers and hangers-on cannot continue, especially if the deprived acquire the power to blow up the vessel. The fact that the line between North and South is also in essence the color line, that the rich are mainly white and the poor are the black and brown peoples, adds to the economic divisions the centuries of discrimination and exclusion based upon racial or ethnic prejudice. The American black and Pan-Africanist leader W. E. B. Du Bois was correct on both social and economic counts when he predicted that the overriding problem of the twentieth century would be the erasing of the line drawn by color.

World Issues: Human Rights

A related but not completely parallel battle is developing over human rights. Soon after it was founded the UN drew up two major codes of rights, a political and a social and economic list. The signatories pledged to promote and implement these rights within their own nations, and the speed with which these covenants were adopted (although not yet, it should be noted, by the United States) was deceptively encouraging. These rosy expectations were buttressed by the end of repressive colonial rule in subsequent decades. A generation later, however, the prospects looked much darker.

A good deal of international tension and debate ensued over the interpretation and implementation of these rights, and over international supervision of such implementation. Most nations regard such scrutiny as infringements of sovereignty—an attitude held by rich governments as well as poor ones, and by democracies as well as dictatorships. Great Britain and the United States have not enjoyed criticism of their penal practices or color discriminations any more than the Soviet Union and China have appreciated external support for dissidents. Moreover, economic and political rights are sometimes perceived as conflicting. Developing nations may argue that the provision of economic security requires temporary abridgment of political freedoms. Some have claimed that economic scarcity and social disintegration are national emergencies that justify the suspension of many rights, as if the nation were under attack. Against this position is the clear evidence that repression in many nations (e.g., Guinea, Uganda, Haiti) has been accompanied by much poorer economic performance and income distribution than that of nations attempting to maintain political freedoms, no matter how poor they are.

This is another debate that has no clear right or wrong, and no simple solutions. Many peoples, governments, and nongovernmental organizations have made the question of human rights a central theme in world affairs. Even if other issues, such as the control of the arms race between the superpowers and their proxies, are seen as more important, disagreements over human rights are not likely to disappear from world politics in the near future.

The Future: More Challenges to the Nation-State

Although we cannot predict the future, we can make some educated guesses about problems that will occur and recur in the world's political future. For instance, there is the worldwide problem of cities, which will be the dominant pattern of settlement for the great majority of the world's people by the end of the century, and which are already staggering under the load. Most cities are nearly powerless creatures of national systems. They have no role in most national political systems, and no place has been found for them in the international political system either. If we do not find some solution, the paralysis of the cities will bring turmoil to large parts of the world. The questions of resource use and conservation are clearly connected to urban development as well.

Another issue is the problem of borders, which have multiplied many times over in this century as the number of nation-states increased. The efforts of both new and old states to behave as though the lines they draw among themselves are impenetrable are contrary to the force of long-standing social, cultural, and economic ties between many of the peoples now separated. Soviet fears of ethnic and religious influence crossing its long border with Iran, the U.S. government's concern about the millions of people crossing the long border with Mexico, and the similar concern in Venezuela about its Colombian border illustrate the impossibility of impermeable divisions. There are hostile contacts between people along borders as well, and the intrusions and skirmishes that occur between neighboring enemies constitute a major source of violence that can rapidly be spread by a network of alliances, as Vietnam and Cambodia demonstrated in 1979.

These two issues, although very different, together bring us back to the original question: In what direction is the world community evolving? What forms will it assume in the future? More specifically, what is the future of the nation-state? Can solutions for such matters as urban crisis and border problems be found within the context of the nation-state? Or do the separatist movements that challenge national authority everywhere, the increasing revival of transborder contacts, the rise of "megacities" that are larger than most national populations, the multinational corporations, and the regional unions forming in Europe, the Americas, and Africa presage the gradual decline of the nation-state? The political ingenuity and innovative ability of the human community as a whole will answer this question. Perhaps the central element in the answer lies in the deeper question facing the human species: Can we create communal identity only by separating ourselves from others? If so, must we not all perish together?

SELECTED READINGS

Aron, Raymond. *Peace and War*. Garden City, N.Y.: Doubleday, 1966.
Barnet, Richard J. *The Giants: Russia and America*. New York: Simon and Schuster, 1977.
_____. *Intervention and Revolution*. rev. ed. New York: New American Library, 1972.*
_____, and Ronald E. Muller. *Global Reach: The Power of the Multinational Corporations*. New York: Simon and Schuster, 1975.*
Bertelsen, Judy S., ed. *Non-State Nations in International Politics*. New York: Praeger, 1977.
Bill, James A., and Carl Leiden. *Politics in the Middle East*. Boston: Little, Brown, 1979.
Blair, John M. *The Control of Oil*. New York: Pantheon, 1976.*
Boorstin, Daniel J. *The Exploring Spirit: America and the World, Then and Now*. New York: Random House, 1976.
Boulding, Kenneth E. *Stable Peace*. Austin: University of Texas Press, 1978.*
Iconoclastic blueprint for reform in world politics, including a "UN Spying Organization which would spy on everybody and publish the results immediately."

*Indicates a paperback edition is available.

Brown, Harrison. *The Human Future Revisited: The World Predicament and Possible Solutions.* New York: Norton, 1978.

Brown, Lester R. *World Without Borders.* New York: Random House, 1973.*

Burchett, Wilfred, and Derek Roebuck. *The Whores of War: Mercenaries Today.* Baltimore: Penguin, 1976.

Cantari, Louis J., and Steven L. Spiegel, eds. *The International Politics of Regions: A Comparative Approach.* Englewood Cliffs, N.J.: Prentice-Hall, 1970.

Cohen, Benjamin J. *Organizing the World's Money: The Political Economy of International Monetary Relations.* New York: Basic Books, 1978.

Dahl, Norman C., and Jerome B. Wiesner. *World Change and World Security.* Cambridge, Mass.: MIT Press, 1978.

Dalton, George. *Economic Systems and Society: Capitalism, Communism, and the Third World.* Baltimore: Penguin, 1974.*

Deutsch, Karl W. *Tides Among Nations.* New York: Free Press, 1978.

Doran, Charles F. *Myth, Oil, and Politics.* New York: Free Press, 1977.

Duchacek, Ivo D. *Nations and Men: An Introduction to International Politics.* 2nd ed.; New York: Holt, Rinehart and Winston, 1971.*

Eldridge, Albert F. *Images of Conflict.* New York: St. Martin's, 1979.*

Galbraith, J. K. *The Nature of Mass Poverty.* Cambridge, Mass.: Harvard University Press, 1979. Some interesting comments on immigrant workers.

George, Susan. *How the Other Half Dies: The Real Reasons for World Hunger.* Denver, Colo.: Allanheld, Osmun, 1977.

Girvan, Norman. *Corporate Imperialism: Conflict and Expropriation.* New York: Monthly Review Press, 1978. A socialist account.

Grant, Ronald M., and E. Spencer Wellhofer, eds. *Challenges to the Nation State: Ethnicity and the Emerging World Economic Order.* Denver, Colo.: Graduate School of International Studies, University of Denver, 1977.

Gordenker, Leon, ed. *The United Nations in International Politics.* Princeton, N.J.: Princeton University Press, 1971.

Hansen, Roger D. *Beyond the North-South Stalemate.* New York: McGraw-Hill, 1979.

Hensman, C. R. *Rich Against Poor: The Reality of Aid.* Cambridge, Mass.: Schenkman, 1972.*

Herz, John H. *The Nation-State and the Crisis of World Politics.* New York: Longmans, 1976.*

Hoffman, Stanley, ed. *Contemporary Theory in International Relations.* Englewood Cliffs, N.J.: Prentice-Hall, 1960.

Hoopes, Townsend. *The Limits of Intervention.* New York: David McKay, 1969.

Hudson, Michael. *Global Fracture: The New International Economic Order.* New York: Harper & Row, 1977.

Kamarck, Andrew M. *The Tropics and Economic Development: A Provocative Inquiry into the Poverty of Nations.* Baltimore: Johns Hopkins University Press, 1977.*

Kaplan, Morton A. *System and Process in International Politics.* New York: Wiley, 1957.

Keohane, Robert O., and Joseph S. Nye. *Power and Interdependence: World Politics in Transition.* Boston: Little, Brown, 1977.

Laqueur, Walter. *Terrorism.* Boston: Little, Brown, 1977*

Laszlo, Ervin, et al. *Goals for Mankind: A Report to the Club of Rome on the New Horizons of Global Community.* New York: Dutton, 1977.*

Lauterpacht, Elihu, and John G. Collier. *Individual Rights and the State in International Affairs.* New York: Praeger, 1977.

Mansbach, Richard, Yale H. Ferguson, and Donald E. Lampert. *The Web of World Politics: Nonstate Actors in the Global System.* Englewood Cliffs, N.J.: Prentice-Hall, 1976.

Mazrui, Ali A. *Africa's International Relations.* Boulder, Colo.: Westview Press, 1978.

McLuhan, Marshall, and Quentin Flores. *War and Peace in the Global Village.* New York: McGraw-Hill, 1968.

Modelski, George. *Principles of World Politics.* New York: Free Press, 1972.

Morgenthau, Hans J. *Politics Among Nations.* 5th ed. New York: Knopf, 1978.

Packenham, Robert A. *Liberal America and the Third World.* Princeton, N.J.: Princeton University Press, 1973.*

Rosecrance, Richard, ed. *The Future of the International Strategic System.* San Francisco: Chandler, 1972.

Rosenau, James W., Kenneth W. Thompson, and Gavin Boyd, eds. *World Politics: An Introduction.* New York: Free Press, 1967.

Sampson, Anthony. *The Arms Bazaar: From Lebanon to Lockheed.* New York: Bantam, 1978.*

Schell, Jonathan. *The Time of Illusion.* New York: Random House, 1976*

Schelling, Thomas C. *Arms and Influence.* New Haven: Yale University Press, 1966.

Steel, Ronald. *Pax Americana: The Cold War Empire and the Politics of Counterrevolution.* rev. ed. Baltimore: Penguin, 1977.*

Stockholm International Peace Research Institute. *World Armaments and Disarmament: Sipri Yearbook 1979.* New York: Humanities Press, 1979.

Tinbergen, Jan, ed. *Rio: Reshaping the International Order: A Report to the Club of Rome.* New York: Dutton, 1976.*

Tucker, Robert W. *The Inequality of Nations.* New York: Basic Books, 1977.

Walton, John, and Louis H. Masotti, eds. *The City in Comparative Perspective.* New York: Wiley, 1976.

Waltz, Kenneth. *Man, the State and War.* New York: Columbia University Press, 1965.

Zartman, I. William. *The 50% Solution: How to Bargain Successfully with Hijackers, Strikers, Bosses, Oil Magnates, Arabs, Russians, and Other Worthy Opponents in this Modern World.* Garden City, N.Y.: Anchor, 1976.*

Zeigler, David W. *War, Peace, and International Politics.* Boston: Little, Brown, 1977.*

Epilogue

The Study of Politics

All problems are divided into two classes, soluble
questions, which are trivial, and important
questions, which are insoluble.
> —*George Santayana*

Knowledge of human nature is the beginning and
end of political wisdom.
> —*Henry Adams*

The study of politics and government is now called political science.
When the ancient Greeks began using the word "science," it simply
meant an organized body of knowledge. Now it often means something
more precise.

First, scientific study of a subject means a systematic and self-conscious attempt to increase knowledge about it. For example, you might
casually notice that students seem to be less interested in politics than
they were last year. To study this scientifically might mean doing a survey—looking at voting records, interviewing students, and so forth. Second, to be scientific is to be empirical, to inquire into what actually is
rather than what is hoped or imagined. Scientific inquiry will actually investigate students' interest in politics, rather than assuming that they
should or should not be interested and speculating about this. To get as
close a look at reality as possible, researchers try hard to keep out prior
assumptions. Otherwise they may find only what they have already decided that they will, or should, find. This is not to say that political (or
any) scientists have no values. Nor can we keep clear of values; even selecting a particular thing for study is a value judgment. But once it is
chosen, we must try to see it as it is, rather than as we prefer it to be.

We also attempt to construct theory in science, so that we can (a)
classify our data and show the differences and similarities; (b) *explain* the

things that happened, say why and how they came about as we have described; (c) *predict* what will happen in the future under similar conditions, or what will probably happen if certain changes occur.

From these characteristics of science, then, we have an emphasis upon empirical knowledge, controlled observation, propositions that can be verified, and quantification—the use of mathematical and statistical techniques borrowed from the natural sciences. The history of political science, especially in the United States, is to some degree a struggle over how much this study of human events can or should follow the same approach that the study of nonhuman events takes.

Political Science as a Discipline

Political science has grown enormously since its early beginnings. It is now divided into several fields, each as complex as an entire discipline. In fact two of them, international relations and public administration, are frequently thought of as separate disciplines in themselves, and are sometimes taught by separate departments. *International relations* is the study of world politics, relations among the nations of the world. It includes the study of international law and international organizations, and international economics, as well as historical and military perspectives. *Public administration* is the study of the management of the public agencies that carry out public policies. It is increasingly important in the industrialized and socialist nations and in the Third World.

In the United States, one basic field of political science is *American government*. This includes not only topics such as governmental structure and function, policy formulation, federalism and intergovernmental relations, interest groups, voting behavior, political parties, campaigns and elections, and the like, but also such matters as constitutional law and civil liberties, which are almost disciplines in themselves. In other nations the study of their own governments will probably form a similar base for political studies. U.S. government then becomes a part of *comparative government*, another of the basic fields, which studies the various national governments and also makes cross-national comparisons. It includes specialization in areas—such as the Far East, the Third World, the British Commonwealth, Eastern Europe—and in a variety of other approaches. For example, one may study comparative judicial process, analyzing and comparing the functions of the judiciaries and related institutions and practices of various nations. The study of comparative administrative systems brings a similar dimension to the field of public administration.

The remaining major subdivision of political science is *political theory* or *political philosophy*. The term political philosophy generally refers to normative studies, those related to goals, the good life, right and wrong, and so on. Political theory may include political philosophy and mean any theorizing about politics, but it now sometimes refers only to the more systematic theories that may apply, for example, to empirical generalizations. Some avoid the difficulty by referring to "political theory and philosophy," but usually the term "theory" is interpreted in the broader sense to mean any formal thought about politics. The discipline of political science is sometimes broken down into more subdivisions than the ones outlined here, but these are the major divisions. Comparative government, American or other national systems, international relations, political theory, and public administration distinguish the primary concentrations and at the same time include all subfields.

The American Search for a Science of Politics

The study of politics has changed significantly in the past hundred years. Throughout much of its history it was confined largely to political theory, with occasional comparative themes included. In the early years of the United States it was largely indistinguishable from history. As the social sciences began to develop independently, the study of government was generally included with that of economic forces in what was called political economy. It was not until the end of the nineteenth century that political science, as a separate discipline, came into being. It coincided with the development of graduate education in the United States and quickly made its way into the undergraduate curriculum.

The most easily identifiable beginning of American political science in more or less its contemporary form was in the 1880s, when John W. Burgess founded a School of Political Science at Columbia University. Reflecting the trends popular in Germany at the time, Burgess strongly stressed the power of the state. A century later this emphasis is still very strong in political science. It is not necessary to sympathize with Burgess's dogmatic doctrines to give him his due as one of the prime movers in establishing political science as an important intellectual force. The Columbia School and Johns Hopkins University, where political science was also developing, were the only two true graduate programs in political science in the United States until the twentieth century, but by then the discipline had increasingly become recognized as legitimately distinct, and many colleges and universities had formed departments of political science. The profession's first journal, the *Political Science Quarterly,* was founded at Columbia University in 1886, and the American Political Science Association in 1903. Soon afterward the association began publishing its own journal, the *American Political Science Review.*

It was not long before American students of political science began trying to establish a "science of politics" modeled as closely as possible upon the examples of the natural sciences. The pioneer in this effort was Arthur F. Bentley, whose *The Process of Government* (1908) attempted to define the core of political science and to limit its boundaries. He called for attention to pressure groups as the prime actors in the political process. The roots of modern political science may also be traced to A. Lawrence Lowell, who became President of Harvard University, and his emphasis upon the importance of public opinion studies in such works as *Public Opinion and Popular Government* (1913). Lowell was also an early advocate of examining function as apart from mere structure, and of the extensive use of statistics and mathematical techniques, though he did not assume the possibility of a completely objective social science.

There were others who did not see a future for a science of politics in the sense of the natural sciences. Among them was Woodrow Wilson, who, in addition to being governor of New Jersey and president of the United States, had taken his Ph.D. at Johns Hopkins and had been prominent as a political scientist in the early years of the discipline. He was elected president of the American Political Science Association in 1910. Wilson did believe that students of politics should deal more with politics as it exists than as people merely assume it to be, but his "realism" was not rigid. He asserted the need for sympathy and insight, and denied that political science was truly a science or that it would ever be. In his presidential address to the APSA, "The Law and the Facts," he said that he did not like the term political science and that human relationships were not suitable subject matter for the scientific approach.

Although there had been calls for a science of politics, its proponents did not have great influence until Charles E. Merriam's work was published in the 1920s. Merriam argued for the intensive application of psychology and statistics to the study of politics. He denied that he wanted to eliminate historical and legal studies, which had constituted virtually the whole of American political science up to the twentieth century, but said that he wished to add to them. In words that sound familiar to the modern ear he called for precise measurement as the foundation of political science, and argued that a science of politics could result in more intelligent control of human affairs and of governmental processes. It would even make possible the conscious direction of human evolution. Despite a greatly exaggerated view of the potential of a science of politics, Merriam admitted that it would be difficult to make sense of the many variables in any human situation or to devise a specific unit of measurement. He was also aware that human beings were unlikely ever to achieve complete objectivity (his own commitment to democracy was a case in point), and he recognized that it might be dangerous to concentrate so much upon method that one lost sight of the subject matter.

Merriam began his campaign to create a new science in 1921 with an article, "The Present State of the Study of Politics," in the *American Political Science Review*. He and his colleagues at the University of Chicago continued their efforts for more than a decade, and produced numerous works, the best-known being his *New Aspects of Politics* (1925). It is ironic that Merriam called so strenuously for a political science, with the accent on "science," but did little to provide the new methodology he sought. Other strong voices called for similar approaches. William Munro, for example, suggested that physics should provide the new model for a science of politics. His presidential address to the American Political Science Association, published in the *American Political Science Review* in 1928, was titled "Physics and Politics." Still further in the same direction was George E. G. Catlin, whose 1927 book, *Science and Method of Politics,* sought to draw a science of politics from the techniques of economics, and attempted to restructure the discipline, much as Bentley had intended years before. None of these efforts succeeded, and the science of politics seemed as far away as ever.

Nevertheless, it would be a great mistake to underestimate the influence of Merriam and the Chicago School. A list of those who studied with him reads like a Who's Who of post–World War II political science—including Harold D. Lasswell, Avery Leiserson, David Truman, V. O. Key, Leonard D. White, Gabriel Almond, Herbert Simon, C. Herman Pritchett, and many others.

Not until this postwar period was the discipline substantially restructured. Earlier, during the 1920s and 1930s, those who opposed the scientific movement argued that its basic impetus was envy of what the natural sciences had accomplished, and that this led to attempts to use scientific techniques where they were not appropriate, by applying them to human affairs. Many opponents accepted the use of statistics and the efforts to eliminate vagueness and bias, insofar as possible, but they deplored suggestions that political scientists should pay no attention to values and goals. Catlin and Munro, especially, invited attacks that pointed out that even the most technical of questions cannot be wholly separated from considerations of policy. We should note here that Merriam, regardless of his position as more or less the father of the movement to construct a new science of politics, agreed that political science should lead toward certain goals and values. Prominent among the critics were Edward S. Corwin, J. Mark Jacobson, and W. Y. Elliott; their attacks hit home by asking just what it was that the scientific movement had accomplished.

Charles A. Beard assailed the advocates of scientific political study from the vantage point of the presidency of the American Political Science Association. His address, "Time, Technology, and the Creative Spirit in Political Science," printed in the *Review* in 1927, blasted both old and new currents of political science. Foremost among his criticisms were those directed at the proponents of the new science for disregarding the central role of ethics. He charged that the new scientific techniques led directly to a cold and mechanistic study that was divorced from the real world and from the purposes of human beings.

There things stood until the 1940s. After a flurry of controversy, the idea of a new science was quiescent. If ever there was a calm before the storm, however, this was it. The rise of behavioralism in the late 1940s represented a reemergence of the idea, coupled with vastly more sophisticated techniques of research and data treatment; but this time there was a difference. Behavioralism struck with such force that during the 1950s and the early 1960s the profession was almost literally torn apart. Although never totally dominant, the adherents of behavioralism came to be a major force in American political science. They occupied a majority of the top posts in the association and were recognized as including many of the leading figures in the discipline. The charge that behavioralism had become a new orthodoxy was an exaggeration, but it had a point.

This being so, it would seem simple to define "behavioralism," but such is not the case. It is easy to identify many who could fairly be labeled behavioralists, at least at certain stages of their careers. There would be agreement upon such figures as Herbert Simon, David Easton, David Truman, Robert Dahl, Harold Lasswell, Heinz Eulau, and many others. On the other hand, many political scientists were clearly outside the movement, including Hans Morgenthau, Leo Strauss, Mulford Q. Sibley, Eric Voegelin, Sheldon Wolin, and others with equal prominence. Many others were difficult, if not impossible, to classify, and there was probably as much disagreement inside the groups opposing behavioralism and those supporting it as there was between them. Behavioralism obviously meant different things to different people.

The term itself was deliberately adopted to distinguish the movement from behaviorism, also a movement of the early 1920s, predominantly in psychology, which stressed an extraordinarily mechanistic approach to human behavior and tended to interpret everything in terms of an oversimple stimulus-response reaction. Behavioralism was not a consistent movement, but certain general principles were widely accepted as its hallmark. Foremost among these was that political science could, and should, become a science akin to the natural sciences, with emphasis upon prediction and the discovery of regularities and laws of human behavior. There was heavy emphasis upon methodology, especially quantitative methodology. Survey research, simulation, game theory, computer technology, and advanced mathematical and statistical techniques became a part of the discipline. Behavioralism tended to stress analysis rather than simple description, and it confined itself to observable phenomena, that is, actual behavior, rather than speculation regarding motives or other considerations not open to direct observation. Probably the heart of behavioralism was the assertion that facts were separate from values, the same positivistic theme that had motivated the early advocates of a science of politics.

Those who opposed behavioralism disagreed on many things, often vehemently, but there was wide acceptance of certain criticisms. They believed that human behavior is not controlled by discoverable laws, and that it is not sufficiently regular to be subject to a high degree of quantification. They argued that the degree of objectivity sought by the behavioralists was not possible, and that behavior itself represents only a part of human life. Generally, they contended, only the more trivial characteristics of human affairs are open to direct scientific verification. A constant theme of their criticism was a need for a moral and ethical dimension to political science that behavioralism denied, and some argued that behavioralism, in confining itself to observable phenomena and rejecting speculation and ethical matters, was a direct underpinning to the political status quo. Criticisms of behavioralism came from many who were strongly conservative politically, and also from elements within the New Left of the 1960s. Both groups attacked behavioralism's rejection of values as a proper concern for political science, and the New Left objected further on the grounds that behavioralism discouraged social and political change. A rather consistent theme among the critics was that the distinction between fact and value is not valid; that values permeate everything, and that it is an error even to consider the two apart from one another.

The disagreements are not dead, and certainly not forgotten, but the bitterness of the conflict is largely a thing of the past. A new generation now has other things with which to concern itself. No longer is one likely to hear such statements from the more extreme ends of the continuum as "Statistics is useless in the study of human affairs," or "If you ain't doing math, you ain't doing political science." A settlement of sorts dates from the presidential address that David Easton, one of behavioralism's pioneers and most closely associated with systems analysis, gave to the APSA in 1969. In it he spoke of the "post-behavioral revolution" and agreed with the critics regarding the impossibility of a value-free social science. Whether the new revolution is truly a revolution, or the natural fizzling out of a controversy, is unimportant. What is important is that the bulk of the political science community now recognizes the value of quantitative techniques where they are appropriate, but also recognizes that they do not present a total picture. There is a general recognition of the importance of an ethical dimension to political science, and most accept the benefits and the limitations of a scientific approach. Thus the political scientist needs to understand basic statistical techniques and be familiar with various methodologies, but also to have an awareness of the value of other forms of study. Behavioralism did an excellent job in exploding many myths about what the "real" situation was by providing description that was documented, but it failed to discover laws of human behavior, and, taken by itself, it limited the subjects open to investigation by the political scientist. It is simpler now for the political scientist to combine approaches and obtain a picture that is somewhat closer to reality, including its implications as well as its physical aspects.

Public Policy into Practice

During this long controversy the field of public administration began to develop as a special study within political science. There is now considerable controversy over whether the study of public administration should remain a branch of political science, as it began, or be treated as a new discipline, as it has been in some places. Such disputes are likely to be matters of empire building, status seeking, or quarrels over words rather than substance. Although they are sometimes entertaining, they are not otherwise of concern to us here.

Public administration as a field grew out of a concern within political science that laws be applied economically, efficiently, and in a manner consistent with legislative intent. The original legalistic orientation has grown into a concentration upon principles of management rather than mere application of the laws. Terms that are fundamental to the modern study of public administration, however, such as management, administration, execution, and even efficiency, are not simple and are not necessarily understood the same way by different persons. Partly because of this imprecision, and partly because the process of administration deals with human beings, all of them different and none of them totally predictable, public administration, like political science itself, is not a "hard" science in the sense of having discovered "laws of human behavior." There is no one orthodoxy or widely accepted approach to the field, although systems analysis, game theory, operations research, and various behavioral techniques have all had an impact, as has the case study method.

The study of public administration in the United States has grown considerably since the American Political Science Association was founded. The concern of many of its early members was that the nations of Europe were far ahead of them, not only in the abstract study of administration but also in the concrete training of public employees. The Progressive period of the early twentieth century was a time of great speculation and study regarding public administration at the municipal level, but the field began to solidify in the 1920s and 1930s and has become almost universal since World War II. Nations of the Third World have concentrated heavily upon the techniques of management as applied to the public sector. India, for example, has an Institute of Public Enterprise affiliated with Osmania University in Hyderabad. Malaysia maintains an institute of administrative studies at its national university; the Philippines have established several such bodies and publish a major journal. In Nigeria there are a number of university-sponsored institutes, several of which publish influential journals, and in addition the government runs administrative colleges for in-service refresher courses. Numerous other examples could be cited. Many of these institutes are sponsoring research and training intended to get at the special problems of *development administration*—establishing and maintaining a political system, while creating economic growth and development, through bureaucratic agencies.

Public administration today has retained many of the currents that motivated the early political scientists and other social scientists who established it, but it has added much as well. It may in fact have dimensions that would startle most of us. Consider the student of public administration in one of the California state universities, who also happened to be a member of a religious group believing that the world would soon come to an end. When asked why he was studying public administration, he replied that the coming heavenly administration would surely require bureaucrats for its divine purposes, and he wished to be prepared.

In a sense, public administration has gone through much of the turmoil that its parent, political science, has experienced. The early effort by many in both fields to separate facts completely from values, or from normative considerations, is now generally recognized as an impossible undertaking—and undesirable even if it were possible. The belated recognition that it is similarly impossible to separate policy making from administration is another example. Most practitioners in both fields would now agree that one cannot study human behavior without some consideration of human motivation and psychology. It is not feasible to understand a part of a human being without also understanding something of the whole person. The earlier emphasis upon public employees as merely employees, cogs in a machine, has therefore generally vanished.

Outlook for the Future

Unfortunately, many other criticisms of both public administration and political science are still valid. Political science has done little to deal with the most pressing social and political problems facing humanity. It has provided little social criticism, and the blame is to be shared by other social sciences as well. Perhaps the concern with methodology has drained too much creative energy. Now that the battle over behavioralism has subsided, it may be possible for the social sciences to start confronting questions such as: Must security and liberty be mutually exclusive? Can the implications of the administrative state be dealt with in a democracy? Can there be institutions that prevent the injustices in individual cases that are inherent in the need to make laws binding upon all? Can nations or peoples establish political orders sufficiently powerful to insure their collective, communal well-being without being so powerful as to trample upon the individuals who make up the community? What are the implications of energy production, consumption, and control for domestic and international politics? Can development be brought about without widening the divisions within society? Can ordinary citizens be allowed—and are they able—to govern themselves? These questions only scratch the surface. Political science has existed in its present incarnation for less than a century, but the study of politics has existed since the beginning of recorded history, and probably before. Aristotle was correct when he termed it the "architectonic" or synthesizing science. At least it should be, and it is time that it began to be.

Much of the work of reshaping or redirecting political science in this direction is now going on outside the United States. Political science in Great Britain followed a similar pattern of development, but the nature of university education there meant a closer concern with philosophical issues and questions of social criticism. The great schools of social philosophy that emerged in nineteenth-century Europe—foremost among which is the class analysis established by Karl Marx—also gave political science there a much different perspective. In the years since World War II greater exchange of research and more frequent exchange of scholars has meant some integration of these perspectives into the rather conservative and narrow vision of American political science, while at the same time introducing a certain amount of pragmatism to the European discipline.

Recent years have also seen the breakup of the great colonial empires and the sudden emergence into the world community of dozens of new and different nation-states. Political scientists in the "old world" have to change their approach in substantial ways if they are to under-

© 1977 United Feature Syndicate, Inc.

stand the political problems and prospects of these nations. Most of the new states have departments and institutes of political studies in their own universities and governments. Many of these were patterned on the models of the colonial power, but they have begun to define political questions and political science in new ways. The circulation of research and scholars around the globe will mean that these new schools will eventually affect the orientation and emphasis in political science among themselves, and in the older programs of study such as the American, British, French, and German. These developments enrich political science. They will make it possible for it to become in fact a truly universal approach to human community.

SELECTED READINGS

Conway, M. Margaret, and Frank B. Feigert. *Political Analysis: An Introduction.* 2nd ed.; Boston: Allyn and Bacon, 1976.

Dahl, Robert A. *Modern Political Analysis.* Englewood Cliffs, N.J.: Prentice-Hall, 1963.*

*Indicates a paperback edition is available.

Deutsch, Karl. *Politics and Government: How People Decide Their Fate.* Boston: Houghton Mifflin, 1970.*

Ellsworth, John W., and Arthur A. Stahnke. *Politics and Political Systems: An Introduction to Political Science.* New York: McGraw-Hill, 1977.*

Eulau, Heinz. *The Behavioral Persuasion in Politics.* New York: Random House, 1963.*

Germino, Dante. *Modern Western Political Thought.* Chicago: Rand McNally, 1972.

Graham, George G., Jr., and George W. Carey, eds. *The Post-Behavioral Era: Perspectives on Political Science.* New York: David Mckay, 1972.

Hacker, Andrew. *Political Theory: Philosophy, Ideology, Science.* New York: Macmillan, 1961.

James, Elizabeth M. *Political Theory: An Introduction to Interpretation.* Chicago: Rand McNally, 1976.*

Meehan, Eugene J. *The Theory and Method of Political Analysis.* Homewood, Ill.: Dorsey Press, 1965.

Rosenau, James N. *The Dramas of Politics: An Introduction to the Joys of Inquiry.* Boston: Little, Brown, 1973.

Sabine, George. *A History of Political Theory.* 4th ed., rev. by Thomas L. Thorson. New York: Holt, Rinehart and Winston, 1973.

Skidmore, Max J. *American Political Thought.* New York: St. Martin's, 1978.*

Spragens, Thomas A., Jr. *Understanding Political Theory.* New York: St. Martin's, 1976.*

Strauss, Leo, and Joseph Cropsey, eds. *History of Political Philosophy.* 2nd ed. Skokie, Ill.: Rand McNally, 1972.

Tinder, Glenn. *Political Thinking: The Perennial Questions.* 2nd ed. Boston: Little, Brown, 1974.*

van Dalen, Hendrik, and L. Harmon Zeigler. *Introduction to Political Science: People, Politics, and Perception.* Englewood Cliffs, N.J.: Prentice-Hall, 1977.*

Glossary

anarchy/anarchism referring to a system of politics with no rulers; a political philosophy of such rule; not to be confused with "chaos."

aristocracy persons of high status by birth; a system of rule by inherited right.

authority/authoritarian rightful or legitimate rule is authority; authoritarian, however, often refers to stern or dictatorial rule.

autonomy independence; self-government; self-sufficiency; absence of control by others, economically or politically.

centrifugal a force pulling parts of a system away from the center.

centripetal a force pulling parts of a system closer to the center.

charisma "gift"; personal grace, charm, magnetism.

class 1. a group or category of similar individuals. 2. in Marxist theory, a self-conscious part of the economic structure of society: e.g., workers (proletariat); owners (capitalists); small businessmen (petit bourgeoisie).

coercive referring to the use or threatened use of force.

colonial/colonialism control by one society over another, by conquest or by treaty, or the system of such control.

community a fundamental unit of human organization, characterized by shared residence and occupational, religious, ethnic, or other affinities and ranging in size from a small locality to nations or even the world.

consensus/consensual rule based upon agreement, through compromise and persuasion.

custom/customary a rule or established practice; often referring to traditional forms of political, legal, or social organization commonly not written down.

197

delegation   1. to confer responsibility or authority on another. 2. a theory of representation holding that the representative merely reflects his constituents rather than making his own judgments.

democracy/democratization   rule by the people; policies to broaden popular participation in decision making.

dependency   a condition of inferior status in political or economic terms; lack of self-sufficiency or self-determination. Often used to describe the international economy today, in reference to the Third World.

developing nation/less developed nation (LDC)   generally, former colonies and other nations, outside Europe and North America, whose economies are less powerful than those of the industrialized states; as a group, referred to as the Third World.

direct democracy   democracy without representation, delegation, or other indirect decision making; direct participation by all.

economy   the system of organization and production of material goods and services; sometimes used to mean "thrift," as in "a program of economy in services."

egalitarian   tending to, or promoting, an equal distribution of power, rewards, or status.

elite   persons of high or favored political or economic status; a privileged minority.

empirical   emphasis on the reality of politics; effort to develop hypotheses and generalizations; contrasts with normative approach.

ethnicity   identity or membership of a particular group of human beings distinguished by language, religion, physical characteristics, or general way of life.

Fourth World   *see* Third World.

franchise   the right to vote.

government   that segment of society which carries out the day to day functions of politics; the system of rule.

grass roots   local; popular; decentralized aspects of politics; sometimes meaning "nonelite."

ideology   an organized set of beliefs about social and political life; a philosophy; may refer to ideas approved by the government in power.

immobilisme/immobility   deadlock; inability to take action as a result of disagreement within the executive branch of government.

imperialism   political behavior oriented toward conquest or control of one group or society by another; may refer to the outward thrust of the Western states from the fifteenth to the nineteenth century.

industrialization   the transformation of an economy and society from one based primarily on agriculture to one organized for mass production and distribution of capital and consumer goods.

instability   extremely rapid change, leading to uncertainty and disorder in social and political life; imbalance; unpredictability.

institution/institutionalize   established, organized pattern of activity, with formalized roles, to carry out a specific function (e.g., a university, factory, or court), and the process of creating such institutions.

interest group   people who have a common concern—general or specific —and organize to advance this concern politically.

law   1. a formalized rule, promulgated and enforced by the political system. 2. recognized, established practice or principle.

lay   nonprofessional; participation without special training.

legitimacy   rightful rule; the recognition, internally or externally, of authority.

linguistic   referring to language; one means of identifying a community.

monarchy   rule by a single person; generally inherited. Examples: king, queen, shah, emir, rajah.

modernity/modernization   referring to a particular pattern of individual or group attitudes and behavior, essentially secular, instrumentalist, future-oriented; associated with literacy, mobility, and industry.

multinational corporation (MNC)   corporations with operations in several countries and probably with multinational ownership and staff as well.

municipal   1. referring to cities. 2. in specialized legal use, referring to national rather than international or "natural" law.

nation   a group of people sharing some or all of the following: a common language, religion, history, territory, and political system. Generally refers to groups of several hundred thousand or more, although there are exceptions.

nationalism   beliefs in, and political action focused on, the establishment and advancement of one's national group as an independent entity; the primacy of national interests over others such as class, race, or international concerns.

nation building policies and actions to promote the integration of those living within a single state as a nation, including a sense of national identity and loyalty.

nation-state the dominant form of political organization in the world; combines the communal entity of the nation with the structural apparatus of the state.

neocolonial referring to the return of colonialism in new guises, through political or economic influence by one nation (perhaps a former colonial power) over another, amounting to control.

New International Economic Order (NIEO) a program to restructure the world economy in more equitable terms, reducing Third World dependency and multinational corporate power, through improved trade and aid.

norm/normative referring to a basic principle, rule, or custom.

oligarchy rule by the few, generally the wealthy; not necessarily by birth.

organic characterized as natural or "living;" a metaphor used to describe certain social theories which hold that social or political systems are more than a mechanical arrangement, and are bound by tradition and status.

particularistic favoritism toward one segment of a plural community, and policies designed to advance their interests to the detriment of others.

partisan taking sides; beliefs and behavior supporting a particular political party, for example, especially when such attitudes are not appropriate.

party an organization of people sharing common political interests, generally for the purpose of capturing political office, or even to challenge an entire government and political system.

patron/patronage a benefactor; advancement or protection through the support of a wealthier, more powerful or more influential person.

plural/pluralism referring to societies composed of several distinct groups, such as linguistic, ethnic or religious groups, under one political system.

plurality in a contest with more than two, the number of votes that is the greatest, but not more than half; hence, less than a majority.

policy a general purpose, which is carried out by specific programs; e.g., a policy of universal literacy may be carried out by free adult education centers.

political machine/machine government a political party organization based on an exchange of services or favors for political support in the form of votes or campaign contributions.

political system the overall pattern of rules, structures, and roles by which a group carries out its political life.

polity the political community; originally referred to the Aristotelian ideal, the city-state.

polyarchy rule by the many; used to describe the idea of plural elites.

proportional representation allocation of legislative representation on the basis of party strength; used in conjunction with multi-member districts.

regime a particular set of individuals holding political power within a political system.

revolution radical and comprehensive change of a political system, altering it in fundamental ways.

secession the attempt by part of a polity (especially the nation-state) to separate itself from the rest, either to become independent or to join another polity. Particularly, but not always, associated with federal systems (e.g., Biafra, Quebec, or the Confederate States of America).

secular institutions, ideas, or behavior not based upon, or promoting, religious principles.

separatism movements by segments of a community to distance themselves politically, up to and including secession; often arising from linguistic or ethnic or religious differences.

SES a common abbreviation for socioeconomic status.

society people living in organized groups and the pattern of their relationships, such as familial, class, or institutional.

sovereignty rule; self-control or self-government.

stability balance or order; change limited to nondisruptive levels; sometimes used erroneously to mean continuation of the status quo without any change at all.

state centralized, territorially defined government, with specialized agencies and personnel for various political functions, with coercive capacity; generally controlling many thousands or millions of people.

state building policies and actions to promote the establishment and maintenance of the state apparatus, such as bureaucracies, courts, legislatures, and its coercive forces, police and military.

status   position or rank; sometimes used as shorthand for "high status."

statute   legislation; a written rule, passed by the formal rule-making body of the state.

structure   a defined pattern of relationships, sometimes established in a set of written rules.

technocracy   rule, or great influence, by experts or learned persons, generally in science or technology, including mass communications.

theocracy   rule by religious leaders; a political system established by, and promoting, a particular theology or religion.

Third World/Fourth World   Third World refers to the states outside the industrialized West and the industrialized part of the Communist countries; generally overlaps with the tropical regions of the world (often former colonies), which are the poorer states; the very poorest among them have been called the Fourth World.

totalitarian   policies or ideologies focused upon total control of a community's beliefs and behavior, often by use of police or military power in a program of terror.

tradition   long-established, generally unwritten, practice or norm, which acquires authority in part through venerability.

transitional society   a group changing from traditional to modern culture; often used as a synonym for "developing nation."

urbanization   1. an increase in the proportion of people living in cities. 2. a cultural shift toward the ideas and behavior associated with cities.

westernization   social change modeled upon the institutions and behavior of the industrialized states of Europe and North America.

Index